To all those who love life, unconditionally!

ORIGINAL TITLE:
Le Guide de l'alimentation saine et naturelle

© LES ÉDITIONS ASCLÉPIADES INC.
  MONTREAL, 1987

Composition by
BERGERON CONCEPTION PUBLICITAIRE

© LES ÉDITIONS ASCLÉPIADES INC.
  MONTREAL, 1994

Legal deposit: Bibliothèque nationale du
Québec, 1994

PRINTED IN CANADA

ISBN 2-9801115-3-8

The GUIDE to Natural and Healthy Eating

by Renée Frappier

Original French version
translated by
BRUCE MURCHISON

ACKNOWLEDGMENTS

Thanks to the dynamic team that
contributed to the translation and preparation
of the English edition.

Translation: BRUCE MURCHISON

Full page illustrations and
cover design: MICHELLE PELLETIER

Other illustrations: ALAIN COURNOYER

Composition: GUY BERGERON

Photos: DANIEL COURNOYER

Food stylists : RENÉE FRAPPIER
ATMO ZAKES

Proofreaders : DENISE ARCHAMBAULT
PATRICIA MARTIN
MARY GRAZIANO

Foreword

The Guide to Natural and Healthy Eating is the fruit of the author's many years of research and teaching.

Its purpose is to promote good health and contribute to the quality of people's lives–values which are essential to the self-realization and the well-being of both individuals and of society as a whole.

An increasing number of people feel the need to change their eating habits, without quite knowing where to begin or how to go about it.

The Guide to Natural and Healthy Eating proposes a winning formula which will bring you pleasure and knowledge in your quest for good health.

To the reader

To open this manual is to open a door to awareness : awareness of yourself, your milieu, and the environment. Opening this book is, in itself, an act of change.

This volume provides an outline of the fundamental concepts that you will surely want to know and master, whether you have already begun to take active steps towards adopting a healthy diet, or you are just beginning.

The expression " a healthy diet " refers to a global concept. It implies that someone has both the desire and the will to change his diet in order to live a healthier life by eating foods which give him the energy (Kcalories) and all the nutritional elements he needs. Eating a healthy diet also implies using a variety of foods which are low in fats and sugar.

The term " natural " is used to describe foods, or ingredients in foods, which have undergone no chemical modifications due to human intervention, after harvesting or when processing is involved; consequently, they contain no chemical additives.

The term «organic» is used to refer to foods which have been grown in soil that has not been treated with chemical fertilizers or other chemical products. " Organic " means " natural [2] ", so to speak!

These three concepts lead us to give more definition to the way we live and they offer us new and stimulating perspectives. They also raise questions about the monotony and deficiencies of our dietary habits, the practices of the food industry, the habits of our contempory society, national and international politics, and, finally, about ecology and environmental equilibrium on a planetary scale.

In order to make this itinerary easier, we have adopted a two-part format for The Guide.

1. THE " THEORY BOOK "

a) **A scientific section** which explains in simple, concise fashion what the body's nutritional needs are as well as how the digestive system works.

b) **A dietary section** describing food products, their nutritional value, and how to prepare them, so that you can learn how to balance menus without meat. In addition, a chapter called " How To Succeed in the Kitchen " is devoted to ways of making these principles an integral part or your daily life.

2. THE " RECIPE BOOK "

More than **150 easy-to-make recipes**, which are both nutritious and appetizing, and which will make your mouth water. In addition, the explanation of several basic techniques, followed by dozens of suggestions, will tempt you into creating tasty recipes of your own.

After all, let's not forget that eating well is an art. Nowadays, we eat too much and too little at the same time : too much, in terms of quantity, and too little, in terms of quality.

" TOO MUCH FOOD IS THE CAUSE OF ALL OUR ILLNESSES ". (Hippocrates)

CHAPTER I

Progressive Changes

It is preferable to change your eating habits gradually, to promote a lasting and harmonious change in you, your family, and your milieu.

1. Eat your food slowly, taking small mouthfuls; chew it well to savor the flavor and make digestion easier.

2. Reduce the quantity of food that you eat at each meal. Listen to your body and do not exceed your appetite nor your needs. Food is fuel, and it is up to us to set our own limits in order to avoid clogging up our system. Eating less keeps the mind and body alert, while maintaining healthy body weight.

3. Avoid drinking during and after meals, so as not to dilute gastric secretions and hinder digestion. Develop the good habit of drinking water **before** meals, or two hours **after** you have finished eating.This will help you to replace stimulants (tea, coffee, alcohol) with healthful beverages (spring water, herbal teas, grain-based coffee substitutes).

4. Avoid eating snacks and junk food.

5. Do not eat before going to bed, so that your body may cleanse itself during the night.

6. Begin each meal with a vegetable or fresh fruit salad. Doing this will increase your intake of vitamins, minerals, and fibers. Moreover, eating raw foods before cooked ones ensures excellent digestion and reduces the sensation of fatigue and drowsiness which is felt after a meal made up of cooked foods only.

7. Start using nourishing whole foods to replace high-calorie foods whose nutritional value is zero or almost zero (empty calories).

   a) **Stop using white sugar.**
   Begin by replacing your desserts with fruit and/or milk-based products in yogurt form, and the habit of finishing off a meal with a dessert will simply disappear. **Desserts** will re-appear only on special occasions; eating them **will no longer be a habit.**

   b) **Eat whole grains.**
   Replace refined grains with whole (i.e., unhulled) grains, which contain more fibers and nutritional elements. It is easy to adopt oatmeal and whole grain bread, rice, pasta, etc., without having to revolutionize your meal menus. And then, gradually introduce less well-known grains such as millet, buckwheat, etc., into your diet.

   c) **Reduce your intake of saturated fatty acids.**
   Replace refined oils and solid fats with non-hydrogenated vegetable oils obtained from the first pressing; they are rich in mono- and polyunsaturated fatty acids. Watch your cheese intake and choose low-fat dairy products. Gradually reduce the amount of meat that you eat and increase your consumption of legumes and grains.

d) Introduce more fresh vegetables and sprouts into the menu.

Reduce your consumption of canned and bottled foods; they contain sugar, salt, and chemical products. When canned, vegetables lose part of their nutritional value because of excess cooking. Using fewer canned goods prompts us to eat more **fresh, nutritious, seasonal foods**.

8. **Always try to choose foods which contain no additives.**

According to the Food and Drug Administration, there are about 2800 food additives. In addition, there are environmental pollutants: pesticides, antibiotics, moulds, organic (i.e., carbon-based) pollutants such as PBCs and DDT, heavy metals, acid rain, etc.[1]

In order **to reduce this chemical potion considerably,** let's stop buying refined and processed foods, delicatessen meats, etc., and instead, **choose whole grains, legumes, nuts and seeds, fresh fruits, and vegetables.**

In so doing, it is important to adopt the following practices:

- Read labels carefully.

- Demand products of organic quality, i.e., grown without the use of chemical products (fertilizers and pesticides).

- Become active in issues relating to the the environment and foods.

LET'S LEARN TO DEMAND QUALITY. NOTHING CREATES MORE LIFE THAN LIFE ITSELF!

Do not forget that eating is a ritual as well as a pleasure to be shared with others.

PROGRESSIVE CHANGES

Adopting each of these new habits is a sucessful accomplishment in itself. Very quickly your body and mind will feel the benefits, and at the same time you will solve certain health problems, including excess weight.

VARIETY, MODERATION, AND
EVOLUTIONARY CHANGE

NOTE : When it is too difficult to give up a certain eating habit, concentrate on acquiring a better one, until the former habit gradually disappears for lack of room in your diet; for example :

- Eat raw fruit or vegetables, or drink water every time you feel the urge for sugar or coffee.

- Eat more vegetable proteins (grains, legumes) in order to reduce your consumption of meat.

- **Drink water instead of nibbling.**

- Before going to bed, go for a walk, instead of eating.

HERE'S AN IDEA FOR KEEPING YOUR BODY CLEAN :

- Spend one day per week on a diet of juice = 52 days per year = 1 year per 7 year period.

- Drink only healthy juices prepared with a juice extractor, every two hours if necessary. Juice can be digested in 15 minutes.

A CLEANSING AND BENEFICIAL REST
FOR THE DIGESTIVE SYSTEM !

CHAPTER 2

A Glance
at Different
Nutritional
Philosophies

As soon as we take an interest in the quality of our diet, we discover that there are different philosophies or doctrines on the subject, and that they often seem to be contradictory.

A healthful nutritional diet implies a global concept of change. Opting for one or the other of these different philosophies makes us take more specific steps; it requires that we seek knowledge through more profound study and research, for we are all different and each of us must come to grips with his or her own heredity, antecedents, energy potential, and milieu.

On the whole, these different dietary theories use the same basic products (grains, legumes, nuts and seeds,

vegetables, fruits, etc.). However, these products are prepared differently (left raw or cooked), distributed throughout the menu in a different way, and are used in different proportions, depending on the diet. All of these philosophies recognize and insist on the importance of air (breathing, exercise), water, and light as health factors.

Here then, for information's sake, is a summary description of each of these philosophies :

VEGETARIANISM

Includes products of the vegetable kingdom only: whole grains, legumes, nuts, seeds, vegetables, fruits. It can be subdivided as follows :

- **Lacto-ovo vegetarianism :** Includes by-products of the animal kingdom such as milk products and eggs.

- **Semi-vegetarianism :** Includes milk products and eggs from the animal kingdom, along with occasional poultry and fish.

- **Strict vegetarianism or veganism :** Excludes all products and by-products which do not come from the vegetable kingdom (meat, milk products, eggs, honey).

HYGIENISM

A vegetarian diet in which the menu is defined according to a set of rules governing the combinations in which foods should be eaten, and where fasting with water plays an essential role in the prevention of disease and in healing. Here it is advocated that food be eaten raw.

MACROBIOTICS

A diet based on grains, mainly whole rice, which is used to balance the yin and the yang. Here milk products are replaced by seaweed; occasionally, fish is eaten. Here it is recommended that food be cooked.

LIVING FOOD DIET

A vegetarian diet based on raw foods: sprouts, nuts, seeds, fresh and lacto-fermented vegetables, wheatgrass juice, other green vegetable juices, rejuvelac, etc. It is also called the " Raw Food Diet ".

IT IS ESSENTIAL TO BE WELL-INFORMED AND
FLEXIBLE AND TO MAKE GRADUAL PROGRESS,
WHEN UNDERTAKING TO CHANGE.

CHAPTER 3

The Needs of the Human Body

In industrialized countries, malnutrition is caused not by a lack of food, but rather by a lack of nutritional elements in the food that is eaten. It is therefore very important to choose the foods you eat in order to avoid any deficiencies.

OBJECTIVE

To inform the reader clearly and simply about the following:

- **The nutritional needs of the body.**

- **The best sources of nutrients as well as the role that they play.**

- **The body's energy (calorific) needs.**

Don't forget that to be in top form and to enjoy all the strength and power that good health brings with it, the following factors must also be taken into consideration: deep breathing, exercise, your ability to relax, and positive thinking: prospectively, an attractive program, don't you think?

Nutrients

Food is composed of nutrients, which the body needs in specific quantities :

1. **Carbohydrates and all the sugars of which they are composed.**
2. **Lipids and the fatty acids which make them up.**
3. **Proteins and the amino acids of which they are composed.**
4. **Vitamins.**
5. **Minerals and trace elements.**
6. **Water.**

ROLES

1. Fuel used to provide energy and heat.
   a) Carbohydrates (starch and sugars).
   b) Lipids (fats).

2. Materials used for construction and maintenance.
   a) Proteins (animal and vegetable).
   b) Mineral salts.
   c) Water.

3. Substances used to regulate body functions
   a) Vitamins.
   b) Mineral salts.
   c) Fiber.
   d) Water.

WHY DO WE NEED TO EAT?

To ensure the following :

- **Full growth and maintenance of the body.**

- **Physical and psychic development.**

NEEDS OF THE BODY

- **Immunity.**

- **The survival of the species.**

It is not just to satisfy our hunger, whence the importance of the QUALITY of the food that we eat.

- The human body is composed of more than 100,000 different substances; 45 of them cannot be produced by the organism. **They must be obtained from food.**

1. Carbohydrates:

Sugar, Starch, and Fiber

DEFINITION

- Carbohydrates are molecules resulting from a specific combination of carbon (C) , hydrogen (H), and oxygen (O). They can be classified into three groups: simple, double, and complex (see the table on the next page).

- Carbohydrates are absorbed by the small intestine in the form of glucose (simple sugar). Double and complex sugars must be transformed by digestion before being absorbed.

- During their combustion (metabolism), carbohydrates release 4 kilocalories/ gram or 17 kilojoules/ gram (metric system).

ROLES

- Main source of energy for the body.

- OUR MAIN FUEL: readily available, economical, and essential.

- Glucose constitutes the only form of energy that can be used by the brain.

- Allow us to make better use of lipids.

- Help the liver function properly.

- Favor the absorption of proteins.

- Favor proper elimination through the favorable action they exert on the intestinal flora (dietary fiber).

  OUR BODY FUNCTIONS ON A COOPERATIVE BASIS.

THE EFFECTS ON HEALTH OF A DIET WHICH IS TOO RICH IN CARBOHYDRATES

- **Obesity may develop.** The body stores only a small part of glucose in the liver and muscles, in the form of glycogen. When the body takes in more calories than it uses, the excess is transformed into fat and stored in the adipose tissues.

- **Overworking of the liver and pancreas.**When normal blood glucose concentration is upset by too high a level of sugar in the blood, the pancreas secretes a hormone, insulin, to reduce the concentration.

- **It causes dental caries**, when substances which stick to the teeth are involved (sweets, bread, dried fruits).

CATEGORIES	SOURCES
1. Simple carbohydrates (monosaccharides) - glucose - fructose - galactose	fruits, vegetables, honey
2. Double carbohydrates (disaccharides) - sucrose or saccharose - lactose - maltose	cane and beet sugar, syrup, molasses milk malt (syrup, powder)

Note: Sugars which are too concentrated are rapidly absorbed and should be avoided because they upset normal blood glucose concentration (100 mg of glucose / 100 ml of blood) and fatigue the liver and pancreas.

3. Complex carbohydrates (polysaccharides) - starch - dextrine	legumes, whole grains starchy root vegetables flours and roasted grains

Note: Starch is an excellent source of glucose, and therefore of energy. If accompanied by fibers, starch is assimilated on a continuous basis, because complex carbohydrates must be broken down into simple sugars before being absorbed. They interfere less with blood glucose concentration.

- Fiber
  (cannot be
  assimilated)
	bran from grains
	vegetables, fruits (peels)
	legumes

REMARKS

- Fresh fruits contain 10 - 20% simple sugars.
- Dried fruits contain 60 - 90% simple sugars.
- Vegetables (except potatoes) 5 -15% simple sugars.
- Honey contains 85% simple sugars.
  N.B.: Simple sugars=simple carbohydrates are absorbed rapidly.

- Sugar contains 99% sucrose.
- Cow's milk contains 4.9% lactose.
  N.B. Refined sugars contain little or no protective elements (vitamins, minerals) nor constructive elements (proteins). They are empty calories.
- Double sugars are also absorbed rapidly.

- Grains contain 65 - 80% starch.

- The bulk of the energy provided by grains comes from their starch content.

- Potatoes contain 20% starch.

  N.B. Starch is absorbed slowly, especially if accompanied by fibers.

- **Fibers**, which are essential to the proper functioning of the intestine, are composed of an ensemble of complex carbohydrates that cannot be assimilated.

CARBOHYDRATES

SOME THOUGHTS ON SUGAR

In North America annual sugar consumption per individual is much too high. This sugar comes in large part from refined, processed products such as candies, commercial biscuits and cakes, ice cream, canned and bottled goods, carbonated beverages, refined grains, etc.

At the beginning of the century, we derived our fuel, or our source of energy, from complex carbohydrates (starch) found in grains, legumes, and potatoes. Today sweet, fatty and refined foods provide for our needs. At what price?

In its eagerness to make profits, the sugar industry puts out massive publicity in order to convince us, both children and adults, that sugar is an excellent source of energy.

Beware of this false, deceptive advertising.

IN FACT, WHAT IS OUR BEST SOURCE OF ENERGY?

STARCH (complex sugar)

It is transformed into a simple sugar (glucose), 90% of which can be used by the body. It is assimilated gradually over a period of 4 to 8 hours (particularly when accompanied by fiber) and thus prevents the blood from becoming overloaded with glucose.

What are our best sources of starch?

Grains, legumes, and root vegetables. These foods also provide proteins, minerals, and B complex vitamins (needed for the absorption of glucose), as well as fiber. Refined sugar is completely devoid of all these nutritional treasures.

What's more, grains, legumes, and root vegetables offer the following advantages:

- They are easy to grow in our climate.

- They are inexpensive to grow or to buy.

- They are veritable natural preserves, which remain in good condition, as is, without cooking or sugar, for a long time.

The habit of eating a great deal of sugar will seriously disrupt a person's physical and mental health.

It is not necessary for us to add sugar to our food, because several foods (grains, starchy foods, fruits) already contain sugar. By eating more whole grains, which contain a large quantity of complex carbohydrates (starch), we can more easily break the dessert habit. In addition, the more fresh foods we eat, the less sugar we eat.

We acquire good and bad eating habits when we are young, whence the importance of making our children aware, of informing them, and of setting a good example for them.

DID YOU KNOW?

- Sugar is the additive which is used most during the industrial processing of foods. It is hidden almost everywhere behind several identities: watch out for all those words ending in "-ose" such as sucrose, dextrose, etc., or in "-ol" such as sorbitol, mannitol, etc.

- Packaged breakfast cereals contain from 0.1% to 56% sugar and often children, as well as adults, add extra sugar.

  - Puffed rice: 0,1%   -   Raisin Bran: 29%
  - Life: 16%   -   Sugar Smacks: 56%
  - All Bran: 19%

- Brown sugar, which is erroneously considered to be less refined, is, in fact, white sugar, coloured with molasses!

CARBOHYDRATES

Just for the record, here is the equivalence, in terms of teaspoons, of the amount of sugar found in a few commonly eaten products.

PRODUCTS	Sugar content in teaspoons
1 piece of chocolate cake with icing	15
10 oz. of soda pop (carbonated beverage)	8
1 chocolate bar	7
1/2 cup of commercial yogurt containing fruit	6 1/2
8 oz. of chocolate milk	6
8 oz. of Kool-aid	6
1/2 cup of ice cream	5 - 6
1 plain donut	4
1 tablespoon of jam	3
1 tablespoon of ketchup	1
1 piece of chewing gum	1/2

All of these data come from studies conducted by the United States Department of Agriculture.

About Fibers

The term fiber refers to those parts of a plant (the vegetable kingdom) which cannot be assimilated by our bodies, because we do not have the enzymes needed to digest them.

They include the following:

Water-insoluble fibers

- cellulose
- hemicellulose*
- lignins

Water-soluble fibers

- pectins
- gums
- mucilages

* Certain kinds of hemicellulose are water-soluble, while others are not.

ROLES

- Fibers prevent constipation.

  - Their volume stimulates peristalsis (movement of the digestive tube); they do away with intestinal laziness and putrefaction.

- Their capacity to absorb water increases the volume of stools and gives them a softer consistency.

- A complete trip through the digestive system, from entrance to exit, takes an average of 36 hours for a bolus which is rich in fibers, and 78 hours, or more, for one which is devoid of fibers.

- According to the Canadian Cancer Society, fibers protect against cancers of the colon and rectum.[1]

- They can help prevent haemorrhoids and sicknesses of the diverticula.

- They reduce the amount of food consumed, while providing an impression of satiety.

- They encourage better mastication.

- The water-soluble fibers permit more regular absorption of glucose into the blood.

- Certain varieties of fiber water-soluble such as oat bran, pectin from carrots and fruit, and the gum found in legumes contribute to reducing cholesterol, because they have the capacity to eliminate biliary salts which are composed of cholesterol.[2, 3]

RECOMMENDED QUANTITY

The Consultative Committee on Fibers, composed of Canadian experts, as well as the National Cancer Institute of the United States, recommends the absorption of 30 g of

fiber per day. Current consumption is about 3 g to 15 g per day. **Consequently, increasing and varying fiber intake is imperative**.

In order to avoid discomfort and intestinal gases, increase your fiber intake gradually and make sure that you drink sufficient quantities of water (6-8 glasses per day). Fibers absorb water.

SOURCES

Whole grains, legumes, flax seeds, raw fruits and vegetables, and sprouts. Vary your sources; bran is not the only source of fiber.

2. Lipids: Fats, Oils, Lecithin, and Cholesterol

DEFINITION

- Lipids (derived from the Greek word *lipos,* meaning "fat") are molecules resulting from a specific combination of carbon, hydrogen, and oxygen (CHO).

- They contain the essential fatty acids.

- They are digested and absorbed in the small intestine, in the form of fatty acids and glycerol.

Bile from the liver breaks fats into fine particles (emulsion) so that the enzymes can digest them (in the small intestine).

KINDS

- There are three kinds of fatty acids: saturated, monounsaturated, and polyunsaturated.

- During their combustion (metabolism) lipids release 9

kilocalories per gram or 37 kilojoules per gram (metric system); that is, over double the energy of carbohydrates and proteins.

ROLES

- To provide a concentrated source of energy (9 kilocalories per gram).

- To aid in the transport and absorption of fat-soluble vitamins (A,D,E,K).

- To ensure that we have reserves of energy (adipose tissue).

- To provide essential fatty acids (EFA).

- To insulate and protect certain organs such as the liver, heart, and nerves.

- To provide a sensation of satiety by slowing down digestion in the stomach.

- To help maintain body temperature.

- To enhance the flavor and texture of foods.

DESCRIPTION

A. Saturated fatty acids

```
      H  H  H  H  H  H
      |  |  |  |  |  |
H- C- C- C- C- C- C- COOH
      |  |  |  |  |  |
      H  H  H  H  H  H
```

- They are mainly of animal origin.

- They are solid at room temperature.

- They contain no double bonds.

- They do not provide essential fatty acids, which are polyunsaturated.

NOTE: Usually, foods which are rich in saturated fats also contain cholesterol.

LIPIDS

Sources of Saturated Fatty Acids

Meat, poultry, butter, chocolate, cheese, milk, egg yolk, palm and coconut oil, and hydrogenated vegetable fat.

B. Mono- and Polyunsaturated Fatty Acids

```
    H  H  H  H  H  H              H  H  H  H  H  H
    |  |  |  |  |  |              |  |  |  |  |  |
H- C- C- C= C- C- C- R       H- C- C= C- C= C- C- R
    |  |     |  |              |              |
    H  H     H  H              H              H
```

1 double bond   2, 3, or 4 double bonds

- They are mainly of vegetable origin.

- They are liquid at room temperature.

- They provide the essential fatty acids.

- They go rancid more easily than saturated fatty acids because of their double bonds which can react to oxygen, heat, and light.

Sources of Mono- and Polyunsaturated Fatty Acids :

Monounsaturated

avocado
canola oil
cashews
peanuts and peanut oil
peanut butter
olives and olive oil

Polyunsaturated

safflower oil
sunflower seeds and
sunflower oil
almonds
soybeans and soy oil
corn oil

About Essential Fatty Acids (EFA)

- Two kinds of polyunsaturated fatty acids—linoleic and linolenic acid–are called "essential" because the body

needs them, but cannot produce them itself. Therefore, they must be obtained from dietary sources.

- They contribute to maintaining healthy skin.

- They regulate the permeability of the membrane of each of our cells.

- They promote a reduction in the level of blood choles-terol.

- Essential fatty acids must be eaten every day; it is also essential to reduce the consumption of saturated fatty acids.

- When eaten in excess quantities, they can be harmful.

- They are fragile, if heated to high temperatures, or if they come into contact with air or light.

Sources of Essential Fatty Acids (EFA)

- Safflower, sunflower, and sesame seeds; flax seeds; soybeans; corn; and cold-pressed oils thereof.

NOTE : Certain authors call the essential fatty acids vitamin F. However, strictly speaking, they are not vitamins.

Needs

- 2 teaspoons (10 ml) per day of a good-quality cold-pressed oil. However, it is best to use nuts, seeds, and butters.

THE EFFECTS ON HEALTH OF A DIET WHICH IS TOO RICH IN LIPIDS
(particularly insofar as saturated fatty acids and cholesterol are concerned).

- Obesity, because lipids release more than twice as many kilocalories (9 kcal/g) as carbohydrates and proteins (4 kcal/g).

- As in the case of cholesterol, they are associated with atherosclerosis, arteriosclerosis, and heart diseases.[4]

- Colon and breast cancers, and endometrium cancers of the uterus are related to the overconsumption of animal fats.

DIFFERENT TYPES OF FATS

Dietary fat	% Total lipids	% Saturated fat	% Monoun-saturated fat	% Polyun-saturated fat
Canola Oil	100	7	**62**	31
Coconut Oil	100	**92**	6	2
Corn Oil	100	13	25	**62**
Flax Oil	100	10	18	**71**
Olive Oil	100	14	**77**	9
Palm Oil	100	**51**	39	10
Palm Kernel Oil	100	**86**	12	2
Peanut Oil	100	18	**48**	34
Safflower Oil	100	9	13	**78**
Sesame Oil	100	15	41	**44**
Soy Oil	100	15	24	**61**
Sunflower Oil	100	11	20	**69**
Walnut Oil	100	10	20	**70**
Milk	3,5	**2,1**	1	trace
Cheddar cheese	33	**21**	10	trace
Butter	81	**50**	24	4
Soft margarine	81	14	29	**35**
Egg	10	3,2	3,8	1,4
Egg Yolk	31	3,2	3,8	1,4
Soybeans	17	3	4	**9**
Tofu	4	1	1	**2**

Source : U.S. Department of Agriculture

NOTE: The overconsumption of meat and animal by-products, which are rich in saturated fats and cholesterol, is a cause for concern; considering the possible consequences of such overconsumption will lead us to change our eating habits without delay. It is worth noting that products from the **vegetable kingdom** contain a large proportion of unsaturated fats; what's more, they **contain no cholesterol**.

LIPIDS

C. CHOLESTEROL

- It already exists in the body (in the brain, liver, blood, etc.).

- It is produced by the liver.

- It comes exclusively from animal sources; vegetables do not contain cholesterol.

- Excess blood cholesterol is associated with the development of arteriosclerosis (hardening of the arteries) and atherosclerosis (thickening of the walls of the arteries).

Roles

- It forms a part of the membrane of cells and certain tissues.

- Cholesterol is one of the constituents of bile, which is used to divide up fats into fine droplets during their digestion in the small intestine.

- It is used to make vitamin D and sex hormones.

Needs

- The liver produces up to 1000 mg (1 g) of cholesterol per day to satisfy the needs of the body.

- It is not necessary to eat cholesterol; however, a maximum intake of 300 mg per day may be tolerated (a single large egg yolk contains 252 mg).

Sources

- There is a very large quantity in giblets (liver, brain, kidneys, etc.). Egg yolks, oysters, and fish eggs contain cholesterol, as do milk products (in lesser quantities).

According to the most recent studies, it is the total quantity of fats that a person eats–especially saturated fats–more than foods which are rich in cholesterol that raises the blood cholesterol level. Let's prevent cardiovascular accidents and other disorders which are linked to heavy consumption of foods with a high saturated fat and cholesterol content. How?

- By reducing your consumption of saturated fatty acids (meat and animal by-products). This will reduce your dietary cholesterol.

- By eating products from the vegetable kingdom, which contain monounsaturated fats and essential fatty acids (olives, nuts, seeds, and legumes), vitamins, minerals, and soluble fibers (vegetables, whole fruits and grains).

- Get lots of exercise.

D. LECITHIN

Roles

- Lecithin forms a part of the membrane of cells and nerve tissues.

- It emulsifies fats in the digestive tract and the circulatory system.

- It facilitates the circulation of lipids in the blood.[5]

Sources

- Soybeans, egg yolks, sesame seeds, and whole grains.

Foods	Quantity	Cholesterol
Beef liver	3 ounces	372 mg
Beef kidneys	3 ounces	315 mg
Hot dogs	2 ounces	112 mg
Pork (lean)	3 ounces	75 mg
Veal (lean)	3 ounces	84 mg
1 egg (yolk)	1 large	252 mg
Chicken (white meat)	3 ounces	65 mg
Canned shrimps	3 ounces	128 mg
Butter	1 tablespoon	35 mg
Cream cheese	1 ounce	31 mg
Hard cheese	1 ounce	24 to 28 mg
Ice cream	1/2 cup	27 mg
Whole milk	1 cup	34 mg

* Source: A study by the United States Department of Agriculture.

THE VEGETABLE KINGDOM CONTAINS NO CHOLESTEROL.

3. Proteins: Amino Acids

DEFINITION

- Proteins (from the Greek word *prôtos* meaning "first") are large molecules made up of smaller molecules called amino acids.

- They are composed of 4 elements: carbon (C), hydrogen (H), oxygen (O), and nitrogen (N), or CHON.

- They may also contain other elements such as sulphur and phosphorus, depending on their nature.

- Our body contains approximately 10,000 to 50,000 different proteins, each of which has a specific role.

- Proteins are digested in the stomach and the small intestine where they are absorbed in the form of amino acids.

- Proteins release 4 kilocalories per gram or 17 kilojoules per gram (metric system) during combustion (metabolism).

ROLES

- Proteins are used for building, maintaining, and repairing cells: bodily growth, the growth of hair and nails, cell renewal, and the repair of injured tissues.

- Enzymes, antibodies, and certain hormones are proteins.

Here are some examples of proteins found in the body:

- immunoglobulin (antibodies),

- hemoglobin (responsible for the transport of oxygen in the blood),

- melanin (pigment found in the skin),

- albumin (present in liquids and tissues),

- insulin (hormone secreted by the pancreas),

- keratin (substance of which body hair and nails are composed),

- pepsin (digestive enzyme found in the stomach),

- trypsin (digestive enzyme found in the pancreas).

Vegetable			Animal	
Legumes	**20-30%**		Cheese	**24%**
Nuts and Seeds	**15%**		Roast beef	**24%**
Cereals	**10-15%**		Meat	**20%**
Bread	**7%**		Fish	**16%**
Dried Seaweed	**7%**	(kombu)	Eggs	**13%**
	20-30%	(dulse)		
	35%	(nori)		

Daily intake: on an average an adult requires 0.8 grams of protein per kilogram of ideal weight.[7]

- In periods of growth, during pregnancy or breast-feeding, or when tissues have been injured, the body's protein and amino acid requirements increase.

- Since the body does not store proteins, it is necessary to eat some every day.

- Animal proteins are complete proteins, i.e. they contain all the essential amino acids.

- Vegetable proteins complete one another. See the chapter on protein complementarity.

DID YOU KNOW?

- Exercise and intense physical work do not increase our need for protein except when the purpose of these exercises is to increase muscle mass (body building). What is most important is to make sure that we get the calories that our body needs by eating a greater number of complex carbohydrates (starch).

It is essential to choose our sources of calories well.

- Meat eaten as a source of protein contains a lot of hidden fat, a few vitamins and minerals, but no fibers.

- Legumes and grains prove to be excellent sources of protein, which are well supplied with complex carbohydrates (starch), vitamins, minerals, and fibers. **They are the logical choice!**

WHY NOT EAT THEM MORE OFTEN?

- The savings obtained through buying vegetable rather than animal proteins will allow you to buy more fruits and vegetables.

- The overconsumption of sugar and meat (excess protein, saturated fatty acids, and cholesterol) is closely linked to the increase of such contemporary diseases as cancer, cardiovascular disorders, hypertension, diabetes, obesity, kidney ailments, etc.

- **The dietary habits of the industrial world bring with them ecological, political, and humanitarian consequences which are very harmful for the planet as a whole:**

  - The use of arable land to support livestock: two thirds of the grain grown in the United States goes into feeding livestock.

  - The wasting of protein resources: six pounds of grain and soya protein are required to produce one pound of beef.

  - Energy-consuming production methods (irrigation, machinery, transportation, etc.).

  - The arable lands used to produce crops for export are controlled by large foreign companies in countries where the population is undernourished. The production of soybeans for American livestock, as well as

sugar and coffee for the American consumer are detrimental to local food-producing crops, which could provide for the nutritional needs of the peoples of these countries.

- It is estimated that in North America each person consumes twice as many proteins as he needs each day.

This means that each individual eats an average of 63 lb (140 kg) of meat and dairy products per year. In underdeveloped countries people scarcely eat more than 2 lb (1 kg) per year![8]

During his lifetime (70 years), a North American with a meat-eating diet eats 12 cows, 29 pigs, 2 lambs, 1 calf, 37 turkeys, 984 chickens, and 910 pounds of fish!

THE EFFECTS ON HEALTH OF A DIET WHICH IS TOO RICH IN PROTEINS:

- Overloading of the liver, which must transform them, and of the kidneys and the intestines, which must eliminate the nitrogenous waste products.

- Poisoning of the blood and cells: they become loaded with uric acid, a nitrogenous waste product from the amino acids.

- Fouling of the large intestine, if too many proteins are not digested.

- Obesity. If too many calories are available, part of the excess changes into fat and is stored away.

- Overconsumption of proteins leads to an increase in the excretion of calcium by the kidneys into the urine, which can contribute to the formation of kidney stones. What's more, the loss of calcium from the bones contributes to osteoporosis (porous bones).[9]

In short, a diet composed of vegetable proteins (grains, legumes, nuts, and seeds) keeps the body's kidneys, liver, and bones in good health.

ABOUT ENERGY NEEDS (KILOCALORIES)

- The quantity and the quality of the energy which we have are closely linked to those of our food (fuel) and combustion (oxygen: breathing, exercise).

$$FUEL + O_2 \xrightarrow[\text{metabolism}]{\text{combustion}} CO_2 + H_2O + ENERGY$$

food + oxygen   carbon dioxide + water + kcal.

- Carbohydrates (4 kcal/g), lipids (9 kcal/g), and proteins (4 kcal/g) from the food we eat provide energy for the body. Vitamins and minerals, which are essential to good health, do not provide energy.

ENERGY

- ensures basic metabolism,
- maintains body temperature,
- allows the muscles, nerves, and brain to function,
- ensures growth.

- We have always used the term "kilocalorie" (British system) to measure energy. Nowadays the term "kilojoule" (metric system) is used in literature.

  1 kilocalorie = 1000 calories = 1 Calorie (large calorie) = 4.14 kilojoules.

- Energy needs vary according to body surface, weight, age, rate of growth, sex, lifestyle, climate, and, above all, physical activity, whence the need to adjust our meals to suit our own reality.

- From the age of 25 to 50, an average intake of 2000 calories (8400 kilojoules) per day is recommended for women, and of 2700 calories (11,200 kilojoules) for men.[10]

- If you eat too many calories, the excess will be converted into fat. It doesn't matter if these calories come from carbohydrates, lipids, or proteins.

- To maintain our body weight, the amount of food (kcalories) we eat must be equal to the energy we expend! Simple, isn't it?

4. Water

Water is indispensable for **life**.

Our body contains about 65% water.

ROLES

- Essential constituent of body fluids: blood, lymph, and secretions of the tissues. It is a part of all tissues.

- Helps the body to regularize its temperature (perspiration, transpiration, respiration).

- Essential for the transport of nutrients and waste products.

- Contributes to excretion of wastes by the kidneys*, the skin, the lungs, and the intestine.

- Improves the quality of tissues such as those of the skin.

- Combats fatigue, headaches, hunger.

* The thousands of filters with which the kidneys are equipped use water to function. This is why it is important to drink lots of water.

NEEDS

- Each day we eliminate an average of 2 quarts (2 liters) of water (through the lungs, skin, intestines, kidneys, lachrymal glands, etc.).

- These losses must be replaced; hence we must drink 6-8 large glasses of water per day.

SOURCES

- Pure spring water.

- Water contained in food.

WHEN SHOULD WE DRINK?

- At least 15 minutes before meals.

- At least 2 hours after meals.

- Spread out water intake over the whole day: when you get up, before and after meals, and at bedtime.

REDISCOVER THE PLEASURE OF DRINKING
WATER. IT IS A QUESTION OF HEALTH!

DRINK TO YOUR HEALTH!

WATER

5. Vitamins

- Vitamins are molecules which we need in minute quantities. They are absolutely necessary to ensure that the body functions properly.

- Since vitamins cannot be produced by the body (except for vitamin D during exposure to the sun), they must be obtained from the food we eat.

NOTE : To a certain extent, the bacteria in healthy intestinal flora can produce the B vitamins (folacin and vitamin B_{12}) and vitamin K.

- Vitamins are classified into 2 groups: those that are water-soluble (B and C) and those that are fat-soluble (A,D,E, and K).

ROLES

- Vitamins have specific functions. Each one plays a particular role.

- They are neither a source of calories nor a construction material, but rather very precise regulators of bodily functions.

- They permit certain reactions to take place; for example, vitamin D allows calcium to be absorbed; vitamin C promotes the use of iron.

- They play an essential role in growth and the protection of the body.

SOURCES

A varied diet which abounds in foods of vegetable origin (grains, legumes, nuts, seeds, fruits, and vegetables) covers all of our vitamin needs.

However, vitamin deficiencies are increasingly frequent for the following reasons:

- Produce being picked before it is ripe.

- Methods and length of storage.

- Refining, processing, and cooking of foods.

- Diets containing too much meat and sugar, etc.

Natural vitamin supplements alone cannot correct a vitamin deficiency. An excess of vitamin pills can be damaging to health, especially in the case of fat-soluble vitamins which the body can stock.

Let's eat a variety of whole, living, organically grown foods. Let's do away with refined, processed, and canned foods.

VITAMINS

VITAMINS	MAIN ROLES
B complex (8)	**They act together.**
B$_1$ thiamin B$_2$ riboflavin B$_3$ niacin B$_5$ pantothenic acid B$_6$ pyridoxine Biotin Folic acid (folacin) B$_{12}$ cobalamin	- They release the energy of carbohydrates. - They are essential for growth and healthy skin and eyes. - They help the nervous system to function properly. - They allow the production of genetic material. - They play a role in the forming of red corpuscles and the fixing of iron in hemoglobin.
VITAMIN C (ascorbic acid)	- It is indispensable for growth. - It plays a role in the formation of bones and teeth. - It contributes to the healing of wounds. - It increases resistance to infections. - It promotes the absorption of iron.
Vegetable source: **PROVITAMIN A** (beta-carotene) **Animal source:** **VITAMIN A** (retinol)	- They promote the health of the skin, hair, and mucous membranes. - They help night vision. - They are essential for skeletal growth, the forming of the teeth, and for reproduction.
VITAMIN D (calciferol)	- It is essential for the growth and health of bones and teeth. - It promotes the absorption of calcium and phosphorus.
VITAMIN E (tocopherol)	- It is an antioxidizing agent which prevents the oxidation of polyunsaturated fatty acids. - It contributes to the formation of red blood corpuscles, muscles, and other tissues.
VITAMIN K	- It is essential for the coagulation of blood. - It contributes to keeping bones healthy.

Water-soluble

Fat-soluble

DIETARY SOURCES

- brewer's and nutritional yeast (B_1, B_2, and B_3)
- whole grains (bran and germ) and whole grain bread
- legumes
- green vegetables
- sprouts
- dairy and animal products (B_2, B_{12})

NOTE : Vitamin B_1, folic acid and vitamin B_{12} can be produced by healthy intestinal flora.

- green peppers
- green vegetables: broccoli, cabbage, parsley
- citrus fruits and the juice thereof
- berries
- yellow fruits

NOTE: 1 cigarette destroys 25mg of vitamin C.

- very colorful green and yellow vegetables: spinach, carrots
- yellow fruits: apricots, cantaloupe
- spirulina
- egg yolks
- dairy products
- liver

- the sun's ultraviolet rays
- fortified milk
- egg yolks
- liver, fish

- wheat germ and the oil thereof
- nuts and seeds and the oil thereof
- whole-grain products
- sprouted grains (wheat)
- egg yolks, butter, liver

- leafy green vegetables
- egg yolks, liver
- soy oil

NOTE: Vitamin K is produced by bacteria in the intestinal flora.

DID YOU KNOW?

- Vitamin A, which is soluble in fats, exists only in the animal kingdom. However, in the vegetable kingdom we find provitamin A in the orangy pigments of carotene; the body transforms it into vitamin A. In green vegetables chlorophyll masks the beta-carotene.

- Green vegetables such as spinach, broccoli, green peppers, cabbage, and parsley as well as orange vegetables like carrots, pumpkins, sweet potatoes, and red peppers are excellent sources of vitamins A and C and of iron. The more intense the color, the more vitamins there are.

- Water-soluble vitamins B and C (except B_{12}) are not stored in the body. Therefore, they must be obtained daily from the food we eat.

- Fat-soluble vitamins (A, D,E, and K) are stored mainly in the liver.

- The best source of vitamin D is undoubtedly exposure to the sun. Go outside as often as possible. During the winter, let your hands and face get some sun.

- Eating sugar, since it is lacking in B vitamins, increases our need for them. It not only supplies no vitamins, but creates a greater need for them!

- B complex vitamins act interdependently with one another. Taking supplements of one of the B group of vitamins can create an imbalance. It is preferable to eat whole grains.

- In order to avoid excessive loss of vitamins, thaw out frozen foods in the refrigerator and not on the counter.

- Potatoes, when cooked whole and unpeeled, retain more vitamin C than if they are cut in two. The more they are cut up, the greater the loss of vitamins.

- Vitamin C oxidizes easily. It is preferable therefore to cut up vegetables at the last minute, using a stainless steel knife or grater. Salads and juices should be covered, and foods, eaten as fresh as possible. Vitamin B_1, (thiamin) and vitamin A are also sensitive to oxidation.

- Vitamins B and C (water-soluble) are more sensitive to heat, cooking, and lengthy storage than are fat-soluble vitamins. Avoid soaking and cooking vegetables in water.

- When exposed to light, certain vitamins (A, B_2 or riboflavin, K) lose their properties; consequently, milk and bread must be stored in opaque containers.

VITAMINS

STORAGE OF VITAMINS

VITAMIN	CONDITIONS OF STABILITY	SENSITIVE TO	DESTROYED BY
Vitamin C (the most fragile)	Freezing Acidity	Storage	Air, heat, cooking, alkalinity, iron and copper from pots, water, light. 1 cigarette destroys 25 mg; stress increases need
B vitamins Thiamin B_1 Riboflavin B_2 Niacin B_3 Pyridoxine B_6 Folic acid B_{12}	B_1: acid environment, freezing, light B_2: heat, acidity B_3: the most stable B_{12}: heat	B_6: light, heat, alkaline environment B_{12}: acidity, alkalinity, air	Air (O_2), heat, cooking, alkalinity, water, caffeine B_{12}: light
Vitamin A	Heat, cooking, freezing		Air (O_2), high temperature, drying, light
Vitamin D	Heat, oxidation	Storage in milk powder	
Vitamin E	Heat, acid environment		Rancidity, alkalinity, air, light, iron, lead, bleaching with peroxides (flour), freezing
Vitamin K	Heat	Oxidation	Alkalinity, UV rays.

6. Minerals and Trace Elements

- Generally, minerals are found in the form of salts.

- About 4% of human body weight is made up of minerals.

- They are essential and are divided up as follows:

    - Those which we need in large quantities: calcium (Ca), phosphorus (P), magnesium (Mg), sodium (Na), potassium (K), chlorine (Cl), and sulfur (S).

    - Those which we need in minute quantities; they are called trace elements (see the table).

- **Our food must provide all of these minerals.**

ROLES

- They play many roles; we are constantly discovering new facts about minerals.

- Certain minerals (sodium, chlorine, and potassium) are responsible for maintaining the body's water content at the right level.

- They neutralize excess acidity, ensuring an acid/base balance.

- They interact with vitamins in order to permit certain bodily reactions to take place.

    IN SHORT, IT'S ALL A MATTER OF TEAMWORK!

MINERALS	MAIN ROLES
CALCIUM chemical symbol: Ca	- The most abundant mineral in the body: used in the construction of bones and teeth. - Promotes correct functioning of the nervous system (relaxation, sleep). - Indispensable for coagulation of the blood and muscle tone. - Maintains cardiac rhythm.
PHOSPHORUS P	- Helps in the construction of bones and teeth. - Involved in the production of energy.
MAGNESIUM Mg	- Constituent of bones and teeth. - Provides resistance to infections and cancer. - Promotes peristaltic activity.
POTASSIUM K	- Regulates the water content of cells (internal). - Plays a role in the control of the blood's pH level.
SODIUM Na	- Regulates the body's water level. - Plays a role in the control of the blood's pH level.
CHLORINE Cl	- A buffer for the blood's pH level. - Is a constituent of hydrochloric acid (HCl) found in the stomach.

DIETARY SOURCES

- dairy products
- butter and whole sesame seeds
- green leafy vegetables: broccoli, savoy cabbage
- almonds and hazelnuts
- tofu

- brewer's yeast
- dairy products
- legumes and whole grains
- nuts

- legumes (especially soy)
- whole grains
- nuts (cashews, almonds), seeds
- dark green vegetables

NOTE: Mg is lost during the processing of grains.

- fresh and dried fruits
- starchy vegetables
- dark-colored vegetables
- legumes, grains

NOTE: Processed foods contains too much sodium.

- salt, tamari soy sauce
- dulse, kelp (seaweed)
- cheese
- olives in brine

- salt (NaCl), tamari soy sauce
- peanuts, hazelnuts
- egg white
- vegetables: broccoli, cabbage, parsley, watercress, onions

TRACE ELEMENTS   MAIN ROLES

IRON Fe	- Essential to the making of hemoglobin, the constituent of red corpuscles which transports oxygen and carbon dioxide. - Increases resistance to stress and disease.
COPPER Cu	- Necessary for the absorption of iron - Present in all tissues.
FLUORINE F	- Mineralization of bones and teeth.
IODINE I	- Essential to the proper functioning of the thyroid gland.
MANGANESE Mn	- An activator of enzymes. - A constituent of bones. - Promotes digestion.
ZINC Zn	- Indispensable for growth and the healing of wounds because it promotes the making of tissues. - Essential to the proper functioning of the prostate gland and the reproductive organs.
COBALT Co	- A constituent of vitamin B_{12}. - Essential to the proper functioning of all cells.

DIETARY SOURCES

- spirulina
- prune juice
- legumes
- parsley, green vegetables
- dried fruits
- seeds, whole grains
- red meat

- nuts
- legumes
- whole grains

- seaweed, seafood
- potato peels[11]
- colored vegetables
- water

- seaweed, fish, seafood
- vegetable plants (depending on the level of iodine in the soil)

- vegetables
- seeds and nuts
- fresh fruits (apples)
- whole grains

- whole grains, legumes
- nuts and seeds
- whole eggs
- meat
- oysters

- seeds
- vegetables
- sprouts

* Trace elements are minerals which we need in minute quantities.

Other trace elements: molybdenum (Mo), **selenium** (Se), **chromium** (Cr), **silicon** (Si), and **nickel** (Ni).

53

- The sun or vitamin D, exercise, and lactose help us to absorb calcium better. Dairy products are the best source of calcium. If we eliminate them from our diet we must find other sources which will satisfy the body's needs.

- During menstruation women need more iron. This is the perfect time to eat spirulina, more prunes, pumpkin and sunflower seeds, and savory green salads to which you have added some parsley, or to cook up some good legume dishes seasoned with seaweed.

ABOUT OUR DIETARY NEEDS

A HEALTHFUL, VARIED DIET BASED ON PRODUCTS OF VEGETABLE ORIGIN, DAIRY PRODUCTS, AND EGGS CAN PROVIDE ALL OF OUR DIETARY NEEDS.

- Whole grains, legumes, nuts and seeds, dairy products, and eggs provide us with the amino acids, essential fatty acids, glucose, vitamins and minerals, water, and fibers which we need.

- Vegetables, fresh fruit, sprouts, and seaweed provide us with an abundance of vitamins and minerals, water, and fibers.

When all is said and done, the closer the food we eat is to its natural state, the better and more long lasting will be our state of health.

ABOUT RECOMMENDED NUTRIENT INTAKES

These figures are based on estimates from tests carried out on one nutrient at a time, in relation to a particular subject or group. Averages and adjustments have been made, but

the fact remains that the whole exercise is of relative value, because each individual has his own previous history, heredetary baggage, digestive capacity, and personal lot of stressful situations that belong to him alone. These figures indicate the minimum quantities of nutrients which are necessary to avoid deficiencies, along with an added safety margin.

The important thing is to consider your own state of health and your personal reality, to learn the basic principles of a healthful diet, to eat a variety of healthful foods, and to make adjustments.

Don't forget that all nutrients interact within our bodies in a truly synergetic fashion, whence the importance—and it's worth repeating—whence the importance of eating a variety of foods, just as nature offers them to us, and of avoiding processed foods.

EXAMPLES OF RECOMMENDED NUTRITIONAL INTAKES FOR AN ADULT (25-49 YEARS OF AGE)

NUTRIENTS	SEX	CANADA RNI Recommended nutritional intake M 74 kg - F 59 kg	UNITED-STATES RDA Recommended dietary allowances M 79 kg - F 63 kg
Energy (Kcal)	M F	2700 2000	2700 2000
Protein (g)	M F	61 44	63 50
Vit A (RE)	M F	1000 800	1000 800
Vit D (mcg)	M F	2,5 2,5	5 5
Vit E (mg)	M 	9 6	10 8
Vit C (mg)	M F	40 30	60 60
Thiamin (mg)	M F	1,1 0,8	1,5 1,1
Riboflavin (mg)	M F	1,4 1,0	1,7 1,3
Niacin (mg équiv)	M 	19 14	19 15
Folic acid (mcg)	M 	220 175	200 180
Vit B_{12} (mcg)	M 	2,0 2,0	2,0 2,0
Calcium (mg)	M F	800 700	800 800
Phosphorus (mg)	M F	1000 850	800 800
Magnesium (mg)	M F	250 200	350 280
Iron (mg)	M F	9 13	10 15
Iodine (mcg)	M F	160 160	150 150
Zinc (mg)	M F	12 9	15 12

These data are based on age and body weight and are expressed in terms of daily intakes.

They are to be used as a guide and are not to be taken as something absolute! The results of these calculations may vary considerably, depending on various factors:

- The mineral content of the soil.

- The agricultural method used.

- Which variety of a particular food is chosen.

- Climatic conditions.

- The time of harvest and the amount of time that goes by between harvest and analysis.

- Cooking and storage methods used, etc.

Various studies confirm this fact. Doctor Michael Colgan, in his book entitled *Your Personal Vitamin Profile,* reveals that the vitamin content of several foods may vary enormously compared to that which is indicated in the tables.

These tables point out the best sources of nutrients and can help us to balance our diet, if necessary.

- There is a direct link between soil quality and agricultural methods, and the nutritional value of foods. That is why it is important to demand organically-grown products.

- The storage of a product, from harvest time to the moment it is eaten, is also important. See the chapter on vegetables, which deals with fresh, whole, organically-grown products!

"LISTEN TO YOUR BODY"

NUTRITIONAL VALUES

ABOUT SERVINGS

What constitutes a serving? How many servings may I allow myself to eat in order to meet my needs, without taking in too many calories? Etc.

To help you answer these questions, here is a chart giving examples of daily servings per category of food for a lacto-ovo-vegetarian diet.

Although these data are very interesting, they should not become an end in themselves. Being attentive to our needs and moods is just as important, when we are making up menus.

Recommended servings must be adjusted to suit age, sex, and activities. They increase during pregnancy and breast-feeding.

FOOD CATEGORY	1 SERVING	RECOMMENDED DAILY ADULT SERVING
GRAINS Grains, whole or in flakes (rolled) Ready-to-serve cereal Slice of bread, muffin Pasta	1/2 cup (125 ml) cooked 1 cup (250 ml) 1 3/4 cup (175 ml)	5 - 12
LEGUMES Cooked legumes Tofu	1 cup (250 ml) 1/2 cup (125 g)	1
NUTS and SEEDS Nuts and seeds Nut butters Vegetable oil (from the first pressing)	1/4 (60 ml) 2 tbsp (30 ml) 2 teasp (10 ml)	1
VEGETABLES Raw vegetables Leafy vegetables + sprouts Cooked vegetables + seaweeds Average-sized vegetables	1/2 cup (125 ml) 1 cup (250 ml) 1/2 cup (125 ml) 1 (potato, carrot, etc.)	3 - 7 including a dark green vegetable and a starchy vegetable
FRUITS Whole fruits Grapefruit, cantaloup, avocado Dried fruits Fruits in salads	1 1/2 1/4 cup (60 ml) 1/2 cup (125 ml)	2 - 3
DAIRY PRODUCTS Milk Yogurt Cheese	1 cup (250 ml) 3/4 cup (175 ml) 50 g	2 - Adults 3 - 4 Adolescents, pregnant or breast-feeding women 2 -3 Children
EGGS	1	1 - 4 weekly
WATER	1 cup (250 ml)	6-8

CHAPTER 4

The Digestive System

In this chapter we are going to embark on a short voyage of exploration and discovery which will enable us to visualize and comprehend the mechanisms of digestion.

This will help us to realize what beneficial effects good eating habits have on our health.

Generally speaking, change takes place more harmoniously and in a more lasting fashion when it is supported by knowledge.

WHAT IS DIGESTION?

- Digestion is the process of change which food undergoes in the digestive system. Thanks to different chemical processes and mechanisms, food is broken down into fine particles, which can then pass through the wall of the small intestine in order to enter the blood and lymph.

- These operations prepare food for absorption.

- **We are able to eat food and absorb nutrients, thanks to digestion.**

- It is a phenomenon of degradation and demolition. The digestive tract fulfils two functions: digestion and absorption.

Digestion is:

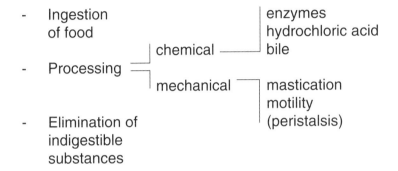

- Ingestion of food
- Processing — chemical → enzymes, hydrochloric acid, bile
- mechanical → mastication, motility (peristalsis)
- Elimination of indigestible substances

WHAT DOES THE DIGESTIVE SYSTEM INCLUDE?

- **Digestive tract:** mouth, pharynx, oesophagus, stomach, small and large intestines.

- **Related organs:** salivary glands, liver, and pancreas.

- From one end to the other, the digestive tract measures about 25-30 feet (9 meters) in length. It begins with the mouth and ends with the anus.

- Related organs are connected to the digestive tract by ducts.

- The inner walls of the digestive tract are covered with mucus, which protects them and keeps them moist.

- The muscles situated along the digestive tract contract to make food advance; this is called peristalsis.

THE DIGESTIVE SYSTEM

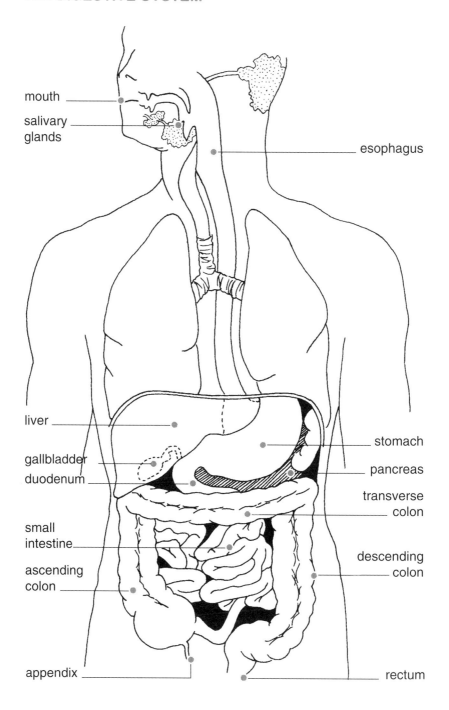

mouth

salivary glands

esophagus

liver

stomach

gallbladder

pancreas

duodenum

transverse colon

small intestine

descending colon

ascending colon

appendix

rectum

Enzymes are substances which facilitate and accelerate all of the body's chemical reactions; among other things, they take care of transforming food, so that it can be assimilated.

In other words, digestive enzymes act like knives which cut up large carbohydrate, lipid, and protein molecules into tiny, little particles capable of going through the wall of the small intestine and passing into the blood.

1. The Mouth

This is where mastication and insalivating take place.

MASTICATION	INSALIVATING
• Mechanical grinding (the only controlled digestive act).	• Moistens food.
• Essential for good digestion.	• The salivary enzyme amylase partially dissolves starch (when cooked, dipped, or sprouted). Try this exercise : Chew a piece of bread for a long time and it will become sweet.
• Regularizes temperature (food, beverages).	
• Increases the quality of teeth and gums; broadens the jaws.	• Up to a 50% proportion of starch can be digested if thoroughly masticated.
• Permits better insalivating.	
• Allows us to prolong the pleasure of tasting (thanks to the tongue's taste buds).	• Drinking while eating or eating foods which are too hot, spicy, cold, or salty interferes with insalivating.
• Helps work done by the stomach.	• Our sense of sight and smell, mastication, and our thoughts promote insalivating.
• Relaxes and calms the atmosphere of meals.	

SO LET'S MASTICATE, MASTICATE, MASTICATE, ETC.

DIGESTIVE SYSTEM

It is advisable to lay down utensils between each mouthful! Concentrate on the flavor, the texture, the colors, and relax.

Food which has been well masticated and well insalivated is half digested. Don't forget that everything we swallow must be in liquid form!

NOTE : Digestion begins in the mouth. The whole process will be influenced by this step, whence the importance of prolonged mastication. **Allow yourself the luxury of eating slowly and savouring your food.** We often eat things too quickly, particularly our favorite dishes: a habit which deprives us of the pleasure of tasting them!

2. The Pharynx

• The pharynx is an intersection which communicates with the nose, mouth, ears, and lungs.

• It is important that food be well masticated and insalivated, and that we swallow it calmly, while remaining silent, in order to avoid having it go down the wrong tube.

3. The Esophagus

• A tube of about 1 foot (30 cm) in length which links the pharynx to the stomach.

4. The Stomach

• This muscular reservoir is a veritable mixer.

• It is located in the left part of the abdominal cavity under the diaphragm.

- It resembles a pleated bag of about 10 inches (25 cm) in depth, in the form of a "J", and it can expand in accordance with the amount of food that has been swallowed.

- Mixing allows the bolus to combine with gastric secretions (hydrochloric acid + enzymes) and become the chyme.

- The digestion of proteins begins in the stomach, a very acid environment.

- Extreme temperatures hinder the action of enzymes, which become active between 100-110°F (38-43°C).

- The digestive process in the stomach lasts about 3 to 8 hours.

- Drinking while eating, or right afterwards, dilutes* the gastric secretions and evacuates them. It is imperative therefore to drink 15 minutes before or at least 2 hours after meals.

NOTE : In order to to make it easier to get rid of the habit of drinking during or immediately after meals, try the following:

- Attempt to visualize enzymes being diluted and disappearing with the liquid you have swallowed. Too bad for the quality of your digestion!

- Salt and sweeten your food less. If you have put a lot of salt and sugar on your food, rince your mouth out well with water, drinking a small mouthful, if necessary. Your thirst will disappear.

- Introducing salads and vegetables into meals will calm your thirst. They have a high water content.

* Milk is the exception to this rule, because it coagulates as soon as it arrives in the stomach. Since it is nourishing, milk will reduce your appetite, when you drink it before a meal. The same thing happens when you drink milk during a meal;

besides, this perpetuates the habit of drinking while eating. Milk should be drunk after meals, then, or as a snack.

5. The Small Intestine

- This is the main seat of digestion and absorption.

- The first part of the small intestine (the duodenum) receives the chyme slowly.

- It is the longest part of the digestive system (10 to 16 feet/ 3 to 5 meters) and is made up of about fifteen loops (flexura).

- This is where the chyme becomes the chyle; it remains in the small intestine for about 4 hours.

ROLES

DIGESTION	ABSORPTION
Digestion is ensured by the following :	**The following nutrients are absorbed :**
- **enzymes from the pancreas**	- **simple sugars (glucose)**
- **bile (emulsifies fats)**	- **amino acids**
- **intestinal enzymes**	- **fatty acids and glycerol**
	- **vitamins**
	- **minerals**
	- **water**

NOTE: In order to increase and facilitate its capacity for absorption, the small intestine is long, and it is covered with minute, velvety, fingerlike projections. These are called villi

and they, in turn, are covered with little hairs (microvilli). This marvelous phenomenon multiplies the surface available for absorption by six hundred, making it as big as a tennis court.[1]

6. The Large Intestine

- The large intestine is about 5 feet (1.5 m) long.

- It includes the ascending colon (on the right), the transverse colon, and the descending colon (on the left), as well as the rectum, which ends with the anus.

- It contains no enzymes, but rather microorganisms, which make up the intestinal flora.

- The chyle spends between 16 and 20 hours here; it may remain even longer if a person's diet contains no fibers.

ROLES

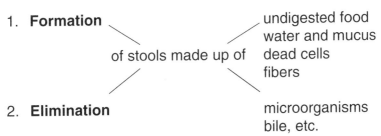

1. **Formation**

of stools made up of

undigested food
water and mucus
dead cells
fibers

2. **Elimination**

microorganisms
bile, etc.

3. **Absorption** of water and a few minerals.

NOTE: More than 700 laxative products are available in North America.This is revealing. Constipation is a long term form of poisoning which creates serious problems. Yet the remedy is simple. Try the following:

- Eat fruits, vegetables, and whole foods, for their fibers.

- Drink lots of water.

- Take the time to stop and eliminate, when you feel the need to do so.

- Walk as much as possible.

- Develop your mental flexibility.

ABOUT INTESTINAL FLORA

- The intestinal flora are concentrated in the ascending colon and contain thousands of bacteria as well as other microorganisms.

- These bacterial flora combat putrefaction and increase our level of immunity to all sorts of infections.

- They produce vitamins such as vitamin K and certain vitamins of the B group (B_1, folic acid, B_{12}).

- They are impaired by antibiotics and chemical products.

- Yogurt, lacto-fermented products, rejuvelac, as well as fibers maintain the normal condition of intestinal flora and can also help to reconstitute them.

- Eating excess quantities of food causes unprocessed food to reach the large intestine; this situation favors putrefaction, especially if the food does not contain fibers.

NOTE: **In order to avoid feeling hungry all the time, we must eat nourishing foods** (whole grains, whole bread, legumes), which provide the body with an uninterrupted supply of glucose (fuel) as well as all the other nutrients essential to health.

The mouth: Digestion of cooked starch (50% if mastication is thorough).

The stomach: Digestion of proteins begins here.

The small intestine: Digestion and absorption of simple sugars; double sugars and composite sugars (starch) must first be broken down into simple sugars before being absorbed.
- final digestion of proteins; absorption of amino acids.
- digestion of lipids; absorption of fatty acids and glycerol.
- absorption of vitamins, minerals, and water.

The large intestine: forming and eliminating of stools;
- absorption of water.

How does our body use the food we eat?

1. It is in our mouth that we masticate our food.

2. Large food molecules are transformed into small molecules (nutrients) by the digestive system in order that they can go through the walls of the small intestine and pass into the blood: this process is called digestion and absorption.

3. Nutrients move on to the liver (that irreplaceable organ) which sorts, transforms, and redistributes nutrients towards each of the cells via the circulatory system (blood).

4. The cells use these nutrients (glucose, fatty acids and glycerol, amino acids) to make their own molecules or to obtain energy and heat.

Digestion — Absorption

ROLES	INGESTED FOOD MADE UP OF	SOURCES	DIGESTED BY	WHERE?	NUTRIENTS ABSORBED IN THE FORM OF
Fuel Energy 4 kilocal./g	**Carbohydrates**	natural sugar (fruits and vegetables) sugar, molasses starch (grains and legumes)	Enzymes	The small intestine The mouth and small intestine	**Glucose**
Heat Energy reserve 9 kilocal./g	**Lipids or fats**	nuts and seeds oil, nut butters fruits (avocado) meat, eggs butter, cream, cheese	Bile Enzymes	The small intestine	**Fatty acids and glycerol**
Growth Maintenance 4 kilocal./g	**Proteins**	legumes nuts and seeds grains, seaweed dairy products meat, fish, eggs	Enzymes	The stomach and small intestine	**Amino acids**

MASTICATION IS OF THE UTMOST IMPORTANCE!!!

CHAPTER 5

Protein Complementarity

OBJECTIVE

To acquire the fundamental knowledge and confidence necessary to make the most of vegetable proteins.

ROLE

Proteins, or nitrogenous materials, take care of the growth and maintenance of the body (construction, repair). They enter into the composition of hormones, enzymes, muscles, and all the tissues of the body.

NEEDS

0.8 g/1 kg (2.2 lb)of ideal body weight. For example: A person who weighs 50 kg needs 40 g of protein per day (50 kg x 0.8).

COMPOSITION

Proteins are composed of an aggregate of 22 amino acids. Among these there are 9 essential amino acids which

cannot be produced by the body; they must therefore be provided by our diet.

The essential amino acids (EAA) are the following:

- Histidine*
- Isoleucine
- Leucine
- Lysine
- Methionine (sulfur)
- Phenylalanine
- Threonine
- Tryptophan
- Valine

* Histidine: Long considered to be nonessential, it has now been added to the list of essential amino acids.

For the body to make the most of EAA, the following conditions must prevail:

1. They must be eaten during the same meal, unless small meals are eaten frequently (every three hours).

2. **A sufficient number of calories** (carbohydrates, lipids) **must be eaten**; otherwise, protein will be used as a source of energy rather than for growth or cell repair.

SOURCES

- Generally, people eat double or even more than double their daily requirement of proteins. This is true for industrialized countries, elsewhere, it's another matter. The majority of these proteins are of animal origin.

- To be complete a protein must contain all 9 EAA in the right proportions.

- Proteins of animal origin are complete. Those of vegetable origin must be completed.
    - **Vegetable sources:** legumes, grains, nuts and seeds, vegetables, and seaweeds.
    - **Animal sources:** meat, fish, seafood, dairy products and eggs.

COMPLEMENTARITY

- Vegetable proteins may be lacking in certain essential amino acids.

- This deficiency reduces the possibility of using the other amino acids which are present.

- Therefore, when one of the essential amino acids is present in insufficient quantity, the quality of the entire protein is reduced.

If a food contains 100% of 8 out of the 9 essential amino acids, but has only 30% of the ninth , the body will use only 30% of the protein, or, in other words, the value of the weakest amino acid. " A chain is only as strong as its weakest link! "

There is a very simple solution to this problem: it is just a matter of eating another food containing the missing amino acid which is limiting the quality of protein intake. In this way you will be able to use the protein to its maximum potential.

In order for you to understand protein complementarity well, here is a small chart which illustrates clearly why one food is used in combination with another to complete it.

FOOD	RICH IN	LOW IN
Legumes	lysine	tryptophane & methionine
Grains	tryptophane & methionine	lysine
Nuts, Seeds	tryptophane & methionine	lysine
Dairy Products	lysine	

PROTEIN COMPLEMENTARITY

It is obvious that if we eat grains with legumes or dairy products, or in like fashion, legumes with nuts or seeds, we will obtain complete proteins.

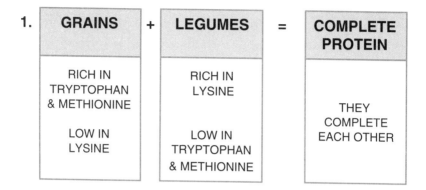

1.	**GRAINS**	+	**LEGUMES**	=	**COMPLETE PROTEIN**
	RICH IN TRYPTOPHAN & METHIONINE LOW IN LYSINE		RICH IN LYSINE LOW IN TRYPTOPHAN & METHIONINE		THEY COMPLETE EACH OTHER

The peoples of the world have long understood protein complementarity; their traditional dishes bear witness to this fact :

- rice + lentils (India)
- rice + black beans (South America)
- corn + kidney beans (Mexico)
- bulgur + chickpeas (Middle East)
- bread + pea soup (Quebec)
- bread + baked beans (Quebec)
- bread + peanut butter (North America)
- rice + tofu (Japan)

Other simple combinations:

- wheat flour + soy flour
- millet + soybeans
- barley + lima beans

NOTE : When we make it a habit to cook large quantities of legumes in advance, we always have some on hand to complete the proteins found in grains in no time at all.

2.	**LEGUMES**	+	**NUTS OR SEEDS**	=	**COMPLETE PROTEIN**
	RICH IN LYSINE LOW IN TRYPTOPHAN & METHIONINE		RICH IN TRYPTOPHAN & METHIONINE LOW IN LYSINE		THEY COMPLETE EACH OTHER

Examples : soybeans + sesame seeds

lentils + walnuts

3.	**GRAINS**	+	**DAIRY PRODUCTS**	=	**COMPLETE PROTEIN**
	LOW IN LYSINE		RICH IN LYSINE		THEY COMPLETE EACH OTHER

Examples: flour + milk powder

cereal-based main course

+ green vegetables + yogurt

oatmeal porridge + milk or yogurt

pasta + au gratin

bread + cheese

IN SHORT:

GRAINS + LEGUMES   = **COMPLETE**
LEGUMES + NUTS OR SEEDS = **PROTEIN**
GRAINS + DAIRY PRODUCTS =

There are also other ways to complete the quality of proteins.

- Since dairy products and eggs contain complete proteins, each time we associate them with any of the vegetable proteins, we can't help but obtain a complete protein.

- Serve nutritional yeast, especially with grains.

- Combine green vegetables with grains.

Proteins contained in a dish made up of 70 to 80% whole grains and 20 to 30% legumes will be used to a maximum extent.

ABOUT PROTEIN COMPLEMENTARITY

Must we complete our proteins within the same meal? This question provokes a lot of discussion. According to the latest research conducted by Frances Moore Lappé and described in the most recent edition of her book *Diet for a Small Planet*, the answer is "Yes!", unless we were to eat more than three meals a day. The fact is that, if necessary, we must complete the essential amino acids within 3 to 4 hours, because the body does not store them for any longer than that.

Be careful. Protein complementarity must not become an obsession or a tiresome juggling act. When our diet is composed of a variety of nutritional foods, proteins are completed naturally.

The following people should pay special attention to protein complementarity: growing children, pregnant women and those who are breast-feeding, people who do not eat any animal products, as well as those who have suffered an injury and have tissues that need repair.

Food for thought

- Today, overconsumption of meat is squandering our society's health. Eating less meat and more vegetable proteins is beneficial not only to the individual but also to the planet as a whole.

- According to a report in the *Journal of the American Medical Association*, a vegetarian diet can reduce the risk of heart disease by 90-97%.

- Scientists from Harvard have discovered that the average blood pressure of vegetarians is significantly lower than that of non-vegetarians.

- Two thirds of grain production in industrialized countries (and almost 90% in the United States) is used to feed animals.

In addition: **8-10 vegetable calories are required to produce 1 animal calorie.**

10 vegetable proteins are required to produce 1 animal protein.

16 pounds (7.264 kg) of feed are required to produce 1 pound (.454 kg) of beef protein.

WASTING ALL THIS ENERGY IS A LUXURY THAT WE CAN NO LONGER AFFORD.

AWARENESS LEADS TO CHANGE.

PROTEIN COMPLEMENTARITY

CHAPTER 6

Grains

Known and used by mankind for thousands of years, grains, the food of foods, form the nutritional base for meals in a healthy diet. Let's rediscover them together, so that we can introduce them to the daily menu.

VARIETIES

1. **Oats**
2. **Wheat**
3. **Corn**
4. **Millet**
5. **Barley**
6. **Rice**
7. **Buckwheat**
8. **Rye**
9. **Triticale**

NUTRITIONAL VALUE

- They are an excellent source of energy. On an average they contain 65% starch (complex carbohydrates), which breaks down gradually into glucose, and is then used in a sustained, on-going fashion by the body.

- Cooking, soaking, sprouting, and light roasting reduce the starch found in grains into simpler sugars and thus make them more digestible.

- They are a good source of proteins (up to 15%). However, their proteins do not contain the 9 essential amino acids and must be completed.

- In order to get a complete protein:

grains + legumes

grains + dairy products

- Grains are rich in B complex vitamins (germ and bran) and vitamin E (concentrated in the germ).

- Sprouting them develops their vitamin A and C content.[1]

- They are a good source of mineral salts and trace elements: iron, sodium, potassium, and phosphorus; since these elements are found near the husk, it is essential that we eat whole grains.

- All grains have similar compositions, with a few small differences.

- Fruits and vegetables that are rich in vitamin C help in the absorption of the iron which is contained in grains. Try eating an orange or drinking some orange juice before eating your breakfast cereal. Prepare some millet with green peppers and tomatoes.

- Whole grains are rich in fibers and help intestinal transport.

- Mastication is essential, because the digestion of grains begins in the mouth, where amalyse, an enzyme found in saliva (and in the pancreas), breaks down the starch which they contain.

Now that you know all of this, there is no point in insisting further on the importance of eating whole grains rather than refined ones.

1. Oats

- Oats grow well in our climate.

- They are used mostly in the form of rolled oats.

ROLLED OATS

- When the grains are rolled once, whole flake are obtained.

- When the grains are crushed and rolled, instant rolled oats are obtained (less nutritious).

- They facilitate lactation and are recommended during pregnancy.

- Oat bran contributes to reducing cholesterol.[2]

Uses

- Porridge: For variety's sake, roast oatmeal before cooking it. Delicious!

- Granola (more digestible when cooked or soaked). See the " Recipe Book " section.

- Muesli: soaked oatmeal along with dried fruit and seeds.

- Croquettes, biscuits.

- For thickening soups and sauces.

- When ground up in a blender, oatmeal provides flour for pancakes, biscuits, etc.

OAT FLOUR

- To make your own ground flour from groats, roast them beforehand.

- Oat flour does not contain enough gluten to be used alone for making bread; the bread will not rise. Use along with wheat flour.

2. Wheat

- Wheat grows well in our climate.

- The use of this grain is very widespread, particularly in the form of flour, in bread (because of its gluten content), pasta, and pastry.

- It may be eaten like rice when cooked whole.

- Eat it raw sprouted, and add to salads and different dishes.

- Since wheat is so widespread, it may be replaced by other grains such as millet, barley, kasha, etc., to provide some variety, or by flour made from these grains.

The Wheat Kernel

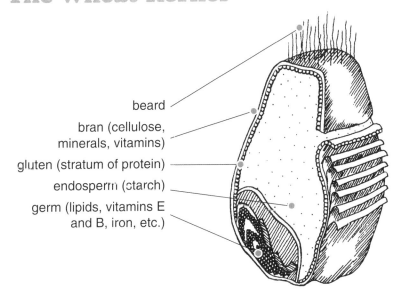

beard

bran (cellulose, minerals, vitamins)

gluten (stratum of protein)

endosperm (starch)

germ (lipids, vitamins E and B, iron, etc.)

THE REFINING OF GRAINS

The refining of wheat removes the germ and bran, and alters its proteins: an unacceptable waste of nutritional resources!

- During this process the majority of its nutrients and fibers are removed, particularly the vitamins and minerals. Afterwards we decide to enrich this very flour that we have just depleted.

- Enriched flours pale in comparison with whole flours, because many of the elements that have been removed are not added back. Since all of these nutrients act together in synergy, the absence of some of them reduces the capacities of the team.

- The costs involved in processing these products, as well as the damage caused in the long run to those who use them, are unacceptable.

- Refining is a doubtful process and all refined products should be eliminated as fast as possible from our diets. **You will live the difference!**

VARIETIES OF WHEAT

HARD WHEAT

- A very small, hard, brown kernel. Fall wheat.

- Its flour is used mainly for the making of bread, thanks to its gluten content. Gluten is a protein-based substance.

- Depending on the degree of bolting, the following are obtained:

    - Whole wheat flour.

- Unbleached white flour: flour from which the bran has been sifted, but that has not been industrially bleached. Peroxide bleaching destroys vitamin E, predisposes people to allergic reactions, and is slightly carcinogenic.[3] But even unbleached white flour has lost a great number of nutrients.

SOFT WHEAT

- A small yellow seed. Spring wheat.

- Its flour is used mainly for making pastry.

- It contains less gluten and more starch than hard wheat.

- Its seeds are used in the making of rejuvelac.

DURUM WHEAT

- Its flour is used to make pasta.

PRODUCTS DERIVED FROM WHEAT

FLOUR

- Should be eaten whole and as fresh as possible.

- Time alters the vitamin E of the germ.

- Do not toast flour and bread too much, because it alters the proteins.

SEMOLINA

- Finely crushed hard wheat kernels.

- Worth discovering as a breakfast cereal.

- May be added to soups, casseroles, bread, pies.

BULGUR

- Pre-cooked, dried, ground hard wheat.

- Cooks in ten minutes.

- Bulgur may be finely, medium, or coarsely ground.

- An outstanding situation-saver, which is delicious hot or cold in salads.

- Replaces couscous because it is more nutritious.

COUSCOUS

- Pre-cooked, dried, hulled wheat or millet semolina.

- Cook like bulgur.

WHEAT FLAKES

- Use as is in granola.

- Serve with sautéed vegetables and a miso béchamel sauce, or use as a base for soups, croquettes, and pâtés.

Minerals are often concentrated near the outer shell. **Let's eat whole foods; let's eat minerals and fibers.**

MALT POWDER

It is sprouted wheat, which has been dried in the oven at 150°F (65°C) for eight hours, and then ground up in the blender.

- Should be stored in a jar in the refrigerator.

- Can replace sweeteners.

WHEAT BRAN

- The outer envelope of the berry; rich in cellulose.

- Helps intestinal transport.

- Taken alone in large quantities, bran irritates the digestive tract. It is better to eat whole wheat.

WHEAT GERM

- Goes rancid very easily. Must be stored in the refrigerator.

- Use whole or sprouted wheat instead, as a source of vitamin E and B vitamins.

WHEAT GLUTEN

- Proteins which are extracted from wheat flour. Used to make seitan.

3. Corn

- It is used mainly as a fresh vegetable.

- Contains a lot of carbohydrates (as sweet in flavor as wheat) and energy.

- Rich in lipids (polyunsaturated fatty acids). We extract oil from it.

- The only grain which is rich in carotene (provitamin A).

- A good way to use whole corn kernels is to dryroast them and grind them up to obtain fresh semolina or flour.

PUFFED CORN

- Equally nutritious; comes from a variety of corn with smaller kernels.

- The seed coat bursts when heated and frees the starch.

GRAINS

- Served without butter, it cannot make you fat! It's a nourishing snack.

- Try new seasonings: a few drops of tamari soy sauce with some nutritional yeast, some sesame salt, cinnamon, or even parmesan cheese.

- May be used as a breakfast cereal.

PRODUCTS DERIVED FROM CORN:

- **Cornmeal:** used for preparing polenta and breakfast cereal. Say goodbye to *Cornflakes*!

- **Corn flour:** delicious and just as nutritious as kernels.

- **Cornstarch:** used as a thickener.

- **Corn oil:** used for making desserts and breads.

- All corn products go rancid quickly because they contain a high level of polyunsaturated fatty acids. Buy small quantities at a time, store them in the refrigerator, and use them up quickly.

4. Millet

- A whole grain in its outer seed coat.

- Serves as the basic ingredient of several main dishes.

- Has alkalizing properties and is easily digestible, nonallergenic, and tasty.

- The gray powder which accompanies it comes from the plant. Wash it thoroughly before cooking.

- Season well, because it has a very mild flavor.

- Well-liked by children. Introduce it into your menus as soon as you begin changing your dietary habits.

COOKING METHOD

- Wash well.

- Dry-roast it. This will enhance its nutty flavor and prevent the grains from sticking together.

- Pour into 1 1/2 times its volume of water. Use very warm water to prevent the grains from bursting.

- Bring the water to a boil.

- Cover and cook over very low heat for 20 minutes.
  or

- Soak (optional) and steam. All the grains will remain separate.

USES

- Baked dishes, soups, desserts, pies, croquettes, pie shells, breakfast cereal.

- Sorghum: from the same family as millet; used in Africa.

5. Barley

- A grain which grows well in our climate.

- A whole grain from which the inedible chaff has been removed.

- Has a mild flavor and crunchy consistency.

- Nowadays it is used in the preparation of beer and for feeding animals. It's high time to introduce it more often into the menu. Cook ahead of time.

- Avoid pearled barley, because it has undergone 6 milling operations, in which it loses its fibers and germ, as well as half its proteins, lipids, and minerals.

- Scotch barley (pot barley) has undergone 3 milling processes.

- Barley may be used in soups, baked dishes, pie shells, croquettes, bread, etc.

- Does not contain enough gluten to be used alone for making bread.

- Use in combination with wheat or rye flour.

6. Rice

- A grain which does not grow in temperate regions.

- The basic food staple of half the world's population!

- Suitable for sedentary people and for those who have a sensitive digestive tract, since it is easily assimilated.

- Contains fewer proteins (7-8%) than the other grains (15%).

- Hulled white rice has lost several of its minerals and B vitamins, particularly thiamine (B_1).

- **Whole long-grain rice:** all the grains remain separate.

- **Whole short-grain rice:** contains more starch; a bit stickier when cooked. Use for croquettes, aspics, soups, or pie shells. Good to eat with chopsticks in cold weather!

- **Whole sweet rice:** has a sweet flavor; recommended for children. It can be moulded easily because it is stickier.

- **Basmati rice:** hulled or whole. Has a characteristic odor and flavor which come from its having aged for 2 years in underground caves before being used.

- **Wehani rice:** whole rice. Its red color gives it an appearance similar to that of meat.

- **Wild rice:** has long black grains. It is considered to be an aquatic plant rather than a grain; it grows in Canada. Manual harvesting methods make it expensive. Mix it in with other varieties.

USES

- Baked dishes, soups, salads, croquettes, pie shells, desserts.

- In flakes: soak and enjoy as is.

7. Buckwheat

- Buckwheat is a hardy plant that is grown without resorting to chemical products. Used as a green fertilizer in agriculture.

- It is recognized as being beneficial in combatting the formation of varicose veins because it contains rutin, which increases the strength of the walls of blood vessels.

- It is a grain that grows in cold regions. It is very popular in the former Soviet Union, where white buckwheat is roasted before being cooked, and is called kasha.

- Why not adopt this delicious, nutritious, quick-cooking grain and rediscover those famous buckwheat crepes?

USES

- Whole grain black buckwheat: used to make flour or grow sprouts on potting soil.

- Hulled buckwheat (white buckwheat) : has a delicate flavor.

- Roasted white buckwheat (kasha): has a more pronounced flavor.

COOKING METHOD

- Wash white buckwheat and dry-roast it, to enhance the flavor. For a milder taste, omit this step.

- Pour into 1 1/2 times its volume of very hot water (boiling hot water causes it to burst and makes it flaky). Bring the water to a boil and cook for 10 minutes or until the water is completely absorbed.

- Use to thicken soups, in spaghetti sauce, shepherd's pie, "meat" pies, salads, and desserts.

- Mix in with breakfast cereal flakes, or serve with bulgur, to enhance the flavor. Makes a delicious mixture.

ALTERNATIVE METHOD

- Wash kasha groats and soak them in warm water for 1 1/2 to 2 hours, or overnight, with muesli. Soaked grains remain crunchy, are more nutritious, and never stick to the pot. They are excellent in salads or added to muffins, bread, and cookies.

- A nutritious, quickly prepared grain with a unique flavor, which is well worth discovering.

At first, use white buckwheat, which is milder in flavor than kasha.

BUCKWHEAT FLOWER

- Used for making those famous crepes!
- Used in combination with other flours in pancakes, muffins, etc.
- Adds a delicious flavor to béchamel sauce.

8. Rye

- A full-energy grain!
- Sprouted rye seeds, ground up in the blender in a hot liquid (water or milk), and spiced with nutmeg, make just the right cereal for a good day of spring cleaning.

RYE FLAKES

- Breakfast cereal (like oat or wheat flakes).
- One of the ingredients found in granola.

RYE FLOUR

- Contains enough gluten to be used alone for making bread.
- Makes denser bread than does wheat flour.
- Use in pancakes, cookies, etc., in combination with wheat flour.

9. Triticale

- A hybrid grain obtained from the crossing of wheat with rye.
- Used with wheat to make bread.

FOUR DIFFERENT METHODS FOR COOKING GRAINS

1. IN WATER, WITHOUT SOAKING

a) Measure out the desired quantity of grains, stir them around in some water to wash them, and strain in a sieve.

b) Grains may be lightly dry-roasted; this increases their flavor and causes them to be less sticky. When whole grains and flour are roasted, starch (a complex sugar) is changed into dextrine, a simpler sugar, and this makes digestion easier.

c) When cooking pasta for recipes in which all the water is not absorbed, add some salt to the required quantity of water, in order to reduce to a minimum the leeching out of minerals into the water. Bring the water to a boil.

d) Add the grains to the boiling water slowly (see the table for the amount of water required); when cooked this way the grains will not be as sticky.

EXCEPTION: Millet and kasha should first be poured into very hot, but not boiling water.

e) Cover when the water returns to a boil; continue cooking over very low heat until the water is completely absorbed (see cooking times in the chart).

NOTE:

- Grains almost triple in volume during cooking.

- Cooking water may be replaced by vegetable stock.

- When cooking is finished, leave the cover on and let sit for 15 minutes; this will give you grains that break apart more easily.

- Do not stir grains while they are cooking; this makes them stickier.

- If the grains are sticky, once cooked, because too much water was used, or for any other reason, rinse them in lukewarm water and then drain them. This will greatly improve the situation. Usually, however, we do not rinse them after cooking.

2. IN WATER, AFTER SOAKING

a) Wash the grains and soak them in cold water for 8 to 12 hours (see the table for the amount of water required). Place them in a cool place to soak.

b) Remove the remaining water, bring it to a boil, and pour in the soaked grains. When the water starts boiling again, cover, and continue cooking over very low heat, until the grains are tender, or for the required cooking time.

NOTE:

- Whole grains: soaking softens the outer coat and shortens cooking time.

- Transformed grains: soaking replaces cooking.

- Oats, wheat, corn, barley, and rye must be soaked for about 8 hours before cooking.

- You can always soak grains before cooking, **as long as you use the same water to cook them in**. In this way the grains re-absorb the B vitamins and the minerals which became dissolved in the water during soaking.

- Grains may even be sprouted a bit after soaking. This makes them easier to digest, increases their nutritional value, and reduces cooking time enormously.

3. STEAMING

All grains can be steamed. The cooking time required is a bit longer.

4. IN A THERMOS

a) In the morning, soak the grains in the quantity of water recommended in the chart.

b) In the evening, bring the mixture to a boil and then pour it into a warmed-up thermos.

c) The next morning, enjoy your cereal the way you like it.

Most people are accustomed to strong and spicy flavors, whether sweet or salty. Consequently, the mild, subtle flavor of grains does not attract them very much. However, herbs, spices, garlic, onion, nutritional yeast, and tamari soy sauce allow us to enhance the flavor of grain-based dishes. A bit of seasoning often makes all the difference.

NOTE: In the " Recipe Book " section, you will find several ideas, techniques, and recipes which will help make learning easier for you.

PREPARING GRAINS TO SUIT YOUR TASTE IS VERY IMPORTANT!

STORAGE AND QUALITY OF GRAINS

- Grains keep very well and for a long time, when stored in well-closed containers in a cool, dark, dry place.

- In plastic bags, grains are not protected from heat and humidity, which change their nutritional quality; nor are they protected from insects.

- Choose preferably whole or processed grains which have been grown organically. It's a question of health!

- Opt for the use of whole grains (rice, millet, etc.), because they are more nutritious than transformed grains (bulgur, flakes, etc.). The latter can be handy in a pinch, however, and allow for some variety in the menu.

COOKING CHART FOR WHOLE GRAINS

Product (1 cup)	Water (cups)	Cooking Time (without soaking)	Cooking Time (after soaking for 8 hours)	Cooked in a Pressure Cooker (water - time)
Oats	4	——	2 hours	1 1/2 cups 1 hour
Wheat	3	——	2	1 1/2 - 1 1/2
Millet	1 1/2	20 min.	15 min.	——
Barley	3	1 1/2 hours	45 min.	2 - 1
Brown rice	2	45 min.	30 min.	——
Wild rice	2 1/2	45 min.	20 min.	——
Buckwheat	1 1/2	15 min.	can be eaten after soaking	——
Rye	3	1 1/2 hours	——	——

PROCESSED GRAINS

Cracked wheat	2	25 min.	——	
Bulgur	1 1/2	10 min.	5 min.	
Flakes	2	20 min.	5 min. or can be eaten as is	
Semolina	4	15 min.	——	
Granola	2	15 min.	can be eaten after soaking	
Bran	——	——	soak for 15 min.	
White basmati rice	2	20 min.	——	

CHAPTER 7

Legumes

Legumes are plants that bear fruit in the form of a pod. Generally they are underestimated, and we do not make sufficient use of them in our menus. In this chapter we will get to know them and learn how to make them an important and integral part of our diet.

They are easy to grow and they are ecological: they fix nitrogen in the soil and consume very little energy for their protein yield, when compared with the amount of energy used to produce animal protein.

VARIETIES

1. **Peanuts**
2. **Fresh and dried beans**
3. **Lentils**
4. **Dried peas**

NUTRITIONAL VALUE

- An excellent source of protein (17- 25%). Soybeans contain 35% protein.

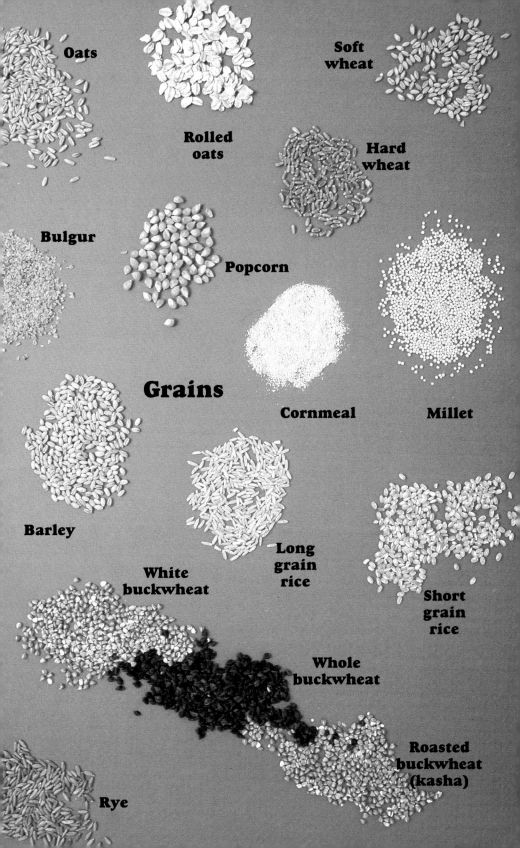

Oats

Rolled oats

Soft wheat

Hard wheat

Bulgur

Popcorn

Millet

Grains

Cornmeal

Barley

Long grain rice

White buckwheat

Short grain rice

Whole buckwheat

Rye

Roasted buckwheat (kasha)

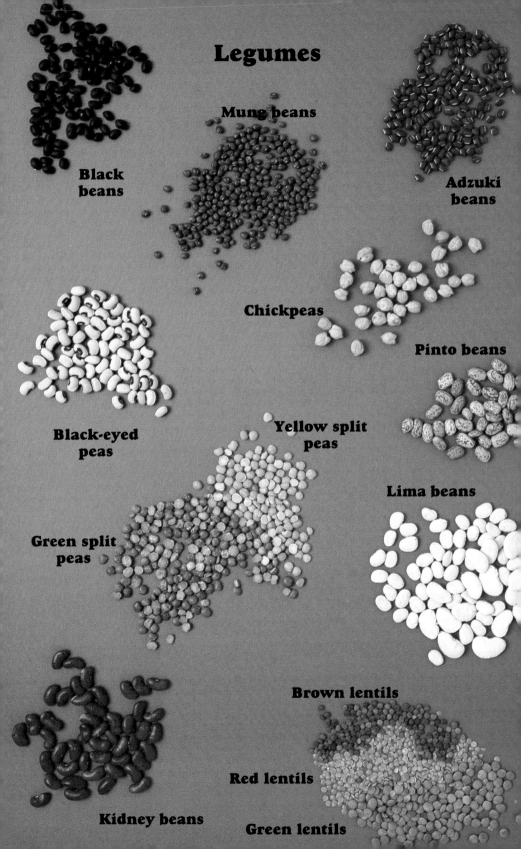

Legumes

Black beans

Mung beans

Adzuki beans

Black-eyed peas

Chickpeas

Pinto beans

Yellow split peas

Green split peas

Lima beans

Brown lentils

Red lentils

Kidney beans

Green lentils

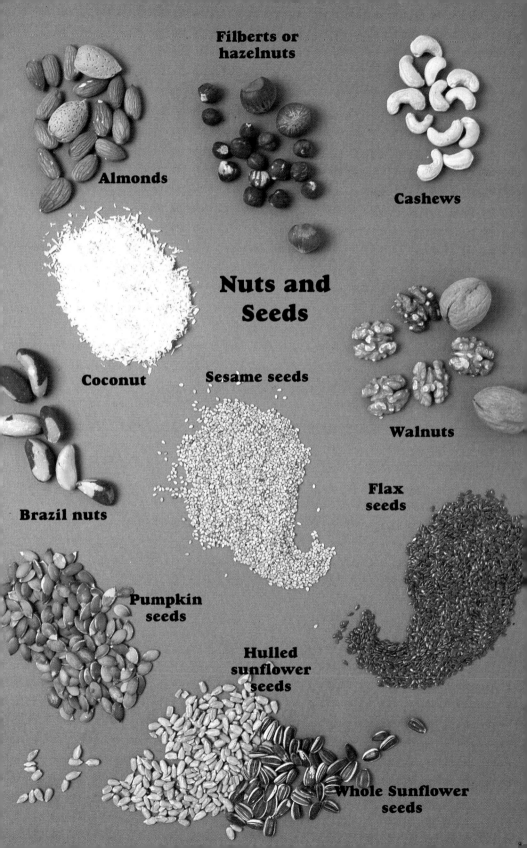

Filberts or hazelnuts

Almonds

Cashews

Nuts and Seeds

Coconut

Sesame seeds

Walnuts

Brazil nuts

Flax seeds

Pumpkin seeds

Hulled sunflower seeds

Whole Sunflower seeds

Tamari

Tofu

Soybeans

Soy milk

Miso

Nutritional yeast

Ginger

Carob

Variety of sprouts

- In order to obtain whole proteins, combine them with grains, nuts, or seeds.

- A good source of energy: up to 56% complex carbohydrates (starch).

- The majority of the lipids they contain are polyunsaturated, and all of them are cholesterol-free.

- A good source of minerals (calcium, phosphorus, and iron) and of B vitamins (thiamine B_1, niacine B_3).

- Sprouting develops their vitamin A and C content and makes them easier to digest.

- A good source of fiber.

- They are concentrated foodstuffs which should be eaten in moderation and in association with vegetable products such as grains and vegetables (tomatoes, peppers, broccoli). The vitamin C in these vegetables helps in the absorption of iron and calcium.

Can Legumes Replace Meat?

LEGUMES ARE GOOD SUBSTITUTE FOR MEAT.

They contain the following:

- Sufficient quantities of protein which must, however, be completed by other groups of food. See the chapter on protein complementarity.

- Few fats and no cholesterol.

- Carbohydrates, minerals (iron and calcium), vitamins, and a great deal of fiber.

% per(/) 100 g of food	Navy beans	Soy- beans	Beef (lean)	Fish (lean)	Eggs	Cheese
Proteins	22.3	34.1	19.00	16.4	12.9	23.2
Lipids	1.6	17.7	13.0	0.5	11.5	30.0
Carbohy- drates	61.3	33.5	0	0	0.9	1.9
Calcium (mg)	144	226	11	25	54	697
Iron (mg)	7.8	8.4	2.3	0.7	2.3	0.9
Vit. B$_1$ (mg)	0.65	1.10	0.07	0.05	0.11	0.02
Fiber	4.3	4.9	0	0	0	0

Obviously, it is very advantageous to replace animal proteins from meat, eggs, or fish with vegetable proteins from legumes.

NOTE: It is important for vegetarians to eat legumes regularly, because they are one of the best sources of iron in the vegetable kingdom. 1 serving = 1 cup (250 ml) of cooked legumes.

1. Peanuts

- Classed amongst the legumes. After pollination, the flowers sink into the soil and form their fruit there.

- Combine with grains and greens.

- Keep unshelled peanuts in a cool place and shelled peanuts, as well as peanut butter, in the refrigerator.

- Avoid hydrogenated commercial peanut butters to which

sugar and salt have been added. Natural or so-called home-made peanut butters are the best.

- For smoother peanut butter, beat in a bit of lukewarm water with a fork. This emulsion should be eaten immediately. See the "Emulsified Nut Butters" recipe in the "Recipe Book" section.

- To make your own peanut butter, dry-roast some raw peanuts and grind them up in a blender, if its motor is powerful enough.

2. Dried Beans

ADZUKI	BLACK	KIDNEY
NAVY	BLACK-EYED PEAS	SOY
BABY LIMA	PINTO	ETC.
MUNG	ROMAINE	

ADZUKI AND MUNG BEANS

- Two small beans: one is red with white stripes (adzuki), and the other, green (mung).

- They can be eaten as sprouts or cooked.

- The adzuki bean is tasty, easy to digest, and diuretic.

- Add sprouts to grain dishes, salads, sandwiches, and chop suey.

- Prepare casseroles, soups, purées, and baked dishes using cooked beans.

NAVY BEANS

- Make traditional baked beans. Can also be used in pies, soups, and purées.

- Try the "Wholesome Beans" recipe from the "Recipe Book" section.

LIMA BEANS

- There are 2 varieties: baby and giant lima beans.

- They have alkalizing properties; they are sweet and digestible, and children like them.

- Delicious in soups, salads, purées, and casseroles.

RED KIDNEY BEANS

- They have the form and color of kidneys.

- Use in salads, croquettes, pies, chili *sin* carne (with to-matoes and spices), and on pizzas. They make good soups in winter.

SOYBEANS

- They have the highest protein content of all beans (35%).

- We will consider them in detail at the end of this chapter.

3. Lentils

- Green, brown, and red.

- They have the highest iron content along with black-eyed peas.

- Delicious and easy to digest, they are among the first beans to introduce into your children's diet.

- In order to obtain better quality proteins, always combine with grains, nuts, or seeds.

- Red lentils are less nutritious and will not sprout, because they have been hulled.

- Best when eaten as sprouts (in salads, soups, pies) or when cooked (in soups, salads, pies, etc. and seasoned with curry or nutmeg).

4. Dried Peas

CHICKPEAS

- Large beige peas with a textured surface. They are delicious and worth discovering.

- Of all legumes, they are the richest in mineral salts; magnesium, iron, calcium, phosphorus, and zinc.

- Used mostly in delicious puréed spreads (hummus).

- Serve in salads, pies, croquettes, soups, or as sprouts.

- Eat in combination with grains to obtain better quality proteins.

YELLOW PEAS

- Use to make soups and purées.

- Add a bit of rice and some onions to the soup to increase the flavor and nutritional value.

GREEN SPLIT PEAS

- Cook rapidly.

- Use to make soups (with carrots, onions, and thyme), in purées, or with a grain.

STORAGE AND QUALITY OF LEGUMES

- You can tell if they are fresh from their shiny appearance. They are fresher in the fall.

- They are natural keepers: can easily be stored for 1 1/2 years.

- As they age, they take longer to cook and are more difficult to digest.

- Store in a dark, dry place.

- When cooked, they can be kept for a few days in the refrigerator, or a few months in the freezer.

COOKING METHOD AND DIGESTIBILITY OF LEGUMES

- Sort them, because often they come mixed with little pebbles (grit); wash them.

- Soak them overnight in 3 times their volume of cold water.

- DRAIN and cover with fresh water to a depth of about 2 inches (5 cm) over the beans.

- Cover, bring to a boil, reduce the heat, and cook over low heat, stirring from time to time.

- Once cooked, they will double or triple in volume, depending on the variety.

NOTE: If you forget to soak them, do the following:
- Place them in cold water.
- Bring the water to a boil.
- Boil for 2 minutes.
- Let sit for 2 hours, so that they can swell up.
- Drain and proceed as you would normally with the steps listed above.

NOTE: **Soaking legumes** makes them easier to digest and

reduces their cooking time. It is a good habit to acquire! Soak for 8 to 15 hours, throw away the water used for soaking, and sprout and/or cook.

The water used for soaking must not be ingested, for it will give you intestinal gases because of the trisaccharides that it contains.

Baking

- Soak overnight or for 8 to 15 hours.

- Throw away the water used for soaking and place in cold water.

- Bring to a boil and simmer for about 15 minutes.

- Then pour into an earthenware or glass crock; add vegetables, seasonings, and enough water to cover. Cover the crock and continue cooking in the oven at 250°F (120°C) for 8 hours.

Pressure Cooking

- Follow the instructions for your pressure cooker.

- Pressure cooking softens the large legumes such as chickpeas and soybeans.

To avoid flatulence

- At the beginning, choose the most digestible legumes: lima beans, lentils, green peas.

- **Eat some every day or almost every day, in small quantities** – about 1/2 cup (125 ml) at a time – in order to accustom your intestines...and your friends!

- Add the following to the cooking stock: herbs (bay leaf

and savory), spices (cumin, ginger), seaweed (pieces of kombu), vegetables (garlic, onion).

- Avoid using bicarbonate of soda (it destroys vitamin B_1), tomatoes, and salt; they harden beans. Add them towards the end of the cooking period.

- Adding sugar (molasses) to legumes makes digesting them more difficult and will not go unnoticed!

- Remove the scum which forms on the surface during cooking.

- Slight sprouting before cooking always makes digestion easier.

- Make sure that they are well cooked and chew them well.

About the Consumption of Legumes

In North America we are not accustomed to eating legumes regularly, with the exception of traditional baked beans and pea soup. They are of great nutritional value and they are both economical and ecological to grow and to use. Now that you are aware of the advantages they offer , you will surely want to learn how you can make legumes a regular part of your daily diet.

IT'S SIMPLE!

1. AUTOMATIC SOAKING

- One evening after supper, when nothing leads you to expect that you might eat some legumes in the next few days, choose two varieties (e.g., kidney beans and

chickpeas) and pop them into some water to soak! It takes 5 minutes, including washing.

2. COOKING IN ADVANCE

- The next day, when you have a minute, drain, cover with fresh water, and cook them.

- You will have a supply for that week or for even longer, if you want.

- Once they are cooked, keep them in the refrigerator to be used in the next few days and freeze the rest in portions which will suit your needs for the following month.

- Then it will be very easy for you to give your inspiration free rein by adding them to a vegetable soup or a salad, using them to garnish a pizza or some bread, or simply adding them to a dish of rice or millet.

- **In this way it will be easy for you to obtain variety and you will develop the habit of eating a serving of legumes every day.**

- Some techniques which will enable you to eat a healthful diet without spending all your time in the kitchen are presented in the chapter entitled " How To Succeed in the Kitchen ".

The Soybean and its Metamorphoses

Greatly appreciated in the East for thousands of years, the soybean is now gaining popularity in North America. A growing awareness of health, of the state of our soils, and of the need to share protein more equitably throughout the world is leading us to discover the many advantages of the soybean.

NUTRITIONAL VALUE

- Soybeans are an excellent source of protein (35%).

- They are good for completing the proteins in grains.

- Their lipids are cholesterol-free and are made up of polyunsaturated fatty acids.

- They contain lecithin, which is essential in all nervous tissues, notably in the brain.

- They are very rich in B complex vitamins.

- Sprouting increases their vitamin A and B content, develops vitamins C and E in them, shortens their cooking time, and makes them easier to digest.

- They contain iron, calcium, phosphorus, and potassium.

- The soy plant adds a large quantity of nitrogen to the soil.

- In order to make soybeans more digestible, soak them for 24 hours before cooking (2 to 3 hours); it is even better to sprout them and then cook them gently (1/2 to 1 1/2 hours).

- Cooking, sprouting, and fermentation neutralize the toxin found in soybeans, anti-trypsin, which interferes with digestion. Do not eat them raw.

The soybean may be transformed in several ways without losing its qualities in the process. It offers us a generous assortment of different products:

SOY NUTS	**SOY OIL**	**SOY MILK**
SOY FLAKES	**SOY SAUCE**	**TOFU**
SOY LECITHIN	**MISO**	**SOY PULP**
SOY FLOUR	**TEMPEH**	**SOY BUTTER**

SOY LECITHIN

- Lecithin is indispensable for nerve cells.

- Egg yolks contain the most lecithin, followed by soybeans.

- To replace eggs in recipes, use 1 teaspoon of lecithin + 2 tablespoons of powdered milk (preferably soy milk) + 1/4 cup (60 ml) of water.

- It is better to ingest soy lecithin from the whole bean rather than in the form of an extract (granules).

SOY FLOUR

- You should develop the habit of always blending a small quantity into your bread, cake, and pie recipes, etc. in order to increase the quality of proteins and to add a pleasant little nutty flavor.

- It should be stored in the refrigerator, because it goes rancid easily.

SOY OIL

- Dark in color, with a nutty flavor (if it comes from the first pressing).

- Contains polyunsaturated fatty acids.

- It is very difficult to find in a cold-pressed form.

TAMARI SOY SAUCE - SHOYU

- The soy sauce used in vegetarian cooking.

- Derived from fermentation, it is a product which is rich in B vitamins such as B_{12}; it is fermented for 1 to 2 years and is available with or without an added grain and sea salt.

- Should always be used towards the end of the cooking process, because tamari sauce must not boil; otherwise, vitamin B_{12} and the bacteria responsible for fermentation will be lost.

- Keep it in the refrigerator.

- Avoid synthetic supermarket soy sauce, which is manufactured from extruded soybeans (the residue of beans from which the oil has been removed) through a process of hydrolysis, using hydrochloric acid; caramel (for coloring) or corn syrup (for flavor) is added.

- Use as a seasoning. Do not use too much, as it is salty! 1/2 teaspoon of salt = 2 teaspoons of tamari sauce = 1 tablespoon of miso.[1]

- A similar product to tamari sauce but in the form of a paste, whereas tamari sauce is a liquid; its fermentation may last for three years. It is available with or without an added grain and sea salt. There is a great variety of miso.
    - Soy + barley = mugi miso
    - Soy + rice = kome miso
    - 100% soy = hatcho miso, etc.

- The fact that it is rich in proteins, B vitamins, and minerals makes it a staple food product among the Japanese.

- Do not boil it; add it at the end of the cooking process in order to maintain its nutritional value.

- Keep it in the refrigerator in a glass jar.

- Tamari sauce and miso can be used to complement grains and facilitate digestion, since they are both products which result from fermentation.

Uses

- You can drink miso; 1 teaspoon (5 ml) in 1/2 cup (125 ml) of warm water.

- For a sauce, combine water, starch, and miso.

- You can add miso to soup, sauce, dressing.

- Dissolve it in a bit of stock beforehand.

SOY MILK

Nutritional Value

- Has a considerable protein content.

- Low in carbohydrates; recommended for diabetics.

- Low in fats.

- Calcium content: 46 mg per cup. Source of iron: 1.8 mg per cup.

- Precious for those who suffer from cardiac disorders and arteriosclerosis, because it contains lecithin and polyunsaturated fatty acids, but no cholesterol.

- Has an alkalizing effect and, therefore, combats acidity; does not contribute to the excessive formation of mucus.

- Extremely economical.

Milk 1 cup (250 ml)	Carbohydrates %	Lipids %	Proteins %	Calcium mg	Iron mg
Cow's milk	4.9%	3,5%	3.4%	307	traces
Soy milk	2.2%	1.5%	3.5%	46*	1.8
Mother's milk	9.5%	4.0%	1.1%	80	0.2

* Soy milk can be fortified with lactate or calcium carbonate, if desired. See the "Recipe Book" section.

Uses

If soy milk is used as a drink, we recommend a progressive change in preference to a radical one; add it gradually to the milk you customarily use. Soy milk has a nutty flavor. To make the change easier add a bit of honey or vanilla, or whip it together with some fruit, in the blender.

For the following reasons, it is possible to use soy milk without restriction when preparing dishes, without creating too many negative reactions:

- Soy milk does not alter the flavor of foods.

- It completes the proteins of other foods (flour, rice, millet, etc.).

- Use it in soups, sauces, béchamels, creams, desserts, pancakes: no one will notice!

- You can make yogurt from soy milk in the same way as with cow's milk. Use a half-and-half mixture at the beginning.

TOFU

- Coagulated soy milk; the curds are pressed to extract the whey.

- Easy to prepare and integrate into the menu; easy to digest.

- Has a high nutritional value. It is a good substitute for meat, eggs, and milk products, because it is an excellent source of vegetable protein, is low in saturated fats, contains no cholesterol, and is very economical.

- Rich in minerals such as calcium (128 mg per 100 g, i.e., 1/4 of a cake or 4 ounces or 1 serving), iron (1.9 mg per 100 g), phosphorus, potassium, and sodium, as well as vitamin B and E. However, it contains no fiber.

Uses

Tofu is one of the most versatile foods. Its flavor is delicate and refined, but not insipid. It's surprising how, when we replace this word with more subtle terms, the flavor changes. Tofu can be used in the preparation of main courses as well as in desserts, and it costs next to nothing.

- Cut into cubes and serve as is, marinated, sautéed, etc.

- Beat in the blender to obtain a simple or sophisticated

sauce, mayonnaise that is "finger-lickin' good", whipped cream, pink icing, etc.

- Crush it with a fork in order to serve it incognito or disguise it by mixing it into scrambled eggs, etc.

- Consult the "Recipe Book" section; it will provide you with inspiration and convince you of the 1001 uses that tofu can be put to.

- Often, with tofu, the secret is in the seasoning and in how the tofu is prepared; as a matter of fact, this is true of all legumes.

It is important to think of adding tofu to grain dishes, which are usually low in lysine (an essential amino acid), because tofu contains an abundance of it. This makes tofu an excellent complement.

Storage

- When vacuum-packed and stored in the refrigerator, tofu keeps for weeks. Once opened it must be covered with water and returned to the refrigerator. The water must be changed as often as possible.

- It can be frozen with no problem. When frozen, tofu takes on a yellowish hue which disappears once it unfreezes; its texture changes and becomes grainy.

- To refresh tofu, if necessary, plunge it into some water and bring it to a boil. Then plunge it into ice-cold water.

OKARA (SOY PULP)

- The pulp which remains after the making of soy milk.

- It has lost a good deal of its proteins (combine with

grains); it still contains 3.5% protein, compared to 35% in the soybean.

Uses

- Roast in a wok with vegetables to make a side dish.

- Add to salads, soups, cookies, bread, pies, etc.

- Can be used to make delicious croquettes, spreads, sausages, etc.

- Can be kept for a few days in the refrigerator. Freeze or dry for longer storage.

SOY MILK POWDER

- Prepare in the blender as you would cow's milk powder (1/4 cup of powder per cup of water).

- When left to stand, the powder readily settles to the bottom. Shake well or filter before using.

- Use as is in recipes. Can be used to replace milk powder, as it is less expensive.

- As a beverage, however, milk made from beans is tastier.

- Here is an example of how to use soy milk powder: whip or mix together 2 eggs, 2 cups of flour, 1/2 cup of soy milk powder, some salt, and 2 cups of water. Makes delicious pancakes!

IT'S INCREDIBLE WHAT CAN BE DONE
WITH THE SOYBEAN!

COOKING CHART FOR LEGUMES

Dried Legumes (1 cup)	Water (cups)	Cooking Time (hours)	Cooking Time after soaking (minutes)	Cooking Time after soaking & sprouting (minutes)	Cooking Time in pressure cooker (minutes)
Adzuki	3	1 1/2	40	30	—
Navy	3	2	60	—	25
Lima	2	1 1/2	30	30	25
Mung	3	1 1/2	45	—	—
Black	4	1 1/2	30	—	never
Kidney	3	1 1/2	30	—	—
Soybeans	3	2-3	105	105	35
Lentils	3	45 min.	15	—	—
Split peas	3	1	10	—	never
Chickpeas	4	2-3	60-90	35	45
Yellow peas	3	3	60	—	—

- This page can be reproduced and placed in a convenient location.

- Legumes are well cooked when they can be easily crushed with a fork.

- In the fall, when they have just been harvested, legumes cook more rapidly. The older they get, the longer it takes to cook them.

- A few examples of how to cook them after soaking or sprouting have been given.

CHAPTER 8

Nuts and Seeds

Nuts and seeds are oleaginous fruits; that is, they produce oil. This term includes all those fruits which are rich in lipids, such as olives and avocados.

NUTRITIONAL VALUE

- A good source of proteins and carbohydrates, they have a high concentration of lipids. They may contain from 3 to 7 times as many lipids as proteins and are high in calories. Avoid overeating!

- A good protein complement for legumes.

- Contain a considerable quantity of mineral salts (calcium, iron, magnesium, zinc) and vitamins (A,B,E).

- Recommended serving: 1/4 cup (60 ml) per day for adults or 2 tablespoons (30 ml) in the form of butter.

SOAKING

- Makes them more tender and digestible.

- Soak in cold water for a few hours or soak overnight. The next day it is easy to add them to your breakfast cereal, to a salad at noon, or to serve them as a snack.

USES

- Soak or serve as is; add to vegetable or fruit salads, yogurt, vegetables, or grain dishes.

- Soak and beat together in the blender with water or rejuvelac to make excellent beverages or sauces, pies, cheeses, etc.

- Dry-roast and grind up for use in different recipes:

    1. Choose a few varieties and wash them.

    2. Dry and then dry-roast lightly in a cast-iron skillet or in the oven on a cookie sheet. What an aroma!

- Let cool and grind up ahead of time into small quantities. Store in small jars in a cool place where they are readily accessible. Should be eaten within a week.

It is better to eat nuts and seeds as a complement within the same meal, rather than nibbling on them between meals.

Nuts

ALMONDS

- They offer good quality protein. Their fatty acids are unsaturated. Oil is extracted from almonds.

- They are a source of calcium and magnesium, which are concentrated in the husk.

A taste treat, when soaked overnight. Make excellent butter.

FILBERTS (CULTIVATED) AND HAZELNUTS (WILD)

- Grow in our temperate climate.
- Delicious, when soaked. Make excellent butter.

CASHEWS

- Fruit of the cashew tree, which grows in tropical regions.
- Contain vitamin A.
- When soaked, they have a creamy consistency.

BRAZIL NUTS

- Very rich in lipids (30% linoleic acid, among others). Among the most calorific of nuts.
- In order to shell these three-sided nuts more easily, freeze for a few hours beforehand or soak for one to two days.

COCONUTS

- Fruit of the coconut palm whose fruit is eaten fresh, or in dried form.
- Contain natural sugars, when dried; there is no need to buy sweetened coconut.
- Can be used fresh, in grated form, in fruit salads and breakfast cereals.
- Diuretic and laxative. Coconut milk is a good vermifuge (pulp + water in the blender).

NUTS AND SEEDS

- Coconut oil (also called copra oil) is a saturated oil, which is solid at room temperature.

WALNUTS

- Grow in temperate climates.

- When shelled, they go rancid quickly. Always store in the refrigerator.

- Keep better in the shell.

  Other varieties of nuts: chestnuts, acorns, pine kernels, pecans, pistachios.

  NOTE: Look for pecans and pistachios which are of a natural color; commercially they are often died red.

Storage and Quality of Nuts

- Unshelled: keep in airtight containers in a cool, dry place, away from the light.

- Shelled: it is preferable to keep them in glass jars in the refrigerator; in this way you can see them and you will use them!

- In their shells, they are less expensive, go rancid less quickly, and keep the children busy!

- Nuts in their shells, when soaked for 1 to 2 days, are easier to shell, and taste better.

- Nut butters should be stored in the refrigerator. They are creamier and more digestible, when beaten together with a bit of lukewarm water (emulsified).

Nuts are harvested in the autumn. It is preferable, therefore, to stock up on them in the fall and to freeze them.

Seeds

PUMPKIN (OR OTHER SQUASH) SEEDS

- Grown in our climate; should be given greater importance and be used more.
- Good vermifuge. Good for the prostate because of their high zinc content.
- Use in dried or ground up form. Add to grain dishes and salad dressings.
- Dry, dry-roast, sprinkle with a bit of tamari sauce, and eat as is, or add to fruit salads or legumes.
- Easy to harvest at home. They make for good eating!
- Green pumpkin seeds are a special variety. They have no shells and can be eaten as is.

FLAX SEEDS

- From a plant with lovely blue flowers and oil-producing seeds, which contain mucilage, a fiber with a laxative effect that is used in foods. This plant's stem provides a fiber used in textiles.
- Used for balancing the intestinal flora (1 tablespoon of ground up flax seeds in water or juice, after getting up in the morning, or at bedtime).
- Flax seeds are good not just for the intestines or when you have something in your eye. Far from it! They are delicious and nutritious. In order to assimilate them better, **eat them in ground-up form**. Add them to breakfast cereal or biscuits.

SESAME SEEDS

- The sesame plant grows to a height of about 1 meter in warm, dry climates and produces white, yellow, brown, or black seeds. Brown ones are more common.

- **Should be eaten unhulled and ground-up;** otherwise, they will not be digested, but rather, eliminated as is.

- Their lecithin and calcium content makes them good for the nervous system.

- Wash well before using; dry them in the oven or in a skillet.

- They make excellent butter. Choose sesame butter made from unhulled seeds which have been lightly roasted, because it has a higher nutritional value than tahini, which is made from hulled seeds.

- Sesame butter is used in chickpea purée, salad dressings, spreads, etc.

- When mixed together with a bit of water, sesame butter can't be beaten!

SUNFLOWER SEEDS
("Helianthus", from the Greek *helios*, meaning the sun, and *anthos*, flower)

- They are grown in cold climates (should be given greater importance) and have very high nutritional value.

- A good source of protein and of polyunsaturated fatty acids, such as linoleic acid, the most important essential fatty acid. They have a very high vitamin B_6 content (pyridoxine).

- Their vitality comes from the sunflower's ability to follow the sun's course from morning until night, and from its

deep roots, which draw trace elements, particularly iron and fluorine, from the soil.

- Remove the black hull before eating. Look for seeds of a beautiful gray color.

- More tender and delicious when soaked overnight before being eaten.

- Dry-roast and sprinkle with a bit of tamari sauce.

- When hulled they yield delicious little sprouts (in a jar); with their black hulls they provide succulent shoots (on potting soil).

- Grind up hulled seeds and add to different dishes.

- Store in the refrigerator, as hulled seeds go rancid quickly.

- Avoid buying sunflower seeds which have already been roasted and salted, because they are often stale. Prepare them yourself.

- Add them to salads, spaghetti sauce, pancake mixtures, cookies, and breakfast cereals; eat them as a snack.

CHAPTER 9

Sprouts

Sprouts are a source of life! They constitute a living food par excellence! Once sprouts have become a part of our eating habits, our health takes an upturn!

THE ADVANTAGES OF GROWING SPROUTS:

- Sprouting increases nutritional value and makes digestion easier.

- It produces vitamins for free!! Vitamin A,B,C, and E content increases from 4 to 10 times.[1] Numerous enzymes are activated during sprouting.

- It makes minerals easier to assimilate.

- It predigests foods: during sprouting starch begins its transformation into simple sugars, which are easier to assimilate.

- It improves the **quality** of proteins; for example, lysine (an essential amino acid lacking in grains) increases by 24% during sprouting.

- It regenerates the body and frees the latent energy of grains.

- It allows us to eat immature plants, which contain anti-carcinogenic elements.

- It is a pleasant, economical, and ecological procedure, which is productive in terms of its nutritional return, and oh, so simple!

- It makes up for dietary deficiencies in northern countries.

- It is an alternative to cooking; sprouts are alive and fresh!

- It is an educational activity for children and adults!

WHAT CAN YOU SPROUT? ANY LIVING SEED!

1. Grains and Legumes

SPROUTING

- Allows us to eat raw wheat, rye, lentils, mung beans, etc.

- Reduces cooking time of soybeans and chickpeas (1/2 hour instead of 2 hours or more).

Green and brown lentils sprout quickly and easily; red lentils will not sprout because they have been hulled.

A) WHEAT SPROUTS

Here we will speak only of sprouting in jars.

- A choice food for overworked people, convalescents, expectant mothers, women who are breastfeeding, and adolescents.

- Chew them well and eat them in small quantities at a time. Try bread made from wheat sprouts also.

- Their sweet flavor will enhance many dishes.

- A revitalizing treatment: Chew 2 tablespoons per day for three weeks (2 teaspoons for children).

- Wheat will sprout in 48 hours. Eat when the sprout is the same length as the wheat kernel; as it grows longer it becomes sweeter.

Nutritional Value

- Sprouting increases wheat's vitamin A (provitamin), B,C,E, and K.

- Wheat sprouts are considered to be a very good source of vitamin E.

- A big increase in minerals can be observed.[2, 3]

B. ALFALFA SPROUTS

Alfalfa sprouts: a precious whole foodstuff.

Nutritional Value

- An excellent source of vitamins, minerals, and essential amino acids.

- A source of chlorophyll in winter.

- Experiments have shown that alfalfa sprouts stimulate lactation, combat the hot rushes of menopause, and soothe people suffering from arthritis.

- Alfalfa sprouts yield greenery, as do fenugreek, cress, spinach, and radish sprouts.

- Alfalfa sprouts are a dietary treasure that we should not

do without. Add them to salads, sandwiches, soups, juices, and salad dressings.

- Children really like alfalfa sprouts.

In winter alfalfa sprouts should be eaten often. Grow them yourself; they are inexpensive and provide a lot of culinary inspiration.

2. Seeds

CABBAGE SEEDS

Combine cabbage seeds with alfalfa and radish seeds to make sprouts. A good source of vitamin C.

FENUGREEK SEEDS

- Fenugreek is a member of the same plant family as alfalfa.

- Young shoots have a sharp flavor which becomes milder as the sprouts grow bigger.

RADISH SEEDS

- Have a sharp flavor; sprout in small quantities along with some alfalfa seeds.

- Good for cleansing the liver.

SPROUTS

SESAME SEEDS

- Hulled seeds will not sprout.

- Whole seeds yield sprouts with a very strong flavor.

SUNFLOWER SEEDS

- Hulled seeds will sprout in a jar.

- Eat these delicious, small sprouts as soon as they are ready, because they will not keep long.

- Have great nutritional value.

- Unhulled seeds will sprout on potting soil.

MUCILAGINOUS SEEDS

- Flax seeds, mustard seeds, cress seeds, etc.

- Sprout differently, without soaking or rinsing.

- Place the seeds, closely bunched together, in a sprouting apparatus or on some screening which has been tightly stretched over a recipient for collecting the water. Water them frequently. They sprout readily and are so delicious!

- They make a marvellous, decorative centerpiece for the table; a delight for the eyes and the stomach!

USES OF SPROUTS

Eat them raw as often as possible in order to take advantage of their full nutritional value.

Raw

- Make excellent, nourishing salads in winter when com-

bined with grated root vegetables or other varieties of vegetables. Sprouted sunflower seeds go very nicely with fruit salads or yogurt.

- Add to sandwiches, soups,dressings, casseroles, etc.

- The blender is an excellent tool for increasing our intake of sprouts! Liquefy sprouts in salad dressings, soups, casseroles, etc.

- Upgrade the nutritional value of juices: lentil sprouts and tomato juice; alfalfa sprouts and tomato, orange, or pineapple juice; etc. Give your imagination free rein!

Cooked

- Tasty in chop suey, chow mein, and various vegetable casseroles.

- Add to bread dough and cookie batter (wheat, rye, or sunflower sprouts).

- Use in main course dishes in place of whole grains: quantities, qualities, and cooking times change.

SPROUTING METHOD

What you need:

- A glass jar with a wide mouth.

- A piece of mosquito netting or of muslin cloth.

- A warm, dark place.

- Fresh water, air, and seeds!

HOW TO PROCEED:

1. Sort the seeds if possible. Damaged seeds will not sprout.

2. Cover the bottom of the jar entirely with seeds, to a depth of 3-4 layers.

3. Fasten the mosquito netting or the cloth over the end of the jar.

4. Wash the seeds thoroughly in warm water, and drain.

5. After washing them, soak the seeds in three times their

SPROUTING

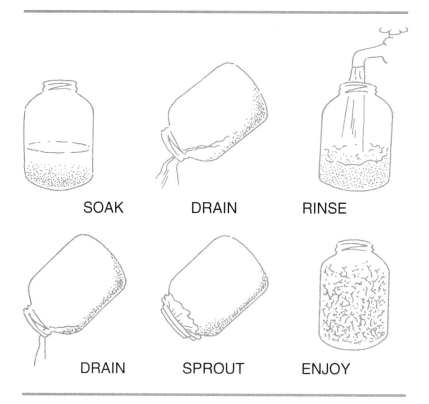

SOAK   DRAIN   RINSE

DRAIN   SPROUT   ENJOY

volume of warm water for 3-15 hours, depending on the size of the seeds. It is customary to soak them overnight.

6. The next morning, pour off the water used for soaking.
   NOTE:
   - This water can be used for cooking or for watering plants.
   - Water used for soaking legumes should not be used for cooking, because it causes flatulence (intestinal gases).

7. Rinse well in warm water and **drain completely**.
   NOTE: Poor draining often causes rotting to occur!

BATHING SPROUTS

BATHE AND REMOVE HULLS

DRAIN

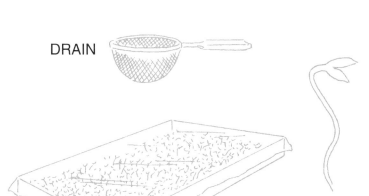

LET GROW

8. Lean the jar up at a 45° angle or lay it down flat, on its side. Put it in a dark place or cover it with a cloth, leaving the mouth of the jar exposed to the air. Leave it at room temperature.

9. Rinse two times a day (in the morning and in the evening).

10. Eliminate as many as possible of the hulls which come loose and float up to the surface of the water during rinsing (particularly mung bean and alfalfa seed hulls).

11. In a few days, depending on the variety of seeds used, the temperature, and the number of rinsings, the sprouts will be ready (see the table).

A FEW SPECIAL DETAILS

1. About alfalfa

Making your own alfalfa sprouts on a daily basis is a simple, pleasant, and profitable activity.

- Alfalfa sprouts must be rinsed twice a day at the beginning but only once a day from the third day on. When prepared in this way, they are crisper and stay fresh longer.

- Alfalfa seeds require lower temperature conditions to sprout than do other seeds: 65°F (16°C).

- To obtain well-developed alfalfa sprouts which keep better, it is recommended to give them a bath!

- After 3 or 4 days of sprouting, when the majority of the hulls have fallen off and two little leaves can be seen, take the sprouts out of the jar, put them into a large bowl filled with warm water, and stir them gently with your hands.

- The hulls will float up to the surface of the water and can be removed by hand or with the help of a sieve.

- Then drain the sprouts in a sieve and place them in a tray, rather than putting them back into the jar. The green plastic sprouting trays sold for preparing garden plants are perfectly suitable for this purpose. Cover the alfalfa sprouts with transparent plastic, which has been perforated here and there to create the effect of a greenhouse. This procedure stimulates growth and the formation of chlorophyll, and prevents the seeds from drying.

- Place the tray in a brightly lit place, but not in direct sunlight. It is not necessary to rinse. In 1 or 2 days your alfalfa sprouts will be ready: superb and delicious!

- They keep very well in a tightly-sealed jar in the refrigerator. **Don't forget to eat some every day.**

This little ritual, which children thoroughly enjoy, is the same for radish, cabbage, and red clover seeds.

2. About mung beans

- Use a large jar with a large opening; this makes it is easier to move the sprouts gently back and forth when rinsing in order to let the hulls rise to the surface for removal.

- In order to obtain longer, fatter sprouts replace the jar with a perforated container or a sieve. Then put a plate, with a weight on top of it, on the beans. This will provide the beans with some resistance while they are growing and stimulate them to grow larger! This technique is not essential; it is a question of choice!

- Mung beans sprout better when rinsed in water which is more than lukewarm: about 80°F (20°C)!

- What's more, if they are rinsed 4 times a day they will sprout faster and will be sweeter and crisper.

- **Be careful of the light**, because it will make the sprouts turn brown.

Seeds	Soaking time (hours)	Daily rinsings	Ready in	Appearance of sprouts
Hard and Soft wheat*	8	2	36-48 hrs.	same length as seeds
Rye	8	2	36-48 hrs.	shorter than seeds
Adzuki beans	8-12	3	4 days	1 inch (2.5 cm)
Mung beans	8-12	4	4 days	1 1/2 inches (4 cm)
Chickpeas	15	3-4	3 days	1/2 to 1 inch
Soybeans	15	3	3-5 days	same length as beans
Lentils	8	2	3 days	hulls fall off, small leaves form at the end of the sprout
Alfalfa	5-8	2	5-6 days	hulls fall off, 2 small leaves appear
Radish	5-8	2	5-6 days	hulls fall off, 2 small leaves appear
Fenugreek	6-8	2	5-6 days	1 1/2 in. (4 cm)
Sunflower	8	2	36-48 hrs.	sprouts appear, seeds open
Almonds	8	2	2 days	sprouts appear

* Millet, oats, and barley, when whole (i.e., unhulled), sprout easily in a jar or on potting soi

Flavor	Comments
sweet	if sprouts too developed, too sweet. Dry and grind up = malt
mild	breakfast cereal: prepare in a blender with warm water
like hazelnuts	diuretic
like green peas	see details in this chapter
diluted	cook for 30 min.
nutty	cook for 30 min., use quickly
like raw potato	let leaves green a few hours in light
mild	see details in this chapter
hot	like alfalfa
hot	let leaves green a few hours in light
delicious when young	eat right away. Do not keep well.
almonds	more digestible

Do you have a problem with rot?

After finding the cause, start again!

- Usually it is due to excesss humidity: poor drainage.

- Lack of air: too many seeds in the jar.

- Seeds are too old or of poor quality: think organic.

- Quality of water- quality of care.

CHAPTER 10

Fruits

CATEGORIES

- **Sweet fruits:** bananas, dates, figs, ripe grapes, dried fruits, etc.

- **Semi-acidic fruits:** apples, apricots, berries, peaches, pears, etc.

- **Acidic fruits:** lemons, oranges, grapefruit, pineapples, kiwis, etc.

- Avocados and olives are the only fruits which are rich in lipids (fats).They should be eaten in moderation, because they are highly calorific. Avocados are neutral fruits which lend themselves to being combined with other fruits and vegetables. They have a very delicate flavor and can be served as is, with a bit of lemon juice, or in the form of a dip or a sauce, etc. Ripe, black olives are delightful in salads, grain dishes, dips, etc.

- An excellent source of vitamins, mineral salts, and water. For example:
    - Vitamin A (in the form of beta-carotene) — yellow fruits such as peaches, cantaloupes, apricots, nectarines, etc.
    - Vitamin C — citrus fruits, strawberries. The acidity of these fruits allows them to keep their vitamin C. Citrus fruits contain calcium; bananas contain potassium; dried fruits contain iron; etc.

- A good source of fructose, a simple sugar which is assimilated directly by the body: 10-20% in fresh fruits, 60-70% in dried fruits.

- A good source of fibers such as cellulose and pectin; they facilitate intestinal transport. What's more, pectin (found in apples) helps to reduce the level of cholesterol in the blood.

Eating 2 or 3 pieces of fruit a day, including an acid fruit (for vitamin C) and an apple (for pectin) is a good dietary principle. The popular saying states the case so well: "An apple a day keeps the doctor away".

EATING FRUITS PROVIDES THE FOLLOWING BENEFITS:

- It ensures that we have a good source of vitamins, minerals, fibers, and water.

- It removes toxins from our body and avoids nutritional overload.

- It requires no culinary preparation.

- It increases our consumption of raw foods.

- It can help us to change certain habits: eating sweet desserts and snacks, drinking coffee, and smoking cigarettes.

HOW SHOULD WE EAT FRUITS?

Raw, ripe, and whole rather than in the form of juice, preserves, or jam.

WHEN?

- When they are in season.

- In the morning to begin breakfast, after drinking 1 or 2 glasses of water!! This allows the body to continue the cleansing process it has undertaken during the night.

- As a snack or with yogurt (at breakfast or as a dessert).

In the summer and fall, eat an abundance of fresh fruits. During the cold season, dried fruits are recommended as, of course, are apples. They are native to North American regions and keep well in cold storage.

NOTE: In general, fruits which are found on the market are non-organic and contain insecticides and even paraffin, which are concentrated on the skin. Always scrub fruits thoroughly in water to which you have added some lemon juice or vinegar. Look for and demand fruits that have been grown organically.

STORAGE

Fruits should be kept in cold storage; however, they should be eaten ripe and at room temperature. Always keep some on hand in a basket but not exposed to direct light.

ABOUT JUICE

- In order to condition children and adults to drink water and eat fresh fruits, it is preferable to serve juice only occasionally.

- Bottles of juice should not be left open or sitting on the counter. Vitamin C is affected by air, heat, and light.

- Fresh juice, prepared in an extractor, oxidizes rapidly, when it comes in contact with air. Drink it without delay. Often, rather than placing a coaster under our glass to protect the furniture, it would be better to place it over our glass of juice. We must protect our health too!

- As often as possible drink fresh juice or reconstituted juice made with spring water and with no sugar added.

- At all cost, avoid carbonated beverages and fruit-flavored drinks. Read all labels carefully, paying special attention to such things as water, sugar, additives, coloring, and in certain cases, caffeine.

Remember that good habits as well as bad ones are acquired at a young age.

Dried Fruits

NUTRITIONAL VALUE

- A good source of vitamins A and B, iron, calcium, and fibers.

- Dehydration concentrates their sugar content. They should be eaten in moderation.

- Soak them before eating in order to diminish the concentration of their sugar content.

- Generally they are treated with sulfur for purposes of conservation. In cooperatives and natural food stores, you can find dried N.S./N.F. fruits (i.e., non-sulfured and non-fumigated). It is preferable to buy this kind of fruit.

Apricots

- N.S./N.F. apricots. They are brown in color and drier than the apricots we are accustomed to using.
- Sulfured apricots are orange-colored and more pulpy than the N.S./N.F. variety.
- Once rehydrated, N.S./N.F. apricots are really good, and they are better for the health.

Dates

- Should be eaten in moderation; one of the sweetest of dried fruits.
- Organic, N.S./N.F. dates are available. They are soft in consistency.

Figs

- Untreated figs can be found.
- Cristals of sugar may form on the surface of this fruit, but this does not affect their quality.

Prunes

- Dried prunes come from blue or purple plums.
- Organic, N.S./N.F. prunes are available.
- A mild laxative. To prepare, soak 3-4 prunes overnight and enjoy them as is, in the morning.

Raisins

- Organic, *Thompson* N.S./N.F. raisins are available.

- There are also Sultana and Malaga raisins, as well as currants.

Other dried fruits: apples, pears, peaches, etc.

USES

- It is best **to soak** dried fruits before using. They will be tasty, not as sweet, and easier to chew. Can be eaten as is.

- Wash, soak in cold water for about 8 hours, and liquefy in a mixer with the water used for soaking (if N.S./N.F.), plain water, or juice.

- If desired, you can add some walnuts, soaked almonds, or a crisp apple, etc. Give free rein to your imagination; the results will be superb!

- Depending on the consistency of the fruits, once lique-fied, you can also obtain sauce, mousse, or fruit butter to be served with fruit, yogurt, pancakes, muffins, cakes, etc., or to be used as a pie filling or as a sauce for the baby.

- May be used to replace sugar and jam.

STORAGE AND QUALITY

- Dried fruits are naturally preserved for the winter.

- Look for organic-quality, N.S./N.F. fruits.

- Keep in glass jars in a cool place, away from light and air.

Vegetables

CATEGORIES

We may call **vegetable** any edible parts of a plant:

- **Fruit** vegetables: eggplants, cucumbers, squash, peppers, tomatoes, etc.

- **Flowering** vegetables: artichokes, broccoli, cauliflower, etc.

- **Leafy** green vegetables: chicory, spinach, romaine lettuce, endives, etc.

- **Stalk** vegetables: asparagus, chard, celery, etc.

- **Root** vegetables: beets, carrots, celeriac, turnips, etc.

- **Tubers**: potatoes, Jerusalem artichokes, etc.

- **Bulbs**: garlic, onions, leeks, etc.

NUTRITIONAL VALUE

- Vegetables provide few calories.

- They are an excellent source of vitamins A, B, and C, as well as minerals such as iron and calcium (green vegetables).

- They are rich in fibers and water.

Eat at least 3 servings per day, one of which is a dark green vegetable. One serving is equivalent to 1/2 cup (125 ml), or 1 cup (250 ml) in the case of leafy green vegetables.

You can increase your consumption of vegetables in the following ways:

- **By beginning meals with raw vegetables.**

- **By always serving a vegetable side dish.**

- **By disguising vegetables in snacks for children.**

The greatest nutritional value of leafy green vegetables lies in their high provitamin A content (beta-carotene), as well as in the vitamin C and folic acid that they contain. These nutritional elements are absent from grains.

This chapter presents a summary description of a few of the most commonly used vegetables. In the "Recipe Book" section you will find a great number of ideas on ways of preparing vegetables.

Leafy Green Vegetables

VARIETIES

Lettuce, chicory, cress, spinach, romaine lettuce, etc. During the winter, don't forget to use **sprouts**, prepared in a jar or on potting soil, to make abundant salads for starting off meals.

Eat an inexpensive green vegetable that is full of iron, at every meal.

- Choose green vegetables that are as dark in color as possible. They are a good source of high-quality protein.

- They are rich in provitamin A (chlorophyll masks the color of the beta-carotene), B vitamins (such as folic acid), vitamin C, calcium, and iron.

- You can count on *dark green* as being a ticket to good health! Long live the color *green*!

- Adding lemon juice to green vegetables makes for better conservation and better assimilation of vitamin C. This vitamin is necessary for the absorption of iron.

Flowering Vegetables

- **Artichokes:** they are worth discovering.

- **Broccoli: a choice vegetable**, because of its nutritional value (proteins, vitamins A and C, and calcium).

- **Cauliflower**, etc.

- Serve raw, as a snack or at the beginning of meals, or cooked, as is or with a sauce.

Fruit Vegetables

- **Eggplant:** an autumn vegetable (ratatouille).

- **Cucumbers:** refreshing; contain a lot of water.

- **Squash:** versatile and nutritious.

- **Beans:** delicious when steamed.

- **Green peas:** delectable, cooked or raw.

- **Red and green peppers:** nutritious and delicious, raw.

- **Tomatoes:** a real treat when in season.

SERVE THEM RAW AS OFTEN AS POSSIBLE!

Squash

- Excellent vegetables; members of the *cucurbita* family.

- Nourishing and easy to digest (simple sugars).

- They come in a large variety: cantaloupes, cucumbers, gherkins, zucchini, spaghetti squash, yellow squash, and winter squash (butternut, buttercup, pepper, pumpkin, etc.).

- Winter squash can be kept for a long time in a cool, dry place.

NUTRITIONAL VALUE

- They contain few calories or proteins, a few carbohydrates (simple sugars), a lot of vitamins (A, B, and C), some minerals (phosphorus, potassium, calcium), and some trace elements (magnesium, iron, copper, manganese, zinc).

- Depurative and diuretic.

USES

- They are delicious, raw! Try finely grated pumpkin salad.

- Cut into cubes and sauté in a wok along with some other vegetables and tofu.

- Bake whole in the oven at 350°F (180°C) for 45-60

minutes, or cut up in order to shorten the cooking time and so as to salvage the raw seeds.

- Use in cakes and cookies.

- Cut into large chunks and steam without peeling. Remove the skin after cooking, if necessary. Use in soups and for making purées.

- Dried seeds, seasoned with a bit of tamari sauce are delicious; dried seeds can be ground up and added to different dishes.

Root Vegetables

- They grow well in the North American climate. Keep well in cold storage. They are eaten mostly in winter.

- They are high-energy foods because of their carbohydrate contents (starch and sugar).

- Rich in vitamins, minerals, and fibers.

- Serve raw in salads and as snacks, or cooked.

Beets

- They contain natural sugars, vitamins B and C, and minerals; their charming color will enhance the flavor and the appearance of your dishes.

- Grate finely and serve in salads or sandwiches; grate coarsely and sauté in a skillet or bake in the oven. They are delightful!

- They make delightful lacto-fermentations.

- Beet leaves can be eaten in salads (provitamin A and calcium).

Carrots

- A good source of provitamin A, calcium, and fibers such as pectin.

- They regularize the intestines; they are effective in treating both constipation and diarrhea (because of their pectin content).

- Serve raw, whole, cut into pieces, or grated, in salads and sandwiches. They can also be cooked. Make excellent juice.

Celeriac

- Nutritious and delicious. Has a celery-like flavor. Good, raw or cooked. Worth discovering.

Rutabagas and Turnips

- A good source of vitamins and calcium.

- Serve raw, julienne, or grated. Steam or bake (along with, or as a substitute for potatoes). Serve in soups.

- If you have a garden, use fresh leaves, raw or steamed. They are rich in vitamins A, B, and C, and in calcium and iron.

- The flesh of rutabagas is yellow, whereas that of turnips is white.

Parsnips

- Long roots of a white, creamy color. Have a diuretic effect.

- Serve raw or cooked–preferably steamed or *à l'étouffée* –

VEGETABLES

because they readily absorb water. Think of adding them to salads, soups, vegetable pies, etc.

Radishes

- A good source of vitamin C and iodine

- They have a depurative effect on the liver.

- Varieties: red, black, and white.

- In winter, radish sprouts add zest to salads and sandwiches.

Tubers

Potatoes

- A nourishing, high-energy food because of their starch content.

- A good source of vitamin C; take special care, as this is a water-soluble vitamin. Potatoes also provide minerals (iron, calcium, magnesium, and potassium).

- Potatoes should not be eaten raw (they contain too much starch), nor should they be eaten green. Color indicates the presence of solanine, a toxin which develops when potatoes are exposed to light.

- In order to avoid losing the water-soluble vitamins (B and C) and minerals, do not soak or cook them in water. This is a habit that we must change.

- Always cook them whole, with the peel left on. Steam or bake. The more they are cut up, the more they lose their vitamins. Peel them after cooking, if necessary.

- Aluminum foil is not necessary when cooking them in the

oven. Simply prick them and bake at 350°F (180°C) for 25-40 minutes, depending on their size.

- A good vegetable; however, do not forget to vary the vegetables you use.

Sweet Potatoes

- They have a very high provitamin A content.

- Cook them like potatoes.

Jerusalem Artichokes

- Not as well known as other vegetables, artichokes are used like potatoes.

- Easy to grow, resistant, and prolific.

- They can be eaten raw, since they do not contain as much starch as potatoes.

Bulbs

Garlic

- A natural antiseptic. Contains sulfur.

- Purifies the blood and combats infections.

- Very good for the intestines and the kidneys.

- Eat raw or lightly sautéed; its flavor enhances any dish. It is a great asset in the kitchen.

Onions

- Onions are also an antiseptic.

- They stimulate the secretions of the digestive (and lach-rymal) glands.

- Serve raw , steamed, sautéed, or baked in the oven, with the skin left on.

Leeks

- Mild and alkaline.

- Diuretic and subtle in flavor; eat raw or cooked.

- Do not forget to use the green part (contains chlorophyll).

All of these vegetables make excellent salads during the winter, or they can be eaten as purées, soups, or oven-baked dishes served with a sauce. When served au gratin they constitute the main course of a light meal.

Do not forget to eat the leaves of these vegetables. They are delightful and nutritious.

HOW SHOULD WE EAT OUR FAVORITE VEGETABLES?

- Insofar as it is possible, vegetables should be home-grown. If you are not able to grow your own, buy them from an organic producer, of whom there is an ever-increasing number.

- Eat vegetables when they are in season:
    - Lots of green leafy vegetables, fruit vegetables, and flowering vegetables in the summer and fall.
    - In winter, sprouts make up for the lack of greenery, and root vegetables, squash, cabbages, etc. complete the menu. There is sufficient variety to satisfy us!

- Vitamins are affected by water and heat. Avoid canned vegetables, which have lost most of their nutritional value. Frozen or dehydrated vegetables are preferable: they provide variety and contribute a bit of color or an

element of surprise; however, they should not form the basis of our winter vegetable diet.

- Finely grating root vegetables makes mastication, digestion, and assimilation easier; however, once cut or grated, vegetables oxidize rapidly when they come in contact with the air, and their vitamins (particularly vitamin C) are destroyed. Therefore, raw vegetables should be prepared just before serving.

A GOOD HABIT TO DEVELOP

- Cover your vegetables with a cloth, after each step in the preparation is completed. A salad, when being prepared, should always be protected from the air and kept cool. Uncover your salads at the last minute to preserve an element of surprise!

- Lemon juice is also effective in combatting oxidation.

COOKING METHODS

When cooking vegetables, do not forget the following:

- Cooking vegetables in water causes a loss of vitamins and minerals. The flavor is also altered.

- Scrub vegetables rather than peeling them, and recycle cooking water, whenever possible.

- Varying cooking methods is an excellent idea!

- Whatever the cooking method used, vegetables should remain crisp in order for maximum nutritional value to be preserved.

In Water

- Cooking vegetables in water is a tradition, and yet it is one

VEGETABLES

of the least efficient cooking methods. From now on, boil vegetables only when making soups—over low heat! See other ways of making soup in the "Recipe Book" section.

À l'étouffée

- Cook vegetables without water, on a bed of onions, in a pot with a heavy cover (so that the steam will not escape). In this way vegetables cook in their own juice. This preserves nutrients.

- You can add 2 tablespoons of water or oil to start the cooking process.

In the Oven

- Suitable for root vegetables, squash, and onions.

- Cook with the peels left on, on the oven rack (they can be wrapped in aluminum foil, if desired); or cook them in just enough liquid or oil to prevent them from sticking. This is a very good method!

Frying

- More difficult to digest.

- Cook as fries (with which everyone is familiar) or as tempura (dip pieces of vegetables in a light batter and fry in oil for a few minutes).

Sautéing

- Heat a wok or a skillet with the burner set at high, add 1 tablespoon (15 ml) of oil, and sauté the vegetables for 5 minutes, stirring constantly.

- Continue cooking over medium heat.

- A bit of water can be added, and the vegetables can be covered to finish cooking, if necessary.

- If you wish to avoid greasiness, sauté your vegetables in water. The flavor is different.

- At the end of the cooking period, add some starch that has been diluted in water, to give the vegetables a shiny appearance. They will be savory and appetizing! Season and serve on a grain dish or as a side dish.

NOTE: **A wok**: The wide-open form and the round bottom of this Chinese pot make it a practical, appropriate utensil for this kind of cooking. It requires less oil, absorbs heat well, allows food to be stirred without making a mess, can be used as a serving dish, etc. It is a very good investment.

Steaming

- Place a stainless steel steamer in a pot or a bamboo steamer basket in a wok.

- Add a bit of water, cover, and bring to a boil.

- In order to avoid a loss of nutrients, place the vegetables in the steamer once the water is boiling.

- In order to preserve the color of the vegetables, remove the cover only when cooking is finished and serve immediately.

- Add a garlic bud to the water in order to give more flavor to the vegetables.

- Wash vegetables in cold water and scrub them with a brush.

- **Do not soak them in water;** this causes a loss of vitamins and minerals. As for broccoli and cauliflower, spread open the fleurets under a stream of water. Cut leeks lengthwise in order to remove any soil.

- **Do not peel or scrape vegetables.** Peel them after cooking, if necessary, since the vitamins and minerals are concentrated near the skins.

- Do not cut vegetables on a board used for cutting meat, because bacteria such as salmonella may be present there.

- Rinse your cutting board and knife in cold water after cutting each kind of vegetable in order not to mix together the flavors.

- The cooking method you use and the cooking time desired will determine how you cut vegetables. Cut into small pieces for rapid cooking.

The way food is presented stimulates the appetite. From one meal to another, vary the colors and the sorts of vegetables that you choose, as well as the way you cut them.

SEASONINGS

Powdered Seaweeds

- A supplementary source of minerals. They look like pepper.

Herbs

- Basil, chervil, tarragon, oregano, parsley. thyme, etc.

Paprika

- A mild variety of peppers; contains vitamin A. It is a beautiful orangey red color. Add towards the end of cooking.

Dill Seeds and Other Spices

- Use occasionally and in small quantities.

Lemon

- Delicious on green vegetables and in salad dressings with oil and garlic.

Ginger

- This is a useful condiment, which adds a great deal of flavor to vegetables. Use fresh, grated ginger.

Garlic

- A bulb used as a condiment. Use raw in salads.

NOTE: Use parsley abundantly for of its nutritional value (iron and vitamin C) and its pleasant flavor. Cut finely and serve in salads; or liquefy it in a blender in juices, salad dressings, soups, etc. It is just a question of remembering to do it.

What About Vinegar?

- Vinegar is a product which results from the acetic fermentation of fruit fructose. The first fermentation is lactic, the second, alcoholic, and the third, acetic.

- Vinegar irritates the digestive tract.

- Use lemon juice, therefore, to make mayonnaise and salad dressings. "Vinaigrette sauces" become "salad dressings".

- In lieu of pickles, try lacto-fermentations.

ABOUT SEAWEEDS

- They are true aquatic vegetables.

- It is so simple and beneficial to incorporate them into your diet.

- A good source of minerals (calcium), trace elements (iron, iodine), vitamins, and proteins (above all nori).

Arame and Hijiki

- Small black filaments. Wash, soak for 5-15 minutes, and serve. They have a very mild flavor. Blend into salads, noodle dishes, and soups or eat as a vegetable side dish.

Dulse

- Dulse looks like red potato chips. Wash, soak for a few minutes, and serve. Delicious with sesame salt (see recipe), béchamel sauce, etc.

Nori

- Small black sheets which should be dry-toasted, over a source of heat until they become green and crispy. Crumble and put in rice, sauces, salads, and soups. Tasty!

Powdered Seaweed

- Using them is like salting without salt and, at the same

time, it ensures a supply of minerals. They constitute a tasty, nutritional seasoning, which is easy to use.

Agar

- Available in the form of flakes, powder, or white filaments. Replaces animal gelatine.

Eating a large quantity and a great variety of vegetables every day is a sure way of providing your body with the vitamins, minerals, and fibers which it needs. The quality of the soil in which fruits and vegetables have been grown, the length of time they are stored as well as the methods used for storage, along with the way they are prepared are all factors which determine their nutritional value, and, therefore, the quality of your diet.

Always store vegetables in a cool place and keep them out of contact with the air.

Leafy green vegetables can be washed and dried in advance. Store them in an airtight container. Eat them as soon as possible and in abundant quantities.

Cutting vegetables can be pleasant. You can have fun cutting them into different shapes, taking advantage of the time you spend to relax or even meditate; or you can consider this work to be a chore. It's up to you!

EATING VEGETABLES IS SO GOOD FOR YOU!

Dairy Products and Eggs

DAIRY PRODUCTS

The nutritional importance of the members of this food group lies in their **protein content** (composed of 9 essential amino acids), since they are of animal origin: 3.5% in milk and 18-24% in cheese.

- They contain vitamins A and D, which are fat-soluble and present, therefore, mostly in milk solids (M.F.), vitamin B_2 or riboflavin, and vitamin B_{12}.
  * Vitamin D is added only to milk that is destined for general consumption.

- An excellent source of calcium and phosphorus, but lacking in fiber, iron, and vitamin C.

- Milk also contains carbohydrates (4.9%): lactose. However, much less is to be found in cheese, because sugar, which is soluble in water, dissolves in the lactoserum or whey.

Fats found in dairy products (3.5% in whole milk and up to 32% in cheese) are saturated and contain cholesterol (34 mg per cup of milk).

You should exercise good judgment in the use of dairy products, especially if you eat other products of animal origin (eggs, meat) which also contain saturated fatty acids and cholesterol.

ROLES

- A source of proteins and calcium.

- They are a good complement to proteins of vegetable source (grains, legumes, nuts, seeds).

VARIETIES

1. **Milk**

2. **Yogurt**

3. **Cheese**

4. **Kefir**

1. Cow's Milk

- Milk is not just a beverage; it is also a growth food. If you drink milk before or during meals, your appetite will decrease. It is preferable, therefore, to drink milk after meals or as a snack.

- Compared to mother's milk, cow's milk contains a high level of calcium and proteins for a baby. Nothing can replace mother's milk!

- Its lipids are made of saturated fatty acids and contain cholesterol. It is recommended that you use skimmed milk, if your diet has a high fat content.

- Light destroys vitamins A and B_2 (riboflavin) in milk. Milk should be put back into the refrigerator immediately after use.

- Milk contributes to the formation of mucus. It should be avoided if you are suffering from a cold, the flu, or any other infection.

- The enzyme which digests the lactose contained in milk is lactase. It is present during childhood but disappears with age. A solution to this problem is to eat yogurt (see later section).

- Raw milk contains lactic fermenting agents which improve digestibility. However, in order to consume fresh, raw milk, rigorous hygiene must be observed, because milk is a medium which favors the development of germs. Milk available on the market is pasteurized.

- Pasteurization destroys all pathogenic germs. However, it does not destroy the residues from antibiotics and pollutants.

- Goat's milk is often used by people with allergies or digestive disorders, because its molecules of fat are smaller than those of cow's milk, and hence are divided up better (natural homogenization), which increases digestibility.

Nowadays you can find raw (very rare), pasteurized, sterilized, or U.H.T. milk, as well as concentrated milk with or without sugar added, and evaporated, and powdered milk. Its composition varies according to the methods used!

MILK PRODUCTS

Cream

- Contains 35% MF (milk fats) (saturated fatty acids).

- Contains vitamin A and, in summer, may contain a bit of vitamin D.

Butter

- Contains 85% MF (saturated fatty acids).

- Rich in vitamin A; in summer, it may contain a bit of vitamin D.

- Contains 2% salt, if salted.

- Keeps in the refrigerator

Powdered Milk

- Made from pasteurized milk, from which the cream has been skimmed off in order for it to keep longer. There is a loss of MF and vitamins A and D in the process. When obtained at low temperatures, it is called "non-instant" milk.

- Stays fresh for a long time, if kept cool and dry.

- Choose non-instant milk powder, because it has kept its vitamin B_6 (pyridoxine) and lysine (an essential amino acid), which is not the case with instant milk powder. It is available in cooperatives and health food stores.

- It is used for making yogurt, cream sauces, etc.

- When added to recipes, it increases their nutritional value.

Clabbered Milk

- This is a means of conservation which our grandparents knew about.

- Lactic fermenting agents develop within 12-24 hours at room temperature.

- They predigest the milk, which suits adults better.

White Cream Cheese

- To prepare, filter clabbered milk.

- Provides mild cheese without cooking.

- Delicious as is, or seasoned to taste.

Kefir

- Originating in the Caucasus, it is still not very well-known and little used.

- It is milk which is fermented at room temperature using a bacterial culture. This produces lactic fermentation and a very slight alcoholic fermentation (1%).

- Digestible and easy to prepare.

Yogurt

- Milk which has thickened because of lactic fermentation caused by a bacterian culture.

- This culture is active at 115°F (46°C), a higher temperature than for natural fermenting agents (clabbered milk).

- Good for the intestinal flora (bacteria for fermentation).

- It has a more acid flavor than clabbered milk.

- MF vary between 1.7% (skimmed milk) and 3,25% (whole milk).

- Particularly suitable for adults because it is already partly digested by bacteria.

- Commercial yogurts containing fruit, as well as frozen yogurt, contain a great deal of sugar. A solution to this problem is to make your own yogurt and add your own fruit. It is so simple.

DAIRY PRODUCTS

NOTE:

- These products can be made with skimmed milk, because it is casein (milk protein) which coagulates with calcium.

- Lactose is transformed into lactic acid through the action of enzymes. The flavor changes from sweet to slightly acid.

- Thanks to lactic bacteria and lactic acid, these fermented products are superior to milk for the following reasons:
  1. Lactose is predigested.
  2. Lactic bacteria have a very beneficial antibiotic effect on the intestinal flora.

Yogurt cheese

- Pour some yogurt into a muslin cloth.

- Let it drain for 24 hours in a cool place or in the refrigerator; it will be less acid this way.

- Season, to taste.

Cheeses

- Formed through a process involving the coagulation of milk protein (casein) brought about by the action of rennet, followed by draining (to eliminate the whey and lactoserum) and maturing.

- Cheeses are a source of fats (23-30%), proteins (18-24%), and vitamins A and B, as well as calcium and phosphorus.

- The quantities of water and lactose contained in cheese determine the consistency: ripened hard cheese (35% humidity), soft cheese (50%), new cheese (80%).

New cheese

- A cottage-type cheese, which is not as fat (4-20%) and more digestible, having a 0.4-4% MF content.

- Can be eaten when new, with fruit, on pancakes, in dips, in salad dressings, in sandwiches, etc.

- It has one disadvantage: high sodium content (salt).

Soft cheese

- Cheeses with mould on the outside: Brie or Camembert (24-26% MF) . Enzymes transform the lactose into lactic acid and certain moulds eat their way from the outside towards the center, creating a white downy covering. These are " good " moulds.

- Cheeses with mould on the inside: Danish Blue, Roque-fort-type, etc.

- Cheeses which mature on the surface and are covered with a hard crust varying from yellow to red: Saint- Paulin, Anfrom, Tomme, etc.

Hard cheese

- Have been drained and pressed longer. The longer a cheese has been drained, the longer it keeps.

- Unripened or semi-ripened: Cheddar, Parmesan, Gouda, etc.

- Ripened:
  Gruyère (has small holes and a shiny surface),
  Emmenthal (has large holes and a dry surface).

Examples of % of Milk Fats in Certain Cheeses

Quark: 0.5%	Brie, Camembert: 17%
Cottage: 0.4 - 4%	Gouda, Oka, Saint-Paulin, Feta: 21%
Ricotta: 10%	Parmesan: 30%
Mozzarella: 16 - 22%	Cheddar, Emmenthal: 32%

Mozzarella is less rich in milk fat than cheddar for au gratin purposes. It is preferable to eat the following types of cheeses: Quark, Cottage (with the cream removed), or Ricotta.

STORAGE

- All milk products should be kept in the refrigerator.

- Bring cheeses to room temperature for about 1 hour before serving.

- Cheeses which begin to go mouldy can be "freshened-up" and used!

- Pay attention to hygiene, as cheeses are very sensitive.

DAILY NEEDS IN TERMS OF DAIRY PRODUCTS

Children (a growth food): 3 servings or more

Adults (a complementary food): 2 servings

Review the " Servings " table.

Often when people decide to reduce their consumption of meat, they eat more dairy products and eggs.

Overconsumption of dairy products and eggs, like overconsumption of meat, can cause the following:

- an excess of saturated fats		**CLOGGING OF**
- an excess of cholesterol	=	**ARTERIES AND**
- an excess of proteins		**OTHER DISORDERS**

BE CAREFUL: It is recommended that these products be eaten in moderation. Develop the habit of varying your sources of proteins, calcium, B vitamins, etc.

• Legumes (soybeans, tofu, kidney beans, etc.).

• Grains.

• Nuts and seeds (sesame seeds, almonds, sunflower seeds, etc.).

• Seaweeds (nori, hijiki, arame, kombu, etc.).

• Vegetables (broccoli, dark leafy green vegetables, etc.).

FOOD	QUANTITY 1 serving	CALCIUM CONTENT
Hard cheese	1 1/2 ounces (45 g)	318 mg
Whole milk	1 cup (250 ml)	307 mg
Yogurt	3/4 cup (175 ml)	348 mg
Soybeans	1 cup (250 ml)	115 mg
Tofu	1/4 cake (100 g)	128 mg
Navy Beans	1 cup (250 ml)	94 mg
Whole sesame seeds	1/4 cup (60 ml)	436 mg
Almonds	1/2 cup (125 ml)	175 mg
Cooked broccoli	1/2 cup (125 ml)	71 mg
Cooked spinach	1/2 cup (125 ml)	88 mg

The recommended daily intake for an adult is 800 mg.

DAIRY PRODUCTS

EGGS

QUALITY

- Eggs should be eaten as fresh as possible. There is an ever-increasing number of producers and retailers who offer quality products.

- Signs of freshness in eggs:
  - the white (albumen) is dense and does not completely spread out or collapse,
  - the yolk is round, firm, and located in the center,
  - the chalazae (bands of albumen which keep the yolk in the center of the egg) are twisted and concentrated.

- The color of the shell depends on the breed of the hen.

- The hen's diet influences the flavor, color, and vitamin A content of the yolk.

- The harder the shell, the higher the mineral content.

NUTRITIONAL VALUE

- An excellent source of complete proteins (13%), which are almost equally divided between the white and the yolk.

- The yolk:	proteins; vitamins A, B (such as B$_{12}$), and D; minerals (copper, iron, phosphorus, and calcium); fats (30%) which contain a high cholesterol level (250 mg); lecithin; and water.
- The white:	proteins, a few minerals (sodium, potassium), and water.

NOTE:
- The proteins found in eggs contain sulfur (methionine),

which is responsible for the odor and the gray color that are characteristic of an egg which has been over-cooked.

- The shell is composed of 94% calcium. You can wash, dry, and grind this calcium-rich shell and add it to your diet as a calcium supplement.

- Egg whites are fat-free. They can replace whole eggs in recipes.

QUANTITY

Eating 1-4 eggs per week is reasonable, depending on the quantity of saturated fats and cholesterol that your diet already contains. Eggs used in the preparation of different dishes are included in this number. However, a greater number of egg whites (fat-free) can be eaten as a source of complete proteins.

As you get to know and begin to use vegetable proteins, which contain little or no saturated fats and no cholesterol, and as you reduce the number of desserts that you eat, eggs will figure less and less on the menu, disguised in the form of quiches, soufflés, or omelets, or simply poached or soft-boiled, which is the way they are best!

**LEARN TO BALANCE AND VARY YOUR MENUS
FOR MAXIMUM HEALTH AND PLEASURE!**

CHAPTER 13

Other Products Worth Knowing

1. Arrowroot
2. Carob
3. Herbal teas and coffee
4. Herbs and spices
5. Honey
6. Molasses
7. Oils, butter, and margarine
8. Sea salt
9. Yeasts
10. Yeast substitute

1. ARROWROOT

- A fine white powder extracted from the tropical arrowroot plant.

- It has mucilaginous properties, which makes it beneficial for the intestinal flora.

- Use for thickening soups, desserts, and sauces.

- Dilute 1 1/2 tablespoons (20 ml) in a bit of cold water. Add this quantity per cup (250 ml) of stock that you wish to thicken.

- Dilute some and add it to vegetables, when they have almost finished cooking, to give them a shiny appearance.

2. CAROB

- Carob comes from a magnificent, large leguminous tree of the same name. Its fruit has the form of long, fat pods containing sweet pulp and seeds. Pulp is dried and ground up to make carob powder.

- Carob is a good substitute for cocoa, instant chocolate milk, and chocolate!

- Carob powder contains no cafeine and little fat–2% compared to 52% in chocolate. It contains carbohydrates, calcium (30 mg of calcium per tablespoon/15 ml of carob powder), and phosphorus.

- Good for the intestinal flora because it contains gums and pectins.

- Used as a beverage and for preparing desserts.

- You will quickly become accustomed to its flavor.

Carob chips

- Quality carob chips, found in good health food cooperatives and stores, are typically composed of roasted carob powder, palm oil, and soy lecithin. No sugar has been added, nor do they contain any other additives.

- Those used in making candies (crunchy bars, carob bars, etc.) may contain up to 30% sugar.

- Add occasionally to cookies, fruit salads, and candies.

3. HERBAL TEAS AND COFFEE SUBSTITUTES

Many people are trying to reduce their consumption of coffee and tea, which are rich in caffeine and theobromine, two alkaloids that are toxic for the body. Here, then, are a few alternatives:

Grain-based Coffee Substitute

• A mixture of beet and chicory roots, barley, and rye. Can be served in instant form or as an infusion.

Ground Barley Coffee Substitute

• A mixture of barley, and dandelion and burr roots. Simmer for a few minutes and filter.

Although these mixtures constitute healthier beverages, it should not be forgotten that they have been roasted at a very high temperature to accentuate their aroma and flavor.

Herbal Teas

There is a wide variety of herbal teas: chamomile, mint, linden flower, verbena, and rosehip, to name only a few. The choice is huge.

Until recently, most herbal teas came from Europe and hence were fumigated for transportation.

However, you can find organic herbal teas to satisfy your needs. Check and read all labels carefully.

Have you considered your garden or natural sources nearby? Here is a fascinating domain just waiting to be discovered.

Herbal teas can be served as follows:

- **As an infusion:** when using the most fragile parts, such

as dried leaves and flowers. Pour on some very hot water and let stand for 10 minutes.

- **As a decoction:** when using stems, roots, and hard fruits. Place in cold water, bring to a boil, boil for 3 minutes, and steep for 10 minutes. For more flavor it is recommended that hard fruits (e.g., rosehips, hawthorns, aniseeds) be slightly crushed before use.

Quantity

- Usually, 1 teaspoon (5 ml) of dried leaves per cup (250 ml) of liquid.

4. HERBS AND SPICES

Here is just a bit of information about that vast field called herbs and spices, and about their qualities.

Herbs

- Basil, chervil, chives, tarragon, fennel, bay leaves, marjoram, oregano, parsley, rosemary, sage, savory, thyme, etc.
- They make indispensable seasonings and tasty herbal teas. Herbs have culinary and medicinal qualities.
- Use large quantities of basil, chives, and parsley, but use only eye-dropper-sized amounts of marjoram, sage, savory, and thyme in the majority of your main dishes.

Here are some examples:

- basil with tomatoes, grains, legumes, and tofu;
- chives with eggs, rice, and potatoes;
- marjoram and thyme in soups;
- oregano with pizzas and tomato sauces;
- an abundance of parsley everywhere ; be sure to add it after cooking;

HERBS AND SPICES

- savory with legumes;
- etc., etc. (See each of the recipes).

• Look for organically grown herbs.

In a healthy diet, those inseparable partners, salt and pepper, are replaced with a variety of herbs and spices. For this reason each dish becomes a new discovery.

Since seasonings are a question of personal taste, do not be afraid to experiment, to sample, or to add more.
BE A GOURMET!

Spices

• Dill, cinnamon, cloves, cumin, ginger, mustard, nutmeg, paprika, cayenne pepper, black or white pepper, and saffron.

• They are used in very small quantities in a whole range of recipes, running from desserts, through eggs and vegetables, to whole grain main dishes.

5. HONEY

• A natural product which has undergone no transformation; it contains a few minerals and vitamins, if it has not been pasteurized!

• It is a concentrated sugar: replace 1 cup of sugar with 1/3 cup of honey.

Honey is superior to all other sugars because of its quality. However, in spite of this fact, it is a concentrated sugar and presents the same disadvantages as other sugars (sugar, molasses, maple syrup, malted barley syrup, etc.).

Blackstrap

- Has the highest concentration of minerals; it is often recommended as a source of iron. However, it is also very rich in chemical residues and it is, above all, a form of sugar.

- A syrupy residue obtained from the crystallization of sugar which comes from sugar cane.

Barbados

- Sweeter and more refined.

- It is not necessary to eat molasses as a source of minerals; there are vegetables, legumes, etc.

7. OILS, BUTTER, AND MARGARINE

Vegetable oils are an excellent source of lipids (100%), depending on the quality of the product from which the oil is extracted as well as the method used!

ROLES

- A source of energy and heat: very calorific (9 kcal/g).

- They transport fat-soluble vitamins (A, D, E, and K).

- A source of polyunsaturated essential fatty acids and monounsaturated fatty acids, whence the importance of using cold-pressed oils obtained from the first pressing.

- Enhance the flavor of foods.

Peanut Oil

- Very stable when heated because it contains mostly monounsaturated fatty acids.

- Suitable for frying foods, because it has a very high smoking point*.

- Keeps well.

* Smoking point: The temperature above which fat decomposes and becomes acrolein (a toxic substance).

Safflower Oil

- One of the best sources of linoleic acid, an essential fatty acid which contributes to lowering the cholesterol level.

- Extracted from hulled seeds.

- It is a beautiful yellow color and has a pleasant taste; easy to incorporate into the menu.

- The all-purpose oil par excellence.

- Has a high smoking point.

Corn Oil

- A good source of polyunsaturated fatty acids (linoleic acid).

- Extracted from the germ of corn kernels.

- It is a vibrant yellow color; contains provitamin A.

- Has a rich, distinctive flavor. Suitable for preparing breads and desserts.

- Has quite a low smoking point and, therefore, smokes easily. It is not recommended for frying foods.

Olive Oil

- Rich in oleic acid (a monounsaturated fatty acid).

- It is green in color and has a flavor similar to that of olives.

- Semi-solid when cold. When left at room temperature for a few minutes before being used, it returns to a liquid state.

- Has a slow oxidization rate; for all-purpose use.

- Generally sold in an unrefined state.

Sesame Oil

- Rich in polyunsaturated fatty acids.

- Has a mild flavor; for all-purpose use.

- Contains sesamoline, which makes it more stable.

Soy Oil

- Rich in polyunsaturated fatty acids and in lecithin.

- It is dark in color and has a nutty flavor.

- It is not recommended for frying foods because it foams up easily.

- Particularly fragile when heated.

Sunflower Oil

- Rich in polyunsaturated fatty acids (linoleic acid).

- For all-purpose use.

QUALITY

The nutritional value of an oil depends on the quality of the initial raw material used to produce it and the methods employed for extraction and storage.

COLD EXTRACTION

- Cold-pressed (86-104°F/30-40°C), filtered, and bottled. These oils are unrefined.

- Rich in polyunsaturated fatty acids, amongst others EFA.

- Each variety has its own particular color, aroma, and flavor, not to mention its nutritional value!

- When stored, should be protected from air, light, and heat.

- These are the best oils to use.

EXTRACTION BY HEATING

- Certain oils, which are called natural, are extracted by

heating the raw material to temperatures ranging from 122-266°F (50-130°C). This alters the quality of their unsaturated fatty acids; however, chemical solvents are not used.

- They are then filtered and bottled.

COMMERCIAL EXTRACTION

- These oils undergo a complex treatment.

- They are extracted by heating raw materials to extremely high temperatures. Chemical solvents are used; this degenerates the final product.

- They are heated and chemical solvents are added (benzene or toluene); then they are washed, deodorized, and bleached, and synthetic antioxidants are added (BHT, BHA).

- These processes result in oils which "are flavorless, odorless, and leave no aftertaste". They are highly refined, it is true. However, they are of little nutritional interest!

QUALITY IS A QUESTION OF CHOICE. SHOP AROUND.

STORAGE

- Its purpose is to slow down oxidization.

- Refrigerate oil in an opaque container away from light.

- Close the container and put it away without delay after using.

QUALITY

- For a healthy diet buy only cold-pressed oils obtained from the first pressing. **Use them raw.**

- Choose unrefined oils that are free of synthetic antioxidants (BHA, BHT: high-risk additives). Oils contain vitamin E, a natural antioxidant which is destroyed during refining.

- Good quality oils are currently sold in natural food cooperatives and natural food stores.

RECOMMENDED INTAKE

A healthy, balanced diet satisfies our daily needs.

For example, 2 teaspoons (10 ml) of oil from the first pressing contains a sufficient quantity of essential fatty acids (EFA) to meet our needs.

ABOUT BUTTER VS. MARGARINE

Butter

- Its fatty acids (81%) are mostly saturated fatty acids (57%). Contains cholesterol.

Margarine

- Its fatty acids (81%) undergo a process of hydrogenation, which reduces the percentage of polyunsaturated fatty acids that were present at the outset.

There are advantages to reducing your consumption of butter and margarine. Here are some ways of doing this:

- Cook with oil, using as little as possible; use utensils with anti-adhesive surfaces (pots, skillets, etc.).

- Use only peanut or other nut butter spreads on your toast in the morning.

- Eat healthy whole grain breads, without butter, and masticate while savoring the flavor.

- Add some lemon juice, sesame salt, or herbs to enhance the flavor of your vegetables.

Animal Fats	Vegetable Oils
1. Rich in saturated fatty acids	1. Rich in unsaturated fatty acids
2. Low in unsaturated fatty acids	2. Low in saturated fatty acids
3. Rich in cholesterol	3. Cholesterol-free
4. Low in essential fatty acids	4. Rich in essential fatty acids
5. Rich in vitamins A, D	5. Low in vitamins A, D (*)
6. Low in vitamins E, K	6. Rich in vitamins E, K
7. Contain traces of iron and copper	7. Contain minute traces of iron, magnesium, copper
8. Contain minute traces of calcium	8. Contain minute traces of calcium
9. Solid at room temperature	9. Liquid at room temperature (**)
10. When eaten in excess: harmful to the circulatory system	10. When eaten in moderation: good for the circulatory system. In excess: can also be harmful
11. Rich in calories and energy	11. Rich in calories and energy
12. Oxidize slowly	12. Oxidize quickly

(*) Except for corn oil and olive oil, which are quite rich in vitamin A.

(**) Except for palm oil and coconut oil, which are rich in saturated fatty acids, and, therefore, solid at room temperature. Coconut oil is also called copra oil.

8. SEA SALT

- Salt is sodium chloride (NaCl).

- It is a source of minerals: sodium, chlorine, magnesium, traces of copper, nickel, etc.

- It contains no iodine; this trace element is necessary to ensure the proper functioning of the thyroid gland. Sources of iodine are seaweeds, all vegetables, depending on the concentration of iodine in the soil, and iodized table salt, in which iodine has been fixed after several chemical manipulations.

- A person's need for salt varies as a function of age, climate, and diet.

- Salt comes either from the sea (*amashio*) or the earth (rock salt).

- In their natural state, several foodstuffs contain sodium: vegetables, dairy products, water. It is not necessary to add more.

- To reduce your habit of salting things, here are a few suggestions for enhancing the flavor of your dishes:

> - Herbs: basil, thyme, marjoram, parsley, etc.
> - Spices: nutmeg, cinnamon, ginger, coriander, paprika, etc.
> - Garlic, onions, lemon juice, dried, ground seaweed, etc. There is no lack of choice!
> - Miso and tamari sauce contain salt. Use them judiciously. Sesame salt can be prepared with or without salt.

- Every American consumes an average of 2-3 teaspoons (10-15 g) of salt per day. To satisfy the body's needs, 300 mg of salt per day is sufficient!

- The link between the excessive consumption of salt and hypertension has been established scientifically. The same is true of the retention of water, pre-menstrual discomforts, and liver diseases.

- We need to change our dietary habits: above all we should reduce the quantity of processed foods that we eat (canned goods, prepared foods of all kinds, etc.), use garlic, onion, and celery powder instead of garlic salt, etc.

- Reading labels carefully will certainly encourage you to eat whole, fresh foods.

- It is easier than you think to get rid of the habit of salting your food. Have confidence in yourself and gradually allow yourself the pleasure of discovering the real flavor of fresh foods. Soon you will be put off by salty foods. The same is true of sugar!

9. YEASTS

Baker's Yeast

- A microscopic mushroom in a latent state. It becomes active if warmed to 110°F (43°C) in a slightly sweet environment.

- A source of B vitamins and minerals.

- It is used to make dough rise. Do not eat raw.

- Yeast feeds off carbohydrates in the dough and gives off CO_2, which makes the dough rise.

- Can be kept for a year in a tightly closed container in the refrigerator.

Nutritional Yeast

- Classified among the microscopic mushrooms, this group of yeasts is grown under different conditions depending on the type.

- The yeasts in this group are deactivated and, therefore, cannot be used to make dough rise.

- A good source of proteins (38%), B vitamins (do not contain vitamin B_{12} unless enriched), and minerals (iron, phosphorus, potassium).

- There are yeasts which are enriched with B_{12} and/or calcium.

- Varieties: brewer's yeast, Torula, Engevita. They are all nutritious but each has a different flavor; they are respectively bitter, medium-bitter, and mild.

- They should be used in moderation and should not be cooked, insofar as it is possible. Sprinkle on soups, salads, grain dishes, etc.

10. YEAST SUBSTITUTE (BAKING POWDER)

- Baking powder is a chemical yeast substitute used for making pastries.

- Contains bicarbonate of soda (baking soda) or of potassium, and cream of tartar. One of its constituents is alkaline while the other is acidic; the two of them react together and give off CO_2, which makes dough rise. Buy baking powder that contains no alum (potassium and aluminum sulfate).

- Do not use more than 1 teaspoon per cup of flour, because vitamin B_1 (thiamine) is destroyed in an alkaline environment.

CHAPTER 14

Storage

The methods used to preserve all these precious food-stuffs have an influence on their nutritional value. When our diet consists essentially of manufactured products which are filled with additives, we lose the habit of paying special attention to the food we eat. In a healthy diet, greater importance is given to fresh, whole, living products; they must be stored adequately from the moment they are harvested or purchased until they are used.

GRAINS AND FLOURS

- Keep them in tightly-closed glass containers.

- Store in a cool, dry place away from the light.

- Avoid plastic bags; they retain humidity.

- Keep soy and corn flour in the refrigerator, because they go rancid quickly.

- Whole grains keep well for a year. When stored for longer

periods, they gradually lose their nutritional value. Wheat keeps longer.

- Here is a test for checking the vitality of grains: prepare a small quantity of sprouts and observe the results; only healthy, vital seeds sprout.

- Wheat germ must always be kept in the refrigerator; it easily goes rancid because it contains a large quantity of lipids.

- Flour is better when fresh. Store it in the refrigerator, if possible; if not, store in a cool place. It will keep for two months.

PASTA

- Store in a cool, dry place in containers or in tightly-closed bags.

- It is recommended that pasta be kept for no longer than 3 months.

LEGUMES

- Use the same method as that used for grains. Legumes keep well: about 1 year, when stored away from the light.

- A shiny bean is a fresh bean.

- After being cooked, they can be kept for 3 to 4 days in the refrigerator, or for two months in the freezer.

TOFU

- Tofu keeps for a long time in the refrigerator, when hermetically sealed.

- After opening a package, keep any remaining tofu in cold water in the refrigerator.

- See the section on tofu in the chapter entitled "Legumes".

NUTS AND SEEDS

- With the shells removed: keep in glass containers in the refrigerator.

- In the shells: keep them away from light, in a cool place. In the freezer they will keep for a long time.

- They keep for 6 months to a year. Buy them in the shells in the fall and freeze. Use as needed.

- Nut butters should be kept in the refrigerator.

OILS

- Oils should be stored in opaque glass containers in the refrigerator. They keep for 4 to 6 months.

- Do not worry about any deposits or strand-like threads which may form; they constitute elements which have nutritional value.

- If the flavor becomes bitter, it is an indication that the oil has gone rancid. Do not use.

YOGURT CULTURES

- When stored in the freezer, they keep for 6 months to a year.

CHEESE

- Keep in tightly-closed plastic bags. Air and fingers are cheese's natural enemies.

- Cheese keeps for several weeks in the refrigerator. In the freezer, it will keep for several months (not cottage cheese).

- For more flavor, place it at room temperature for about an hour before serving.

YEASTS (both nutritional and baker's yeast)

- In tightly-closed containers in the refrigerator or freezer they will keep for 6 months to a year.

MISO AND TAMARI SAUCE

- Keep in a cool place in glass containers.
- Unpasteurized miso should be kept in the refrigerator.

SALT

- Store in a dry place.

HERBS AND SPICES

- Store them in a dry place away from light. Do not keep them over the stove; there is too much light and heat there.

FRUITS AND VEGETABLES

- Store them in the refrigerator away from air; use them up quickly to avoid losing large quantities of vitamins.
- Fruits with the peels on can be left at room temperature for the eye to behold. This will stimulate you to eat them!
- Leafy green and other green vegetables rapidly lose their vitamin C. Always store them in the refrigerator in airtight containers.

DRIED FRUITS

- Keep them in tightly-sealed glass containers in a cool place.

SEAWEEDS

- Store in glass containers or plastic bags in a dry place.

IN SHORT

There are certain recurrent principles which pertain to the storage of food products.

- Keep them away from air, light, heat, and dampness.

- For better quality, practice the rotation of stocks.

When you adopt a healthy dietary regime, the refrigerator, your cupboards, and " grandma's pantry " will be filled with lovely jars and well-labeled containers.

An efficient, well-organized storage system helps preserve the quality of foods.

STORAGE

CHAPTER 15

How To Succeed in the Kitchen

ORGANIZING WEEKLY MENUS QUICKLY

Now you know that to eat a healthy diet, you must prepare grains, legumes, vegetables, etc. You must invest time, energy, and knowledge.

However, this need not be a chore; it is just a question of organization! Here, then, are a few means which can help you to simplify any difficulties that may arise. They are proof that taking an interest in the task at hand and having a sense of organization are the keys to success.

1. Do a weekly inventory of the pantry

- Make a note of the staple products which you still have on hand.

- Also note those which are depleted.

2. Roughly determine what constitutes the chief ingredient of each of your main course dishes.

- In order to achieve variety, take into account what the menus were the week before.

- Set aside the varieties of legumes which you will be soaking.

- Note which dishes have to be prepared in advance.

3. **Make a list of complementary products that must be purchased.**

- Vegetables, fruits, etc.

4. **Leaving things to soak: a habit worth developing.**

- A simple gesture which increases the digestibility of certain foods such as nuts, seeds, and dried fruits, and shortens the cooking time of legumes and grains.

- Hopefully, soaking will become a reflex action—a mechanical gesture—that you engage in before going to bed or in the morning, depending on your timetable.

- **The systematic soaking of one or two varieties of legumes each week will prove to be the best, if not the only way, of adopting these foodstuffs as a part of your menu.**

- Cold water is required for long periods of soaking. Ideally, soak legumes in glass jars in the refrigerator. It is sufficient to use 2-3 times their volume of water; too much water causes a greater loss of vitamins B and C, which are water-soluble.

- Several grains and legumes do not need to be soaked (rice, lentils, etc.). Nevertheless you will benefit from adopting the habit, because soaking offers the following advantages:
    - It reduces cooking time.
    - It increases digestibility.
    - It saves energy.

ORGANIZING MENUS

- **Dried Fruits:** Soaking reduces the concentration of sugar and makes fruit more tender. Eat fruit as is, or in the form of butters, mousses, or sauces.

- **Nuts and Grains:** When soaked, they are more digestible and easier to chew. Eat them as is, in sauces, milk, or pies.

- **Legumes:** They will be more digestible and their cooking time will be shortened. Cook or prepare them as sprouts; eat them as is, or in different preparations.

- **Grains:** Soaking shortens their cooking time. Use soaking water for cooking. Sprout if desired.

- **Grains in the Form of Flakes:** Prepare them for breakfast.

5. Cook things in advance:

- In the morning, soak a sufficient quantity of the following to suit your needs:
  - 2 varieties of legumes (chickpeas, black beans, or other varieties of beans).
  - 2 varieties of grains (barley, rice, etc.).

- **In the evening, cook them and keep them on reserve for meals to come.**

Use part for the next meal, store another part in the refrigerator (for a maximum of 4 days), and freeze the rest in appropriately-sized containers; when frozen, precooked grains or legumes will keep for 1 month. In this way you will not monopolize all your time cooking basic foodstuffs every day of the week.

When you have a supply of precooked grains and

legumes on hand, it is quick and easy to prepare nutritious meals and lunches.

LONG LIVE GOOD HABITS!

For example, having cooked kidney beans on hand will incite you to add some to a rice dish, a soup, or a salad, or to prepare them in the form of croquettes or a spread. If you had to prepare them every day, you would eat them only rarely. When you have developed the habit of soaking different varieties of legumes, you eat more of them, which guarantees that you get an adequate intake of proteins: carbohydrates, B vitamins, iron, and fibers.

6. Take time out for cooking

- We have all dreamed about ready-to-eat foods one day or another, when our schedule was particularly busy. Fortunately, the possibility of eating a healthy diet can be a very simple matter. There are always sprouts, yogurt, fruits, raw vegetables, nuts and seeds, bread, and tofu to help you out in a pinch. And, if you want to have a stock of ready-made foods on hand, you just have to prepare them in advance, either by yourself or in the company of others!

- WHY NOT MAKE THIS INTO A FAMILY ACTIVITY? SINCE EVERYONE EATS, EVERYONE PITCHES IN!

- Use this time to prepare yogurt, dried fruit butters (soak the fruits beforehand), salad dressing, and a few cooked dishes according to your needs. Cook double quantities and freeze the surplus: this will constitute a greatly appreciated reserve stock.

  For example, 2 vegetable pâté recipes, 2 millet pies, 2 pizzas, a double recipe of spaghetti sauce, 1 large potful of soup.

7. Freeze Foods

- This procedure suits short-term conservation purposes (a maximum of one month).

- Quickly cool cooked dishes and freeze them.

- Thaw them quickly or slowly in the refrigerator.

Freezing is a modern compromise to help us cope with hectic schedules.

8. Explore and Vary Your Menus

- Cooking can become a special a time, and occcasion to relax and be aware of your body and your gestures; It can even become a pleasure, particularly if you listen to your favorite music at the same time. It's a question of attitude.

- If you work standing up, it is important that you pay attention to your posture, distributing your weight evenly on both feet. Relax your jaw and breathe deeply. Why not hum a tune?

- Discover the pleasure of colors and forms. Make beautiful salads. Create a variety of dishes. And since practice makes perfect, the more you practise, the more your imagination will be stimulated.

You will be so resplendently healthy that the people around you will certainly want to follow your example and cook with you!

9. Get the Children to Participate

These steps to success can also open up new perspectives and initiate a dynamic change in your family. This approach lends itself to conducting educational activities with the children. Here are some suggestions:

- Write out some slogans and post them in the kitchen.
  - We chew our food well.
  - An apple a day keeps the doctor away.
  - Good health is precious.

- Organize and conduct small cooking workshops and have the children participate: make bread and cookies; prepare and rinse alfalfa sprouts, etc. Have the children make drawings based on the theme of good health.

- **Finally, always keep in mind that humor and creativity are ingredients which are essential to good health.**

A Typical Menu

Breakfast

- 1-2 glasses of water when you get up in the morning (take little sips, if possible!!!).

- Juice, if desired; or, better still, fresh fruit or soaked dried fruit.

- Grains in the form of bread, pancakes, muffins, or a bowl of cereal. Serve with a nut butter or a dairy product.

Breakfast, the first meal of the day, is comforting and it provides sustenance. Take a couple of minutes the night before to set a welcoming, friendly table for the next morning. Take turns, for fun!

- **Breakfast is the most important meal of the day.** It should be nourishing.

- The best way to get children to eat a really nourishing breakfast is to set a good example yourself. Give up the habit of buying boxes of sweetened breakfast cereal

(READ LABELS CAREFULLY); when there are none on hand, everyone will have to eat something else! Work fresh fruits, hot cereal, and whole grain bread into the menu.

- Preparing the breakfast table before going to bed greatly stimulates the appetite and puts people in a good mood the next morning.

- Give yourself time to eat breakfast by getting up a bit earlier.

- Avoid eating before going to bed in order to fell hungry in the morning.

SUGGESTIONS

- A piece of sliced fruit, alone, or with yogurt, to which you have added nuts, seeds that you have soaked (if you think of it the night before), or ground seeds (prepared in advance).

- A dried fruit sauce served with bananas, pancakes, or a muffin.

- A serving of muesli, either hot or cold (see the " Recipe Book " section).

- Hot oatmeal porridge accompanied by fruits, seeds, or nutritional yeast.

- Granola (see the "Recipe Book" section).

- Cream of wheat, rice, millet, or cornmeal. Grind up the cereal you choose and cook it in 3-4 times its volume of water until thick. Serve with fruit, nutmeg, cinnamon, or carob powder.

- Whole wheat bread with nut butter: almond, sesame, peanut, etc. Try emulsified nut butters.

- Muffins, pancakes, or crêpes. For a quick breakfast, prepare the mixture the night before; it takes only a few minutes. Cover and let stand overnight on the counter; fermentation will begin. If you add eggs, put the mixture in the refrigerator. Serve with yogurt and grated apple.

- A whole range of juices and milkshakes:
  - orange juice, alfalfa sprouts, and peanut butter.
  - apple juice and soaked prunes.
  - milk, bananas, and carob powder or vanilla.
  - orange and pineapple juice along with yogurt.

Lunch

- **Always begin with raw vegetables:** a green salad in summer; sprouts, shredded root vegetables or cabbage in winter. A variety of raw vegetables is available.

- A pièce de résistance made with a grain, legume, nut, or cheese base, and accompanied by colored vegetables, either steamed or sautéed, Chinese-style, in a wok.

The amount of food you serve at this meal will vary depending on what you served for breakfast, the morning's activities, and those yet to come.

Supper

- **This is the lightest meal.** It may be made up of fruits and cottage cheese, a selection of vegetables with a sauce, a salad, and a soup; or it may be just a soup which serves as a complete meal.

- To aid the body's nightly regenerative efforts and prevent clogging up the system, avoid overloading on food; i.e., eat supper at least 4-5 hours before going to bed and eliminate those bedtime snacks.

Pièces de Résistance

- Pièces de résistance will vary according to the amount of time available for preparation, your activities, the time of day, and your appetite. Here are a few general ideas:

- The main course is generally preceded by a raw vegetable appetizer and accompanied by cooked vegetables; however, it is not necessarily followed by a dessert!

SUGGESTIONS

- Legumes (such as tofu) and grains can be prepared in casseroles, soups, croquettes, pâtés, pies, salads, etc.

- There are numerous pasta-based dishes.

- Dishes whose main ingredient is eggs (quiches, soufflés, omelettes) will be transformed according to the vegetables you choose.

- The same recipe can be served in different forms. See the " Recipe Book " section.

AS A GENERAL RULE, **PEOPLE EAT 21 MEALS PER WEEK**. THEY COULD BE DIVIDED UP AS FOLLOWS:

7 GRAIN-BASED BREAKFASTS

- Accompanied by fruits, dairy products, soaked nuts and seeds, a nut butter, or an occasional egg.

5 GRAIN-BASED MEALS, INCLUDING PASTA

- Soups
- Croquettes
- Salads
- Pies

4 LEGUME-BASED MEALS

- Side dishes (to complete grain dishes)
- Casseroles, croquettes, salads

3 TOFU-BASED MEALS

- Dips
- Cubed or sliced tofu: serve as is, with vegetables or on grains; with bread or in soups; in sauces or salads

1 MEAL BUILT AROUND DAIRY PRODUCTS

1 EGG-BASED MEAL

> **All of these possibilities provide ample proof that eating a healthy diet will lead you to discover new flavors and a variety of forms and colors. It will get you away from monotony. In a word, it represents an investment in balance, pleasure, and good health!**

ORGANIZING MENUS

Snacks (for children)

Snacks vary according to how big a breakfast children have eaten, their activities and their appetites.

- The simplest ones are the best ones: some apples, carrots, or stalks of celery; some strips of cabbage, green peppers, or turnips; some lettuce leaves, alfalfa sprouts, or seasonal fruit.

- A nourishing snack: a slice of bread, peanut butter, and alfalfa sprouts.

- Cottage cheese with fruits or vegetables.

- Sunflower seeds, which have been soaked and sprouted for a few hours, or roasted with tamari sauce. Very nourishing!

- Popcorn.

- Milkshakes or juiceshakes.

- Fruits.

LONG LIVE CHANGE!

There are

9	VARIETIES OF **GRAINS**
24	VARIETIES OF **LEGUMES**
40-50	VARIETIES OF **COMMONLY-USED VEGETABLES**
20	VARIETIES OF **FRUITS**
12	VARIETIES OF **NUTS**

The vegetable world overflows with nutritional riches!

THE CHOICE IS UP TO YOU!

CONCLUSION

CHANGE

AWARENESS

KNOWLEDGE

COMMUNICATION

Communication is the key to **K**nowledge,

Knowledge awakens **A**wareness,

Awareness leads to **C**hange!

Let's be receptive to Hope, by assuring the health of each individual, humanity, and the planet!

PRACTICE SECTION

Recipe Book

From Theory
to the Kitchen

It is in our mouth, when masticating our food thoroughly, that we derive pleasure from its flavor.

It is through practical experience, when cooking, that we make new dishes our own and discover our hidden talents.

It is through the careful choice of nutritional foods that we build good health for ourselves and our families.

Products in Review

Agar:
Extract taken from seaweed, natural gelatin for jellies and aspics.

Bulgur:
Whole wheat, crushed and precooked. Cooks rapidly.

Carob:
Powder, rich in minerals, obtained by grinding the beans of the Carob tree. It is the healthful substitute for cocoa.

Kasha:
Buckwheat, hulled and roasted. Excellent grain which cooks rapidly.

Malt:
Wheat or barley which has been sprouted, dried, and ground. Replaces sugar.

Meal (corn or wheat):
Grain, dried and ground more coarsely than flour. Used at breakfast in the form of porridge, and in cakes and breads.

Millet:
Grain which cooks rapidly and has a mild flavor.

Miso:
Soy paste, fermented with a grain. Used in soups, sauces, and spreads.

Okara:
Residue of soybeans that have been used to make soy milk.

Safflower:
Plant whose seeds provide an oil which is rich in polyunsaturated fats.

Tahini:
Butter from hulled sesame seeds. Paler and less nutritious than sesame butter made from whole sesame seeds.

Tamari:
Soy sauce, naturally fermented. Enhances grain dishes.

Tofu:
Cheese made from soy milk. Source of protein; contains no cholesterol. Mild in flavor, it can be used in many ways.

Recipes

FOR BEST RESULTS ALWAYS READ THE ENTIRE RECIPE BEFORE BEGINNING.

Experiment, be creative, and savor the results by adopting our approach to good health.

Objective:

- To become acquainted with the products which form the basis of a healthy diet.

Contents:

- More than 150 recipes chosen for
  - their nutritional value,
  - their flavor,
  - their simplicity, and
  - the popularity they are sure to enjoy with the whole family.

- The basic techniques for using the ingredients.

- Numerous ideas that will make you want to create your own culinary masterpieces.

INTRODUCTION

A RECIPE IS AN INSPIRATION AND A GUIDE.

With 150 recipes, you can create 1000 different meals by varying the vegetables, the grains, the seasonings, and the presentation. Good luck!

May the kitchen become an enjoyable place to work, where all the necessary utensils are close at hand and where experimenting and working together to prepare a meal become a pleasure.

Initially, changing our eating habits requires that we invest some time because everything is new to us.

Be perseverant! You will learn by experimenting and soon, cooking with whole, fresh foods will become second nature. Your health will improve and the enjoyment you get from cooking will increase. Be confident!

- The majority of these recipes yield 4-6 servings. If that is too much, divide the recipe in two and freeze the second half for a later occasion, or use it to make lunches.

- The appearance of the food we eat stimulates our appetite. Take a few extra minutes to devote special attention to the presentation of meals. The more appetizing the dishes, the better they will be appreciated and digested. An attractive presentation adds to the pleasure of eating!

- Seasonings are recommended for each recipe. However, always sample a dish before serving it; often it is necessary to make some adjustments to suit particular tastes and eating habits. As time goes by, discovering new flavors, other than "salty" and "spicy", will be part of the change. Seasonings make all the difference.

- The choice of dishware is also an important consideration in making new dishes attractive. It affects adults and children alike. A prune mousse and tofu whipped cream will meet with more success served one on top of the other in a glass cup rather than mixed together in a bowl.

- Imagination and creativity can be developed. In no time you will find you have a talent for coordinating flavors and colors. Cooking will become a source of both pleasure and self-esteem.

- In order to master all of the cooking techniques as fast as possible, whether it be for grains, legumes, or vegetables, frequently read over the descriptions in the "Theory Book" section of this guide.

Groceries First... Naturally:

You will need to change the staples on your grocery list.

White bread	*should be replaced by*	**whole wheat bread.**
White flour	"	**whole wheat flour.**
White rice	"	**whole-grain rice.**
Pearl barley	"	**hulled barley.**
Packaged breakfast cereal		**rolled oats or granola..**
White pasta	"	**whole wheat pasta.**
Commercial soy sauce	"	**tamari soy sauce.**
White sugar	"	**honey.**
Hydrogenated peanut butter		**natural peanut butter.**
Refined commercial vegetable oils		**vegetable oils obtained from the first pressing.**
White vinegar	"	**lemon juice.**
Cocoa and chocolate milk powder		**carob powder.**
Cubes of chicken or beef bouillon		**cubes of vegetable or soy stock**
Salt	"	**sea salt and herbs.**
Tea and coffee	"	**herbal teas or coffee substitutes made from grains.**

As Time Goes By...

Introduce new products into the traditional menu gradually.

- Grains: millet, bulgur, buckwheat, etc.
- Legumes: kidney beans, lima beans, lentils, chickpeas, tofu, etc.
- More nuts and seeds.
- Nutritional yeast.
- Agar instead of commercial gelatin.
- A few varieties of seaweed: arame, hijiki, nori.

Concerning Protein Complementarity

- In order to make up menus which contain complete proteins, carefully reread the chapter entitled " Protein Complementarity " in the " Theory Book " section.

- The majority of the recipes contain complete proteins. In those that do not, suggestions as to complementarity are included.

- In order to have fun while getting some practice with protein complementarity, try underlining the examples that you find in the recipes.

- If a recipe contains milk products or eggs, complementarity of vegetable proteins is automatically ensured.

In short, follow the *Guide:* it will help you to succeed in your efforts to change your nutritional habits. It will assist you in exercising good judgment in the use of a complete range of healthful foods; in discovering, appreciating, and searching for more nutritional and savory food products; and in achieving a good state of *health* for yourself and your family. And ultimately, it will increase the *quality of your life*.

CHAPTER 1

Grains

COOKING METHOD FOR GRAINS

Detailed cooking methods as well as a cooking chart may be found in the chapter on grains in the " Theory Book " section.

A reminder:

1° Wash and drain the grain.

2° Measure the quantity of water required and bring it to a boil.

3° Add the grain, cover, reduce heat, and cook over low heat until all the water is absorbed.

Grains may be lightly dry-roasted in a hot cast-iron skillet. Wash, stir while roasting, and add to the cooking water. Roasting makes grains less sticky, accentuates their flavor, and begins the transformation of starch into simpler sugars, which makes digestion easier.

USES IN RECIPES

- Cooked or sprouted grains may be served:
  - as is, accompanied by vegetables.
  - in casseroles with baked vegetables.
  - in soups with vegetables and/or legumes.
  - in salads with vegetables and/or legumes.
  - in croquettes with vegetables and sauce.
  - in aspics with vegetables.
  - in puddings or desserts.

DID YOU KNOW?

- 1/2 cup of a cooked whole grain constitutes a single serving. It is suggested that anyone following a lacto-ovo vegetarian diet should eat 5-12 servings of grains per day.

- You can develop your interest and gain confidence by frequently rereading the theory concerning grains and how to cook them.

GRAINS	+	LEGUMES	
GRAINS	+	DAIRY PRODUCTS	= **COMPLETE**
GRAINS	+	EGGS	**PROTEIN**

- Adding a grated apple or other fruit to breakfast cereals will help you to break the habit of sweetening them with sugar.

- When cooking grains you may replace water with a more nutritional or tasty stock such as vegetable stock, mint tea, or a powdered soup base mixed with water.

- Lightly dry-roasting grains with a bit of garlic and/or onion brings out their flavor.

- Soaking grains before cooking rehydrates them and reduces cooking time.

IMPORTANT: Cook grains in the water used for soaking in order to recover the B vitamins which it has absorbed. B vitamins are water-soluble.

- Copy the " Grain Cooking Chart " and put it in a practical place for quick consultation, such as on the inside of a cupboard door.

- When cooking grains, the amount of water you use will determine their consistency. The more water you use, the more the grain will swell or expand. Adjust to suit your taste.

- It is taken for granted that all recipes are made with unrefined whole grains.

- Grain-based recipes for soups, pancakes, breads, and desserts can be found in their respective chapters.

- Most grain recipes may be used to stuff vegetables.

Since grains are the cornerstone of healthful nutrition, choosing organically grown grains is a positive gesture not only for one's personal health but also for that of the planet.

All About Preparing Croquettes

Here is a selection of foods which may be used in the preparation of croquettes. They may be used individually or in combinations.

MAIN INGREDIENT:

- Cooked grains and/or flakes and/or semolina.

- Cooked, crushed legumes (lentils may be used whole), tofu, or okara (soy pulp).

- Bread which has been reduced to crumbs in a blender or a food processor.

ADDITIVES:

- Seeds or ground nuts.

- Grated raw vegetables or cooked vegetables.

- Grated cheese or milk powder.

- A bit of oil to prevent drying.

SEASONINGS:

VERY IMPORTANT

- Garlic, onions, or finely chopped green onions.

- A choice of herbs.

- Nutritional yeast.

- Seaweed powder, gomashio, miso, or tamari soy sauce.

- A bit of powdered soup concentrate.

BINDING AGENT:

- Egg. The quantity varies with the size of the egg and the consistency of the mix.

- Thick béchamel sauce.

- A bit of flour to thicken. Other varieties of flour such as rice, oat, or barley may be used instead of wheat flour.

METHOD:

- Combine the ingredients so as to obtain a mixture of thick consistency.

- Make into croquettes by hand or with a spoon.

COOKING:

- Bake at 180°C (350°F) on a lightly oiled cookie sheet without turning over, or cook on both sides in an oiled skillet.

GRAINS

The same recipe may be prepared in the following forms:

- **A loaf:** Place in an oiled loaf pan and bake in the oven. Serve plain or accompanied by a sauce. With the latter the mixture may be a bit more liquid. For example, add tomato juice, stock, or another liquid.

- **Small individual patties:** Place the mixture in an oiled muffin tray.

- **Griddle cakes:** Cook whole over medium heat in a skillet or bake in the oven. Make sure that they are well cooked inside. Cut into pieces and serve like a pie.

- **Pie, deep-dish pie, tart, or double-crusted pie:** Place in a piecrust.

- **Balls:** Form the mixture into balls and cook for 15-20 minutes in a sauce or a soup of your choice. In this case the mixture must be very firm.

THERE IS NO END TO THE POSSIBILITIES!

1. Oats

- Oats are used mainly in the form of rolled oats.

- Rather than instant oats, that have been cut up, choose whole oats, since they are more nutritious.

- Rolled oats are served at breakfast in the form of muesli, porridge, or pancakes, and at lunch or supper as croquettes, and in soups, pies, or desserts.

- They will thicken a soup in no time at all.

- Grind them up in a blender to make flour.

Muesli *Serves 1*

1/3 cup (75 ml) whole rolled oats

Add sunflower or pumpkin seeds, buckwheat seeds, coconut, or dried fruit, as desired. Soak the mixture overnight in just enough water to cover.

Serve hot or cold with milk and/or yogurt. Do not sweeten with sugar! Add a grated apple instead.

Muesli is a simple, nourishing dish which is so easy to prepare in small or large quantities: a particularly healthful breakfast. Soaking preserves the nutritional value better than cooking. The bran in the oatmeal and the pectin in the apple can reduce the cholesterol level in the blood.

Granola *Serves 10-12*

3 cups (750 ml) rolled oats	1/4 cup (60 ml) sesame seeds
1 cup (250 ml) coconut	1 cup (250 ml) fruit, dried and cut
1 cup (250 ml) sunflower seeds	1/4 cup (60 ml) safflower oil
1 cup (250 ml) almonds, split	1/4 cup (60 ml) honey

- Heat the honey and the oil in a large saucepan until thin in consistency.

- Add all ingredients except the dried fruit. Mix well.

- Put the saucepan in the oven at 350°F (180°C) and stir every ten minutes, making sure to scrape the bottom and sides thoroughly, since they cook faster. Do not overtoast.

NOTE:

- To make it more digestible, soak or cook the granola before serving.

- An infinite variety of ingredients may be used.

GRAINS

VARIATION: Brown on top of the stove over medium heat, stirring constantly. Add dried fruits, let cool, and keep dry in a well-sealed container.

Granola Bars

- Bind the granola together with eggs - 2 to 4 eggs, depending on their size and the size of your cookie sheet. Use 4 cups of granola per cookie sheet.

- Bake at 350°F (180°C) for 30 minutes.

- Cut and let cool. An excellent snack!

Porridge   *Serves 1*

1/3 cup (75 ml) rolled oats   2/3 cup (150 ml) boiling water

- Cook over low heat for 20 minutes. Serve with milk and/ or yogurt. Sprinkle with a bit of cinnamon if desired. A grated apple or fresh fruit, when in season, adds to the pleasure.

- For a different kind of porridge, dry-roast the rolled oats in a cast-iron skillet, pour in the water, and cook. All the flakes will separate.

- Accompany with nuts or your choice of seeds.

VARIATION: One of these fine mornings, try porridge made with rye or wheat flakes!

Oat Croquettes   *Makes 8 (see photo)*

1 cup (250 ml) rolled oats
3 eggs, beaten
1 onion, finely chopped
3 cloves garlic, finely chopped

1 tablespoon (15 ml) tamari soy
   sauce
1 teaspoon (5 ml) basil
1/4 teaspoon (1 ml) thyme

- Mix all the ingredients together thoroughly. Let sit for 20 minutes.

- Spoon into an oiled skillet and cook on both sides, or bake at 350°F (180°C) for 20 minutes on a lightly oiled cookie sheet.

Serve with tomato sauce or onion gravy, etc. and accompanied by a side dish of stewed carrots or Brussels sprouts.

VARIATION: Add 1/2 cup (125 ml) grated cheese or ground seeds to the basic mixture.

2. Wheat

COOKING METHOD

- Wash and soak the wheat kernels for 8 hours in three times their volume of cold water.

- Drain, bring the water used for soaking to a boil, add the kernels of wheat, and cover.

- Cook in the water used for soaking for 1 1/2 to 2 hours.

When cooked, wheat kernels remain crunchy. Serve in casseroles, baked in the oven; add to bread dough; etc.

Wheat and Lentil Pilaf   *Serves 4*

1 onion, finely chopped
1 carrot, cut into fine strips
1 stalk celery, sliced diagonally
1 tablespoon (15 ml) safflower oil
1 1/2 cups (375 ml) cooked wheat
 (1/2 cup uncooked wheat)

1 cup (250 ml) cooked lentils
1 teaspoon (5 ml) caraway seeds
A pinch of thyme, a hint of sage
1/2 cup (125 ml) tomato juice

- Sauté the vegetables in the oil until tender.

- Add the wheat, lentils, caraway seeds, herbs, and juice.

- Cover and cook over low heat for 15 minutes.

Serve hot after an appetizer of raw vegetables.

VARIATIONS: Use wheat sprouts or wheat flakes, and lentil sprouts. Use whole rye or rye flakes.

Bulgur: COOKING METHOD

- Wash the bulgur and pour into 1 1/2 times its volume of boiling water.

- Cook over low heat for ten minutes.

Tabouli *Serves 4-6* **(see photo)**

Lebanese salad made of parsley, mint, tomatoes, and bulgur. Refreshing and quick to prepare. A very popular meal, especially during the summer.

1 1/2 cups(375 ml) bulgur	3 medium - sized tomatoes, cubed
2 1/2 cups (625 ml) water	4 green onions, finely chopped
1 1/2 cups (375 ml) cooked chick-peas	1/2 cup (125 ml) lemon juice or less, to taste
1 1/2 cups (375 ml) fresh parsley, finely chopped	1 1/2 teaspoons (7 ml) sea salt
1/2 cup (125 ml) fresh mint or 2 tablespoons (30 ml) dried mint	2 cloves garlic or more, to taste
	1/4 cup (60 ml) olive oil

- Bring the water to a boil and pour in the bulgur. Bring to a boil again and reduce to low heat. Cook for 10 minutes.

- Cool by plunging the saucepan used for cooking into cold water or refrigerating it.

- Mix together the bulgur and the other ingredients.

- Let the mixture sit for one hour in the refrigerator before serving on a bed of romaine lettuce.

This is a delicious dish that everyone loves.

Spanish Bulgur   *Serves 4-6*

1 onion, sliced
1/2 green pepper, cut into strips
2 cloves garlic, crushed
1 cup (250 ml) uncooked bulgur
4 tomatoes, diced
2 tablespoons (30 ml) oil
1 cup (250 ml) water

1 tablespoon (15 ml) tamari soy
   sauce
1 teaspoon (5 ml) basil
1/2 teaspoon (2 ml) oregano
Paprika, a pinch of thyme, ground
   seaweed (kelp + cayenne pepper)

- Brown the onion, garlic, green pepper, and bulgur in the oil until the bulgur is saturated with oil.

- Add the tomatoes and seasonings.

- Add the water, cover, bring to a boil, reduce heat, and cook until the water is completely absorbed.

Serve with slices of tofu or add a milk product to the meal in order to complete the proteins.

RECIPE IDEAS

- Cook some bulgur with kasha for 10 minutes. It's delicious. Serve as is with a sprinkle of finely chopped fresh parsley.

- Use bulgur for stuffing vegetables. Chilled, it makes excellent salads.

- Bulgur is practical because it cooks quickly. It is good when you are in a hurry or when making light meals.

- There is fine, medium, and coarse bulgur. Use coarse bulgur for best results.

3. Corn

Corn is most often eaten fresh, as corn on the cob. When dried it becomes a grain which is used in the form of popcorn, cornmeal, and flour.

Popcorn

- Heat a thick-bottomed saucepan. Oil it with a brush.

- Spread out the corn in the bottom and cover.

- Shake the saucepan with a circular movement until all the kernels have burst.

- Season with nutritional yeast and tamari soy sauce or a bit of parmesan cheese.

Serve as a breakfast cereal, as a nourishing snack for children, or in a soup!

Cornmeal Casserole *Serves 6-8*

1 cup (250 ml) cornmeal
3 cups (750 ml) water
Herbs and vegetables (optional)
2 cups (500 ml) tomato sauce

2 zucchini, sliced
1 tablespoon (15 ml) olive oil
1 tablespoon (15 ml) tamari soy
 sauce

- Bring the water to a boil in a thick-bottomed saucepan and sprinkle in the cornmeal.

- Bring to a boil again and cook over low heat for 20 minutes, stirring frequently until thickening occurs.

- Pour into an 8 x 10 inch (20 x 25 cm) baking dish. Let cool.

- Add the herbs and assorted vegetables to the tomato sauce, unless they have already been mixed in.

- Pour the tomato sauce over the cornmeal.

- Sauté the zucchini in the olive oil. Season with the tamari soy sauce.

- Lay the zucchini on top of the sauce. Bake at 350° F (180° C) for 30 minutes.

- Sprinkle with parmesan cheese or nutritional yeast before serving.

Polenta *Serves 6*

You will like the color, the texture, and the versatility of polenta. And it's so easy to make. Try it!

4 cups (1 L) water   1 cup (250 ml) cornmeal.

- Bring the water to a boil. Sprinkle in the cornmeal while stirring with a wire whisk.

- Cook over low heat until thickening occurs.

- Spread out in a pan and pack to a thickness of approximately 1 inch (2-3 cm). Let cool.

- When it cools, the cornmeal becomes firm. Cut into squares.

USES

- Spread with almond butter and serve with bananas at breakfast.

- Serve hot, drenched in tomato sauce.

- Sauté cubed polenta and serve with beans in a casserole.

- Brown, add herbs, and cook au gratin.

- Use as a side dish instead of bread.

GRAINS

- Add cheese while the cornmeal is being cooked.

- Use as a piecrust by pressing the mixture into a pie plate.

4. Millet

COOKING METHOD

- Always wash millet and drain it.

- Lightly dry-roast millet in a cast-iron skillet. This accentuates the flavor and prevents the grains from sticking together.

- Put the grains in 1 1/2 times their volume of very hot water. Boiling water makes the grains swell too quickly.

- Bring to a boil, reduce heat to a minimum, cover, and cook for 20 minutes.

Millet and Oatmeal Pie *Serves 6 (see photo)*

1 cup (250 ml) uncooked millet
1 1/2 cups (375 ml) very hot water or 2 1/2 cups (625 ml) pre-cooked millet
1 large onion, finely chopped
1 cup (250 ml) mushrooms, sliced
3 cloves garlic, finely chopped
1 tablespoon (15 ml) safflower oil
1 cup (250 ml) rolled oats

2 teaspoons (10 ml) basil
2 tablespoons (30 ml) fresh parsley
2 tablespoons (30 ml) nutritional yeast
1/2 teaspoon (2 ml) paprika
1/4 teaspoon (1 ml) cloves
1/2 teaspoon (2 ml) thyme
1 cup (250 ml) liquid: vegetable stock, miso dissolved in water, or béchamel sauce.

- Heat the water until piping hot. Wash the millet and put it into the water. Bring to a boil, reduce heat to a minimum, and cook for 20 minutes; or, use 2 1/2 cups (625 ml) of precooked millet.

- Using a wok or a skillet, lightly sauté the vegetables in the oil. Add the rolled oats and stir well.

- Add the cooked millet and season as you would a traditional meat pie.

- Add sufficient liquid to obtain the consistency of a meat-pie filling; the mixture must not be dry.

- Pour the preparation into a 10 inch (25 cm) piecrust, cover with a top crust, in which you have made vents, and press the edges together firmly.

- Bake at 350° F (180° C) for 20 minutes. For a browner top crust, brush on a bit of egg yolk.

Serve as is, with gravy, or with spaghetti sauce, accompanied by green vegetables.

VARIATIONS: Blend some cooked lentils and/or a cubed potato into the mixture.

Millet-Tofu Dish with Vegetables   *Serves 4-5*

1 cup (250 ml) uncooked millet	1 leek, cut into strips
1 1/2 cups (375 ml) very hot water	1 red pepper, cut into strips
or 2 1/2 cups (625 ml) precooked millet	2 tablespoons (30 ml) safflower oil
	2 tablespoons (30 ml) tamari soy
1/2 16-ounce package (225 g) tofu, cut into large cubes (225 g)	sauce
	1 teaspoon (5 ml) tarragon
2 cloves garlic, finely chopped	Seaweed, and garlic powder,
2 stalks celery, sliced diagonally	paprika

- Wash the millet and put it into the hot water. Bring to a boil, reduce heat to a minimum, and cook for 20 minutes; or, use 2 1/2 cups (625 ml) precooked millet.

- Using a wok or a skillet, heat the oil and sauté the vegetables. The vegetables must remain crisp.

- Add the cooked millet, season, and taste. Adjust the seasoning if necessary.

Serve with a salad of green vegetables and carrots.

VARIATION: Replace the tofu with 1 cup (250 ml) of cooked legumes (kidney or soybeans, etc.)

Millet Croquettes *Makes 8*

2 cups (500 ml) cooked millet
1 clove garlic, finely chopped
1 green onion, finely chopped
1 cup (250 ml) mushrooms,
   chopped
1 carrot, finely grated
1 teaspoon (5 ml) basil

2 tablespoons (30 ml) tamari soy
   sauce
1/2 teaspoon (2 ml) seaweed
   powder
1/2 teaspoon (2 ml) thyme
1 egg, as a binding agent

- Sauté the garlic, the green onion, and the mushrooms.

- Add the carrot, the millet, the tamari soy sauce, and the seasonings.

- Bind together with one egg, or two, if necessary.

- Cook on both sides in an oiled skillet, or bake on a cookie sheet at 350° F (180° C) for 20 minutes.

Serve with mushroom sauce and steamed carrots. Don't forget to begin the meal with a raw vegetable salad.

RECIPE IDEAS

Broth, soup, or cream soup.

- Cook in the same way, only longer. Use more water and vegetables. The grains will burst and you will obtain a more velvety texture.

- When cooking is completed, season to taste.

- To thicken any soup, a handful of millet is all you need.

Croquettes

- To give consistency to cooked millet, add either flour, ground seeds, or breadcrumbs, and bind together with an egg.

Dessert

- Goes well with aspics of fresh summer fruit.

- Cook the millet and pour into a mold, adding fresh fruit. Take out of the mold and serve.

Salad

- Millet, after being cooked and cooled, makes a delicious salad with greens, vegetables, or sprouts.

Piecrust

- Use cooked millet leftovers by pressing them into an oiled pie plate. Ideal as a piecrust for quiches.

Flour

- Grind uncooked millet in a blender or a coffee grinder and use to make pancakes.

Filling

- Mix together cooked millet and small cubes of vegetables. Use to stuff peppers, zucchini, eggplants, and tomatoes.

5. Barley

COOKING METHOD

- Wash barley and let it soak overnight. Cook in a saucepan in 3 times its volume of water.

GRAINS

- Bring the water used for soaking to a boil, add the barley, cover, and cook over low heat for about an hour.

- The grains burst, providing a soft, fluffy texture.

Barley Roast   *Serves 4-6*

1 cup (250 ml) uncooked barley
or 3 cups (750 ml) cooked barley
3 cups (750 ml) water
1 large onion, chopped
2 cloves garlic, finely chopped
2 1/2 cups (625 ml) chopped
   vegetables of your choice

2 tablespoons (30 ml) safflower oil
2 tablespoons (30 ml) tamari soy
   sauce
2 teaspoons (10 ml) nutritional yeast
1 tablespoon (15 ml) basil
1 teaspoon (5 ml) thyme
2 eggs, beaten

- Wash, drain, and lightly dry-roast the barley in a cast-iron skillet.

- Bring the water to a boil. Add the salt and barley. Reduce heat, cover, and cook over medium heat for about 1 hour.

- Sauté the vegetables in hot oil for about 5 minutes. Add them to the cooked barley. Season to taste.

- Blend in the beaten egg, place in a loaf pan, and bake at 350°F (180°C) for 40 minutes.

VARIATIONS:

- Serve, bathed in a simple tomato sauce.

- Form into croquettes and bake at 350°F (180°C) for 20 minutes.

- Place between 2 piecrusts and bake at 375°F (190°C) for 40 minutes. This dish resembles a meat pie.

- Leave out the eggs and call it a " Barley Dish with Vegetables ".

- Leave out the eggs and replace the vegetables with 1 cup (250 ml) of mushrooms. Now you have a " Barley Dish with Mushrooms ".

6. Rice

COOKING METHOD

- Wash rice well.

- Dry-roast lightly in a cast-iron skillet (optional). This enhances the aroma and prevents the grains from sticking.

- Put rice into two times its volume of boiling water.

- Bring to a boil again, reduce heat to a minimum, cover, and cook for 45 minutes.

OTHER POSSIBILITIES

- Soak rice for 8 hours in twice its volume of water.

- Bring the water used for soaking to a boil, add the rice, reduce heat to a minimum, cover, and cook for 30 minutes.

- Cook rice in the oven to obtain well-separated, loose grains. Place washed rice in a baking dish, cover in twice its volume of boiling water, and bake at 350°F (180°C) for 45-60 minutes.

Spanish Rice   *Serves 4*

In this recipe, the choice of spices gives a characteristic hot flavor to the rice.

1 cup (250 ml) brown rice or whole-grain basmati rice
3 stalks celery, chopped
1 green pepper, cubed
1 onion, cut into narrow strips
2 cloves garlic, crushed
1/2 teaspoon (2 ml) cumin seeds

1 tablespoon (15 ml) safflower oil
3 medium-sized tomatoes, cubed
1/2 teaspoon (2 ml) salt
1/2 teaspoon (2 ml) chili powder
1/2 teaspoon (2 ml) oregano
1/2 teaspoon (2 ml) seaweed powder

GRAINS

- Wash the rice and put it into boiling water. Bring to a boil again, reduce heat to a minimum, and cook for 45 minutes; or, use 3 cups (625 ml) of precooked rice.

- In a wok, sauté the cumin seeds and all the vegetables except the tomatoes. When tender, add the tomatoes and the seasonings.

- Add the rice and mix together. Serve hot.

Some grated cheddar cheese may be added to the mixture.

Green Rice *Serves 6*

This is an easy-to-prepare dish when you are invited out to friends' for a bring-your-own-food community supper.

3 cups (750 ml) brown rice, cooked	1 teaspoon (5 ml) sea salt
1/3 cup (75 ml) parsley, chopped	1/3 cup (75 ml) parmesan cheese
1/2 cup (125 ml) raw spinach, chopped	1/4 cup (60 ml) or less oil
	2 eggs, beaten
2 tablespoons (30 ml) onion, finely chopped	1 cup (250 ml) milk

- Mix together all the ingredients and pour into a 9 x 9 inch (23 x 23 cm) cake pan.

- Bake at 350° F (180° C) for 45 minutes.

- Cool and cut into squares.

RECIPE IDEAS

- Make a cold rice and colorful vegetable salad with red and green peppers and bright yellow corn. Season and pour on a trickle of olive oil.

- Serve short-grain rice (rice with a sticky texture) with pink coloring obtained from beets. Form into balls with an ice cream scoop. Place them on a large plate with arame

seaweed and bouquets of broccoli which have been cooked until just tender.

Being playful with forms and colors whets the appetite. For example, you can serve pink, green, or yellow rice according to your inspiration and the season.

Green Rice: rice to which green onions, green peppers, parsley, chives, etc. have been added.

Yellow Rice: rice to which curry, nuts, and yogurt (optional) have been added. Encircle with grated carrots when serving.

- Try serving rice with onions, celery, apples, and nuts. Sauté the vegetables and serve the mixture hot, or cut them into pieces and serve them raw in a salad with the rice. The flavor is exquisite and surprising.

7. Buckwheat

COOKING METHOD

- Wash the grains and place them in 1 1/2 times their volume of very hot water. Boiling water causes them to expand too rapidly.

- Bring to a boil, cover, reduce heat to a minimum, and cook for 10 minutes until all the water is absorbed.

NOTE:

- Buckwheat can also be eaten without being cooked, after being soaked along with other ingredients. See the " Muesli " recipe.

GRAINS

- Buckwheat is found in the following forms:
  - Whole grains with a black hull. When planted in potting soil they produce sprouts.
    They are also ground into flour to make those incomparable thin buckwheat crêpes.
  - White buckwheat, with a flavor everyone enjoys.
  - Roasted buckwheat (kasha), even more flavorful.

- Buckwheat cooks in 10 minutes. It is worth including often on the menu. Its texture and color make it a good substitute for ground meat in traditional recipes.

Shepherd's Pie with Buckwheat   *Serves 4-6*

1 cup (250 ml) white buckwheat
1 1/2 cups (375 ml) very hot water
1 onion, chopped
1 green pepper, cubed
1 cup (250 ml) mushrooms, sliced
2 cups (500 ml) kernels of corn
   (off the cob or frozen)

2 tablepoons (30 ml) safflower oil
1 tablespoon (15 ml) tamari soy
   sauce
1 teaspoon (5 ml) basil
1/2 teaspoon (2 ml) seaweed
   powder
1/2 teaspoon (2 ml) thyme

- Wash the buckwheat and add it to the very hot water. Bring to a boil, cover, reduce heat to a minimum, and cook for 10 minutes.

- Sauté the vegetables in the oil. Keep them crisp.

- Mix together the buckwheat and vegetables. Season.

- Place this mixture in a baking dish.

- Add the kernels of corn.

- Cover with a purée of steamed vegetables: potatoes, carrots, rutabaga, or, for variety, winter squash (pumpkin, pepper squash, buttercup squash, etc.). Squash purée is a delightful color and has a sweet flavor.

- Sprinkle with nutritional yeast and heat in the oven for 15 minutes so that the flavors blend together.

Serve with steamed broccoli after a crispy salad.

VARIATION: Add some cooked lentils to the buckwheat mixture.

Easy-as-Pie Buckwheat   *Serves 4-6*

1 cup (250 ml) white buckwheat **or** kasha, as desired
1 1/2 cups (375 ml) very hot water

A large quantity of parsley, chopped
Tamari soy sauce, to taste

- Wash and cook the buckwheat as in the preceding recipe.
- Garnish with parsley and season with a bit of tamari soy sauce.
- Serve as is with a vegetable (e.g. broccoli which has been steamed for a few minutes) and accompanied by 1 or 2 slices of roasted tofu.

NOTE: In general, children like to eat simple dishes rather than mixtures.

8. Pasta

A pasta-based dish made from organic whole-grain flour constitutes a nutritious, enjoyable main course which is greatly appreciated by the whole family.

COOKING METHOD

Cook pasta in 3 times its volume of boiling salted water. The salt reduces the transfer of minerals from the pasta to the

cooking water. Conserve this water and use it as a stock.

NOTE: 1/2 pound (250 g) of uncooked pasta yields 4 cups of cooked pasta or 4 servings.

Lasagna with Béchamel Sauce *Serves 8*

1/2 pound (250 g) lasagna or 6-8 ribbons, depending on their width
Boiling hot salted water
4 tablespoons (60 ml) safflower oil
6 tablespoons (90 ml) wheat flour
3 cups (750 ml) soy or other milk
1 tablespoon (15 ml) parsley, chopped
1/2 teaspoon (2 ml) sea salt
A pinch of nutmeg

1 cup (250 ml) Gruyère or other cheese, grated
3 cloves garlic, finely chopped
1 onion, chopped
1 green pepper, cubed
1 carrot, grated
1 cup (250 ml) broccoli
1 cup (250 ml) mushrooms
1/2 cup (125 ml) breadcrumbs
1/4 cup (60 ml) parmesan cheese
2 tablespoons (30 ml) olive oil

- Cook the pasta in the salted water.

- Make a béchamel sauce with the oil, flour, and milk. Cook until thick. Add the seasonings and the cheese.

- Brown the garlic and the onion in a bit of oil and add the other vegetables. Cook for just a few minutes.

- Build up the lasagna in layers in a rectangular baking dish. Start with the sauce. Then add some pasta and, after that, some vegetables. Repeat the same procedure, finishing with the sauce.

- Thoroughly mix together the breadcrumbs, parmesan cheese, and oil. Cover the lasagna with this mixture and bake at 350° F (180° C) for 35 minutes.

Garlic and Parsley Spaghetti *Serves 4*

1/2 pound (250 g) spaghetti
Salted water or vegetable stock
3 cloves garlic, crushed
2 tablespoons (30 ml) olive oil
1/2 cup (125 ml) parsley, finely
   chopped

A pinch of cayenne pepper
A few drops of tamari soy sauce
   or 1/2 teaspoon (2 ml) seaweed
   powder (kelp and cayenne
   pepper)

- Cook the spaghetti noodles al dente in a large volume of boiling salted water (or stock).

- Heat the olive oil and sauté the garlic.

- Add the seasonings and 6 tablespoons (90 ml) of cooking stock.

- Add the parsley. Pour this sauce over the well-drained spaghetti noodles.

Serve with parmesan cheese and strips of black olives along with a side dish of steamed carrot medallions.

Macaroni with Spinach *Serves 4*

3 cups (750 ml) cooked macaroni
1/2 pound (250 g) raw spinach
2 tablespoons (30 ml) tamari soy
   sauce

1 teaspoon (5 ml) oregano
1/2 teaspoon (2 ml) paprika
1 tablespoon (15 ml) olive oil

- Pour the precooked macaroni noodles into a baking dish and mix in the chopped spinach.

- Season and blend in the olive oil.

- Cover and bake at 350° F (180° C) for 15 minutes. Cook au gratin with 1/2 cup (125 ml) of grated cheddar cheese if desired.

Jiffy-Quick Pasta Shells *Serves 4*

2 cups (500 ml) pasta shells
6 cups (1.5 l) salted water or stock
2 onions, finely chopped
2 cloves garlic, crushed
2 tablespoons (30 ml) oil
14 ounces (400 g) canned
   tomatoes, drained

1/2 teaspoon (2 ml) marjoram
1/2 teaspoon (2 ml) oregano
1/2 teaspoon (2 ml) basil
1 cup (225 g) cottage cheese
  or creamy ricotta cheese
Seaweed powder to taste

- Bring the water or stock to a boil, add the pasta shells, and cook al dente.

- Heat the oil and sauté the onion and garlic. Cut the tomatoes into pieces, add them to the onions, and season.

- Beat the cottage cheese until creamy smooth and season with the seaweed powder and herbs.

- Place the pasta shells in a bowl and add the tomato mixture. Garnish with the cheese.

Rotini with Tofu *Serves 4-6*

2 cups (500 ml) rotini
6 cups (1.5 l) boiling hot salted
   water
1 16-ounce package (450 g) tofu,
   coarsely cubed
A 1-inch piece fresh ginger, grated
1 onion coarsely chopped

2 tablespoons (30 ml) safflower oil
1/2 broccoli (flowers and stem), cut
   into pieces
1 red pepper, cut into strips
Tamari soy sauce, basil, and
   seaweed powder, to taste

- Cook the rotini al dente in the boiling salted water.

- Heat the oil in a wok. Sauté the garlic, ginger, onion, and tofu. Add the broccoli and cook for 5 minutes.

- Add the green pepper and finish cooking. Keep crisp.

- Add the rotini to the other ingredients in the wok and season to taste.

Serve after a plentiful green salad or a salad of sprouts and grated carrots, depending on the season.

VARIATIONS:

- Marinate the cubes of tofu before sautéeing them, in order to accentuate the flavor. See the " Marinated Tofu " recipe.
- Use the " Chinese Vegetables " recipe.
- Prepare the tofu as in the " Roast Tofu Sticks " recipe.
- Add a béchamel sauce with cheese.

RECIPE IDEAS

Pasta exists in various forms and may be served in many different ways... even without sauce!

- Soba noodles (buckwheat spaghetti) make excellent soup with miso and selected vegetables.

- Build up your lasagna in different ways:
    - tomato sauce, pasta, cottage cheese, spinach, parmesan cheese, tomato sauce, etc.
    - tomato sauce, squash medallions, cubes of tofu, pasta, tomato sauce, etc.

- Serve macaroni as a salad with kidney beans, peppers, and garlic sauce.

- Serve pasta with finely chopped fresh herbs and 1 tablespoon (15 ml) of fresh cream.

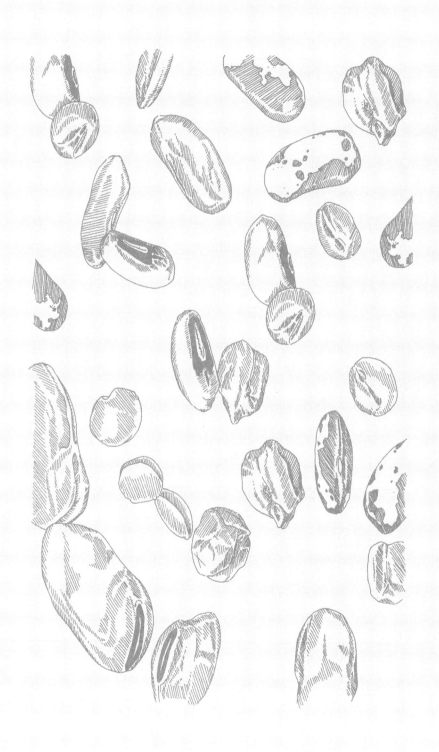

CHAPTER 2

Legumes on the Menu...

Always keep in mind that the simplest way to put legumes on the menu once a day to ensure sufficient protein intake is to routinely soak and cook them in advance.

WHAT DOES THIS MEAN?

Wash - soak - cook - refrigerate - freeze.

In this way you can quickly prepare nutritious meals simply by adding some legumes to a soup, a grain dish, or a salad, or by serving them in a casserole with vegetables and bread, or crushing them to make a spread.

COOKING METHOD

For details, reread that part of the " Theory Book " section dealing with legumes.

IN SHORT:

- Sort and remove any foreign substances.

- Wash and soak legumes for 8 to 12 hours in 3 times their volume of cold water.

- Do not cook them in the water used for soaking. It will contain trisaccharides, which contribute to the production of intestinal gases and, if the legumes were not grown organically, it will contain chemical residues as well.

- Put the legumes in a saucepan, cover with water to a depth of 2 inches (5 cm), bring to a boil, and cook over low heat until they can be crushed easily with a fork. See the table of cooking times in the " Theory Book " section.

- Legumes double or triple in volume during cooking. Once cooked they can be kept for 4-5 days in the refrigerator. Remember to freeze some in small quantities for use over the next month.

- In order for the body to get used to eating legumes, a daily intake of 1/2 cup (125 ml) is recommended at the beginning.

**1 serving of legumes per day =
1 cup (250 ml) cooked legumes (adults)
or 1/2 cup (125 ml) cooked legumes (children).**

Adzuki Bean Pie *Serves 4*

1 cup (250 ml) adzuki beans	1/2 teaspoon (2 ml) basil
1 onion, chopped	1/4 teaspoon (1 ml) marjoram
2 carrots, grated	A pinch of sage
1 stalk celery, chopped	4 tablespoons (60 ml) tomato paste
1 tablespoon (15 ml) oil	2 tablespoons (30 ml) water
1/2 cup (125 ml) nuts, chopped	2 tablespoons (30 ml) tamari soy
1 teaspoon (5 ml) parsley, chopped	sauce

- Soak the beans for 8 hours. Drain.

- Transfer to cold water, bring to a boil, reduce heat, and let simmer for 45 minutes (1 1/2 hours if the beans have not soaked). Yield: 3 cups once cooked.

- Heat the oil, sauté the vegetables, and season.

- Mix all the ingredients together and pour them into an uncooked, 9-inch (23 cm) whole wheat pie shell.

- Cover with aluminum foil or a top crust and bake at 350°F (180°C) for 35 minutes.

VARIATIONS:

- Prepare au gratin.

- Serve the adzuki bean filling over a cooked grain rather than in a pie shell.

- Place in a pie shell made of rice, millet, or cornmeal.

Wholesome Beans   *Serves 6-8*

2 cups (500 ml) dried navy beans
1 medium-sized onion, chopped
2 cloves garlic
5 cups (1 1/4 L) unsalted vegetable stock
1 bay leaf
1 onion, chopped

1 cup (250 ml) tomatoes, puréed
  or chopped
2 teaspoons (10 ml) dry mustard
1 teaspoon (5 ml) ginger, ground
4 carrots, cut into small medallions
2 teaspoons (10 ml) salt
2 tablespoons (30 ml) olive oil

- Soak the beans overnight in 6 cups (11/2 L) of water. Throw away the water used for soaking. Cook the beans in 5 cups of vegetable stock along with the onion, garlic, and bay leaf. To prevent the beans from hardening, begin cooking them in cold stock. Bring them to a boil and then let them simmer gently for 20 to 30 minutes, or until the beans are tender, but not completely cooked. In the fall when beans are fresh, it may take only 10 minutes.

- Add the chopped onion, olive oil, tomatoes, and all the other ingredients. Mix together. Place in a bean crock or a large glass casserole dish. Cover well. Bake at 225°F (105°C) for 6 to 8 hours. The beans will be ready for supper. Halfway through cooking, check to see if there is enough liquid. Add a bit of stock (or water) if necessary.

NOTE: To brown the beans you may remove the cover for the last hour of baking.

Auntie's Navy Beans   *Serves 2*

1/2 cup (125 ml) navy beans
2 cloves garlic
1 large onion, finely chopped
1 large carrot, sliced into medallions
1 large tomato, cut into pieces
1 green pepper, cubed
1 clove
1 tablespoon (15 ml) oil

1 bay leaf
Thyme, basil, oregano
A pinch of cayenne pepper
1 1/2 tablespoons (20 ml) tamari
  soy sauce
1 tablespoon (15 ml) nutritional
  yeast

- Soak the beans overnight. The next day, cover them with

cold water, boil for three minutes, and simmer for 15 to 20 minutes.

- Add the clove, bay leaf, and herbs. Cook for 1 hour.

- Heat the oil in a frying pan and sauté the garlic, onion, carrots, tomato, and green pepper.

- Add the beans and let simmer for 15 minutes.

- Add the tamari soy sauce and nutritional yeast.

Serve with bread on noodles or cooked grains.

Lima Rapido   *Serves 2*

2 cups (500 ml) cooked lima beans
1 onion, chopped
1 green pepper, cubed
1 stalk celery, sliced diagonally
1 tablespoon (15 ml) oil
1 or 2 tomatoes, diced

1/2 teaspoon (2 ml) thyme
1/2 teaspoon (2 ml) seaweed
  powder
1/2 teaspoon (2 ml) basil
1/3 cup (75 ml) fresh parsley

- Heat the oil and sauté all the vegetables except the tomatoes.

- Add the tomatoes, the beans, and the herbs. Cook for 5 minutes.

Serve with bread and salad.

Lima Bean Salad   *Serves 2* **(see photo)**

1 1/2 cups (375 ml) cooked lima
  beans
2 cups (500ml) fresh spinach
1 tomato, cut into quarters

2 tablespoons (30 ml) green
  onions
1/2 teaspoon (2 ml) dill
1/2 teaspoon (2 ml) paprika

- Mix all the ingredients together.

Serve with garlic salad dressing on a bed of rice or another cooked grain, or with rye bread.

A Potful of Kidney Beans   *Serves 4-6*

2 cups (500 ml) kidney beans
2 onions, chopped
2 cloves garlic, finely chopped
2 stalks celery and 3 carrots, sliced
  diagonally
1 teaspoon (5 ml) paprika
1 bay leaf
1 teaspoon (5 ml) celery seeds

1 teaspoon (5 ml) seaweed
  powder
1 teaspoon (5 ml) basil
1/2 teaspoon (2 ml) cumin
1/2 teaspoon (2 ml) oregano
A pinch of chili powder
1 cup (250 ml) tomato purée
1 tomato, cut into quarters

- Wash and soak the beans for 8 hours.

- Drain and put them into a saucepan with the bay leaf.

- Cover with cold water, bring to a boil, reduce heat, and cook for 1 1/2 hours; or, use 4 cups (1 L) of precooked beans.

- In a wok, sauté the vegetables with the paprika in 1 tablespoon (15 ml) of hot oil.

- Add the beans, purée, and seasonings.

- Simmer over low heat for 30 minutes and add the quartered tomato.

Serve with bread, or a grain such as bulgur or rice.

Red Croquetteburger   *Serves 4*

2 cups (500 ml) cooked kidney beans
1 cup (250 ml) breadcrumbs
  (or cooked millet or buckwheat)
2 onions, chopped
2 tablespoons (30 ml) tomato paste

1/2 teaspoon (2 ml) thyme
1/2 teaspoon (2 ml) seaweed
  powder
1 egg, beaten
1 tablespoon (15 ml) oil

- Mash the beans with a fork or in a food processor. Add the rest of the ingredients.

- Form into croquettes and cook on both sides in an oiled frying pan, or bake at 350°F (180°C) for 20 minutes.

Serve with cooked vegetables and a salad or serve on a hamburger bun with a slice of tomato and some lettuce or alfalfa sprouts.

VARIATIONS:

- Leave out the egg and use the mixture as a spread or to stuff vegetables.

- This recipe can also be cooked in a rolled-out pastry dough.

Lentil and Rice Salad *Serves 5*

1 1/2 cups (375 ml) cooked green lentils
1 1/2 cups (375 ml) cooked long-grain brown rice
2 green onions, chopped
3 cloves garlic, finely chopped

1/2 cup (125 ml) parsley, chopped
2 tablespoons (30 ml) olive oil
2 tablespoons (30 ml) lemon juice
1 teaspoon (5 ml) basil
1 teaspoon (5 ml) curry
2 tablespoons (30 ml) tamari soy sauce

• Mix all the ingredients together thoroughly. Let stand for 15 minutes. Serve with a carrot and alfalfa sprout salad. May also be served hot.

Variations on Lentils *Serves 6*

3 cups (750 ml) cooked lentils
2 cups (500 ml) tomatoes, crushed
1 onion, chopped
1 green pepper, chopped
1 teaspoon (5 ml) wheat flour

1/2 teaspoon (2 ml) salt
1 teaspoon (5 ml) basil
1/2 teaspoon (2 ml) celery seeds
Nutritional yeast

• Mix all the ingredients together in a frying pan. Cover.

• Cook for 15 to 20 minutes. Sprinkle 1 teaspoon (5 ml) of nutritional yeast on each portion when serving.

Lentil Loaf with Tomatoes   *Serves 4*

1 cup (250 ml) onions, finely chopped
1 clove garlic, finely chopped
1 teaspoon (5 ml) safflower oil
1 tablespoon (15 ml) wheat flour
1 teaspoon (5 ml) tamari soy sauce
3/4 cup (200 ml) tomato sauce

1 1/2 cups (375 ml) cooked
   lentils (2/3 cup if uncooked
   or 2 cups if sprouted)
3/4 cup (200 ml) breadcrumbs
3/4 cup (200 ml) nuts, chopped

- Sauté the onion and garlic in the hot oil, add the flour, and cook a bit.

- Add the tomato sauce, stir, and then add the rest of the ingredients.

- Mix together, pour into an oiled mold, and bake at 350°F (180°C) for 35 minutes.

- Decorate with green peppers cut in rounds and serve accompanied by carrots with dill, and a salad.

VARIATION: Add 1/4 teaspoon (1 ml) of ground cloves or cinnamon to the mixture if desired. Then place between two pieces of rolled-out pastry dough as if you were making a meat pie. Bake at 375°F (190°C) for 40 minutes.

Hummus: Chickpea Purée   *Serves 4* (see photo)

2 cups (500 ml) cooked chickpeas
1/3 cup (175 ml) sesame butter
4 cloves garlic
1/2 teaspoon (2 ml) sea salt

4 tablespoons (60 ml) lemon juice
1 teaspoon (5 ml) basil
1/2 teaspoon (2 ml) coriander or
   cumin (optional)

- Reduce all the ingredients to a purée in a mixer or a food processor, adding 1/4 to 1/2 cup (60 to 125 ml) of water, depending on the consistency desired.

- Add a trickle of olive oil, decorate with parsley, and serve as a dip or a spread.

Felafels: Chickpea Croquettes   *Makes 10*
(Spicy Croquettes or Balls)

2 cups (500 ml) cooked chickpeas
4 cloves garlic
3 tablespoons (45 ml) sesame butter
1 green onion, finely chopped
1 onion, chopped
1 egg, beaten
1 teaspoon (5 ml) tamari soy sauce

2 tablespoons (30 ml) fresh
    parsley, chopped
1/2 teaspoon (2 ml) coriander
1/4 teaspoon (1 ml) cumin, ground
1/4 teaspoon (1 ml) cayenne
    pepper
1 teaspoon (5 ml) basil

- Purée the chickpeas in a food processor. Blend in all the remaining ingredients.

- Form into croquettes or small balls, add a bit of water if necessary, and cook on both sides in an oiled frying pan; **or**, brush with oil and bake at 350°F (180°C) for 15 minutes. Traditionally, they are fried in a large quantity of oil.

Serve in pita bread with tomatoes and cucumber salad with yogurt, or drenched in tahini sauce. See the recipe for " Tahini Salad Dressing " which may be served hot or cold.

NOTE: You can increase the quantities of spices in order to approximate the traditional flavor of felafels.

Chickpea Loaf   *Serves 4* **(see photo)**

2 cups (500 ml) cooked chickpeas	1/2 cup (125 ml) breadcrumbs or
1 carrot, grated	cooked bulgur
1 stalk celery, chopped	2 eggs, beaten
1/2 green pepper, cubed	1 tablespoon (15 ml) tamari
1 onion, finely chopped	soy sauce
2 cloves garlic, finely chopped	1/2 teaspoon (2 ml) salt
1 tablespoon (15 ml) oil	1 tablespoon (15 ml) basil

- Heat the oil and sauté the vegetables. Purée the chickpeas in a food processor. In a bowl, mix together the vegetables, chickpeas, and the rest of the ingredients.

- Place in an oiled mold and bake at 375°F (190°C) for 30 minutes.

Slice and serve with plain tomato sauce and a plentiful salad of Chinese cabbage, alfalfa sprouts, and filberts.

Green Split Pea Purée   *Serves 4*

1 cup (250 ml) green split peas	1 teaspoon (5 ml) basil
3 cups (750 ml) water or stock	1/2 teaspoon (2 ml) salt
2 cloves garlic, finely chopped	

- Cover with water and cook over low heat for about 45 minutes.

- Once cooked, the peas can be easily puréed. Season.

- Serve as a purée. Add a little milk if desired.

RECIPE IDEAS

When cooked and allowed to cool, all legumes make excellent salads. Mix them with raw vegetables,and pour on a fine stream of oil and lemon juice to which you have added some herbs.

Add a grain such as rice or millet, or serve with some tasty bread. In this way you can prepare a complete, appetizing meal in just a few minutes.

- Salad made of rice, kidney beans, green peas, and green peppers.

- Salad made of adzuki beans, green onions, green peppers, and apples.

- Salad made of lentils, sautéed onions and garlic, green onions, and tomatoes.

- Salad made of chickpeas, kidney beans, green peppers, celery, and black olives.

- Salad made of lentils, garlic, curry, a pinch of cayenne pepper, and ginger.

- Salad made of millet, black beans, broccoli, and greens.

- Salad made of chickpeas, carrots, celery, and green onions.

NOTE: You can transform all of these salads into hot dishes by sautéeing or steaming the vegetables and heating the mixture. Precooked legumes can help you to prepare quick, nourishing meals. Add them to spaghetti sauce or soup; put them on pizzas or in pâtés; purée them to make a spread; or, use them as the main ingredient in " Shepherd's Pie ".

LEGUMES

Soy Milk *Makes 8 cups (2 L)*

1 cup (250 ml) soybeans   8 cups (2 L) water

- Cull and wash 1 cup (250 ml) of soybeans, removing damaged beans, little stones, etc. Soak the beans for 24 hours in the refrigerator in three times their volume of cold water.

  1 cup (250 ml) of dried beans will yield 2 1/2 cups (625 ml) of beans after soaking.

- Measure out and then heat 8 cups (2 L) of water. This water will be used when grinding up the beans.

- Grind the soaked beans in a blender or a food processor, doing 1/3 of the beans at a time in at least 2 cups (500 ml) of very hot water. Pulverize them and pour the mixture into a large saucepan.

- When all of the beans have been ground up, add any remaining water to the milky mixture in the saucepan.

- Slowly bring the liquid containing the pulp (*okara* in Japanese) to the boiling point.

  - Be careful! Soy milk froths up easily and will spill over almost immediately on reaching the boiling point.

  - The soy milk and pulp (*okara*) must be cooked in order to destroy the anti-trypsin which is found in the beans and which hinders the digestion of proteins.

  - Soy milk has a nutty flavor. For those who prefer a milder taste, separate the pulp from the milk before cooking.

- Place a sieve or a strainer which has been lined with a cloth over a saucepan or a large bowl, and then filter the milk through it.

- Squeeze well in order to extract the greatest amount of liquid possible. About 2 cups (500 ml) of soy pulp residue, called *okara*, will remain.

- Pour the warm milk into preserve jars and close the lids tightly. It keeps longer this way: from four days to more than a week.

  - Both soy milk and *okara* keep well when frozen.

- To obtain soy milk which is fortified in calcium, add 1/2 teaspoon (2 ml) of calcium carbonate per cup (250 ml) of milk.

HOW TO USE THE MILK

Cooked:

- As a substitute in all of those dishes where milk is usually used (béchamel sauce, quiches, pancakes, creams, etc.), it will go unnoticed.

- Very economical, nutritious, cholesterol-free, etc.

- Review the " Theory Book " section.

Uncooked:

- With cereal in the morning or as a beverage. In this case 1 tablespoon (15 ml) of honey and 1/2 teaspoon (2 ml) of vanilla may be added.

- Whipped in a blender with fruit or carob, it makes a delicious milkshake.

TRANSFORMATION: TOFU

- Soy milk which has been coagulated, drained, and pressed into a cake.

- Of very great nutritional value. Review the " Theory Book " section, which deals with this subject.

Tofu-based Recipes

Generally,
1 cake = 16 ounces = 454 g
1 serving = 125 g
A suggestion: 1 serving of tofu, 3 days a week.

Scrambled Tofu with Herbs *Serves 4*

1 onion, chopped
2 cloves garlic, finely chopped
1 stalk celery, chopped
1 tablespoon (15 ml) olive oil
16 ounces (454 g) tofu
1 tablespoon (15 ml) parsley

1 teaspoon (5 ml) chives
1 teaspoon (5 ml) basil
1 tablespoon (15 ml) tamari
  soy sauce
1 tablespoon (15 ml) nutritional yeast

- Heat the olive oil and sauté the onion, garlic, and celery.

- Crush the tofu with a fork or in a food processor, add to vegetables, and season.

Serve as you would scrambled eggs, with baked potatoes, green vegetables, and slices of tomato.

"Special Texture" Tofu *Serves 5*

- Take 1 cake (454 g) of frozen tofu and let it thaw in the refrigerator for one day.

- Cut it into thick slices, place it between two cloths, and lay a board on top. Place a weight on the board in order to extract as much water as possible.

- In an oiled frying pan, roast the slices of tofu, which has been garnished with sliced tomatoes, selected herbs, and cheese; or, garnish the tofu like mini pizzas and bake at 375°F (190°C) for 15 minutes.

Serve with a plentiful salad of Chinese cabbage and black olives.

NOTE:

- Frozen tofu takes on a yellow color which it loses when it thaws. It has a grainy texture. It can be served in slices or mashed with a fork or in a food processor.

- It can also be sliced before freezing, ready for use when needed.

VARIATIONS:

- For those of you who must use tofu incognito, crumbling it is a good trick. It can be used this way with rice, millet, spaghetti sauce, or in croquettes.

- As for the others, crumbled tofu can be used to stuff vegetables or, when mixed with a bit of mayonnaise, herbs, and a green onion, it becomes a sandwich spread.

- You can also use crushed tofu as the main ingredient in " Shepherd's Pie ".

Express Spread *Serves 4*

8 ounces (225 g) tofu	1 teaspoon (5 ml) tamari soy sauce
2 tablespoons (30 ml) mayonnaise	Basil and seaweed powder, to taste
1 tablespoon (15 ml) nutritional yeast	Paprika, if desired

- Mash the tofu with a fork. Add the rest of the ingredients.

- Use as a spread.

Serve in a sandwich or in a pita bread with alfalfa sprouts and grated carrots. A simple, nutritious meal!

VARIATION: Add some yogurt and a finely chopped green onion, and you will have a delicious dip.

TOFU

Macaroni Salad with Tofu   *Serves 4*

2 cups (500 ml) cooked macaroni
1 cup (225 g) firm tofu, cubed
1 green pepper, cubed
1/2 red pepper, cubed
1 stalk celery, cut into pieces
1 teaspoon (5 ml) basil

A trickle of olive oil
Lemon juice
A few drops of tamari soy sauce
1/2 teaspoon (2 ml) seaweed
   powder

- Mix the ingredients together. Garnish each serving with one teaspoonful (5 ml) of nutritional yeast.

Tofu Spaghetti Sauce   *Serves 6-8*

3 onions, chopped
5 cloves garlic, finely chopped
2 tablespoons (30 ml) safflower oil
2 green peppers, cubed
1 cup (250 ml) broccoli, cut into
   pieces
2 stalks celery, sliced
1 cup (250 ml) carrots, cubed
2 large tomatoes, cubed
16 ounces (500 ml) canned
   tomatoes

2 cups (500 ml) tomato sauce
5 1/2 ounces (156 ml) tomato paste
1 16-ounce package (450 g) firm
   tofu, cubed
1 tablespoon (15 ml) basil
1 teaspoon (5 ml) oregano
1/2 teaspoon (2 ml) thyme
1 bay leaf
1/4 teaspoon (1 ml) cayenne
   pepper

- Heat the oil in a large saucepan and brown the onions, garlic, and herbs to bring out the flavor. Add the remaining vegetables and stir.

- Add the rest of the ingredients.

- Simmer over low heat for 30 minutes. Serve over pasta or a hot whole grain.

VARIATION: Spread the sauce on a pizza crust or on slices of bread.

Marinated Tofu *Serves 4-6* *(see photo)*

3/4 cup (200 ml) tamari soy sauce
11/2 cups (375 ml) water
3 cloves garlic, crushed
1-inch piece ginger, grated
or 1 teaspoon (5 ml) ground ginger

1 teaspoon (5 ml) basil
1/2 teaspoon (2 ml) thyme
A 16-ounce package (450 g)
  tofu

• Mix together all the ingredients except the tofu.

• Cut the tofu into small slices or cubes, and marinate it for at least 2 hours. Tofu can be marinated for several days in the refrigerator.

Serve as is, or place in an oiled baking dish. Pour on a trickle of oil and brown at 450°F (230°C) for a few minutes.

Delicious and easy to prepare. Goes well with vegetables, pasta, or grains.

VARIATIONS:

- The marinating sauce may be thickened with 1 table-spoon (15 ml) of arrowroot and then added to the tofu dish of your choice.

- The remaining sauce can be used a second time.

- You can also marinate vegetables in it.

Hot Tofu Sandwich   *Serves 1*

2 slices of tofu
1 tablespoon (15 ml) safflower oil
1/2 onion, finely chopped
1 green onion
1 teaspoon (5 ml) tamari soy sauce

1 teaspoon (5 ml) nutritional yeast
1/2 teaspoon (2 ml) seaweed
  powder
2 slices of bread
Sesame butter (optional)

- Sauté the tofu in the oil until it takes on a slight color.

- Add the onion, green onion, and seasonings.

- Toast the bread lightly in a toaster.

- Spread a bit of sesame butter on the bread (optional).

- Place the tofu and the vegetables between the 2 slices of bread and cover with brown sauce(see Chapter 6).

Serve with green peas and cole slaw.

Tofu and Curried Rice Salad   *Serves 5* *(see photo)*

A REAL DELIGHT!

16 ounces (450 g) firm tofu,
  mashed in a food processor
2 1/2 cups (625 ml) cooked
  long-grain brown rice
1 onion, finely chopped
1/2 cup (125 ml) fresh parsley,
  chopped
2 green peppers, cubed

6 tablespoons (90 ml) olive oil
1/4 cup (60 ml) lemon juice
2 cloves garlic, finely chopped
1 teaspoon (5 ml) sea salt
1 teaspoon (5 ml) curry
1/4 teaspoon (1 ml) cayenne
  pepper

- Mix together the first 5 ingredients.

- Make the salad dressing with the remaining ingredients and add it to the salad.

- In order to let the flavors blend together thoroughly, let sit for a few hours in the refrigerator.

Serve on a bed of lettuce on a large plate. Garnish with red peppers cut into strips and sliced in rings.

Vegetables with Tofu   *Serves 2*

A VERY QUICK AND DELICIOUS MEAL.

1 carrot	1/2 teaspoon (2 ml) basil
1/2 rutabaga	1/2 teaspoon (2 ml) seaweed
1 onion	powder
2 tablespoons (30 ml) safflower oil	Nutritional yeast
8 ounces (225 g) tofu	Tamari soy sauce

- Coarsely grate the carrot and rutabaga, and chop the onion.

- Cut the tofu into large cubes. Dip it in the tamari sauce and sprinkle it with yeast.

- Heat the oil in a skillet or a wok, and sauté the onions.

- Add the cubes of tofu and cook for a few minutes.

- Add the grated vegetables, season, and savor the result.

Serve with a delicious green salad, sliced tomatoes with garlic sauce, and garlic bread.

VARIATION: Cut the vegetables into match-sized sticks and sauté them until they are cooked. Add 2 tablespoons (30 ml) of water to the vegetables. Cover and cook for a few minutes until tender.

TOFU

Roast Tofu Sticks

16 ounces (450 g) tofu, cut into thick strips	2 tablespoons (30 ml) nutritional yeast
2 tablespoons (30 ml) oil	1/4 teaspoon (1 ml) onion powder
1/4 cup (60 ml) tamari soy sauce	1/4 teaspoon (1 ml) garlic powder

- Heat the oil in a wok and sauté the tofu until it is lightly roasted. Be careful! If the tofu contains a lot of water, begin by placing the slices between two cloths and pressing down on them with a weight; then cut into strips and brown.

- Mix the strips of tofu with the rest of the ingredients and sauté again.

Serve as is with steamed vegetables, or on top of pasta or millet.

VARIATIONS:

- Cut the tofu into slices, proceed with the recipe, and serve in sandwiches.

- After coating the strips with sauce, dip them in bread-crumbs (made in a blender) and bake them in the oven.

Tofu Chow Mein   *Serves 6*

3 cups (750 ml) celery, cut diagonally	1 cup (250 ml) tofu, cubed
	1 cup (250 ml) mushrooms, sliced
2 cups (500 ml) Chinese cabbage, cut diagonally	2 cups (500 ml) mung bean sprouts
	1/4 cup (60 ml) parsley
1 large onion, chopped	

- Heat a wok and add 2 tablespoons (30 ml) of oil.

- Heat the oil and sauté the vegetables along with the tofu, stirring constanly.

Prepare the following sauce:

1/2 cup (125 ml) water
1 tablespoon (15 ml) arrowroot

1 tablespoon (15 ml) tamari soy
sauce

- Pour the sauce over the sautéed vegetables, and stir until thickened.

- Add the sprouts and parsley.

Serve with rice.

RECIPE IDEAS

Tofu has a neutral flavor. It takes on the taste of the ingredients with which you prepare it.

- Dip it in tamari sauce, sprinkle it with nutritional yeast, and roast it; or, eat it as is.

- Coat it with granola or whole wheat breadcrumbs.

- Crumble and blend with peanut butter to obtain a creamy mixture. Use as a spread. It is delicious and more nutritious.

- **Tofu Kebabs:** Use large cubes of marinated tofu, and vegetables. Bake in the oven on skewers and serve on top of rice.

- **Tofu Vol-au-vent:** Use small cubes of tofu to replace the chicken.

- **Tofu Chop Suey:** Use strips of tofu to replace the meat.

- **Tofu Shepherd's Pie:** Use crumbled tofu with cooked vegetables. Season well. Serve with corn and mashed potatoes.

- **Tofu Pâté:** Use crumbled tofu with vegetables and a cooked grain (rice or millet). Season as you would a meat pie and bake between two crusts.

OKARA

Soy pulp by product resulting from the making of soy milk. It is used mainly to complement recipes. Reacts well to freezing. Review at the " Theory Book " section, which deals with this subject.

Okara Croquettes *Makes 8*

2 cups (500 ml) okara
1 onion, finely chopped
2 cloves garlic, finely chopped
1 carrot, grated
1 tablespoon (15 ml) tamari soy sauce

3 tablespoons (45 ml) wheat flour
1/2 teaspoon (2 ml) sea salt
1 teaspoon (5 ml) basil
1/2 teaspoon (2 ml) thyme
1 egg, beaten

- Mix together all the ingredients.

- Form into croquettes with a spoon and cook in an oiled skillet, browning on both sides; or, bake at 350°F (180°C) for 25 minutes.

Serve with a vegetable purée and a beet salad.

VARIATIONS:

- Replace the okara with 2 cups (500 ml) of soy or other beans, which have been cooked and mashed.

- Pour this mixture into a baking dish, cover with slices of tomato, and bake au gratin.

Okara Pâté *Serves 4*

3 tablespoons (45 ml) safflower
3 tablespoons (45 ml) wheat flour
1 1/2 cups (375 ml) soy or other milk
1 cup (250 ml) mushrooms, sliced
2 onions, finely chopped
1 1/2 cups (375 ml) okara

1/2 cup (125 ml) cheese, grated
3 tablespoons (45 ml) tamari soy sauce
1/4 cup (60 ml) breadcrumbs
2 tablespoons (30 ml) parmesan cheese

- Make a béchamel sauce with the first 3 ingredients.

- In an oiled skillet, sauté the onions and mushrooms for a few minutes.

- Remove from the heat and blend in the béchamel sauce, okara, cheese, and tamari sauce.

- Pour into an oiled loaf pan; sprinkle with breadcrumbs and parmesan cheese.

- Bake at 350°F (180°C) for 30 minutes.

Serve with tomatoes and lots of greens.

Nicole's Okara Sausages   *Serves 4-6*

1 cup (250 ml) okara (soy pulp)
1/2 cup (125 ml) wheat flour
1/4 cup (60 ml) rolled oats
2 tablespoons (30 ml) nutritional yeast
1/4 cup (60 ml) safflower oil
1/4 cup (60 ml) soy milk (the quantity may vary according to the moisture content of the pulp after squeezing)
1 tablespoon (15 ml) tamari soy sauce

1/2 teaspoon (2 ml) oregano
1/2 teaspoon (2 ml) sea salt
1/2 teaspoon (2 ml) Jamaican pepper
1 1/2 teaspoons (7 ml) garlic powder
1 teaspoon (5 ml) dry mustard
1/2 teaspoon (2 ml) basil
1/4 teaspoon (1 ml) paprika
A pinch of cayenne pepper, to taste

- Mix together all the ingredients. The mixture will be of a thick consistency.

- Knead with your hands in order to develop the gluten from the wheat. This will allow you to obtain sausages which are easy to slice.

- Steam for 1 1/2 hours in an oiled tin can measuring 3 inches (6 cm) in diameter, which you have covered with aluminum foil.

- Remove from the can while still hot.

OKARA

Slice and serve as hamburgers. You can also roast the slices in a skillet, bake them in the oven, or use them as a spread.

VARIATION : Soy Sausage with Carrots

Add the following to the first seven ingredients in the above recipe :

1/4 cup (60 ml) carrots, grated
1/2 onion, finely chopped
1 1/2 teaspoons (7 ml) paprika
1 teaspoon (5 ml) chili powder
1 teaspoon (5 ml) garlic powder
1/2 teaspoon (2 ml) oregano

1/2 teaspoon (2 ml) sea salt
1/2 teaspoon (2 ml) coriander, ground
1/4 teaspoon (1 ml) basil
Cayenne pepper, to taste

Prepare and cook in the same way.

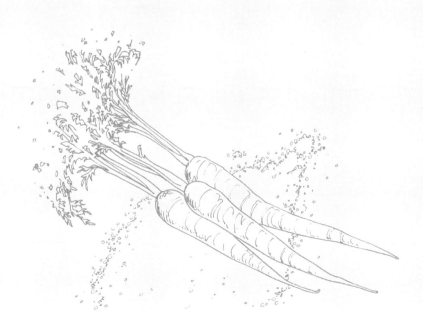

CHAPTER 3

Salads
Salad Dressings
Sprouts
Beverages

Salads are rich in fiber and promote good digestion. They are indispensable and should be eaten at lunch time and at supper. A creatively stimulating dish par excellence, salads are served at the beginning of the meal instead of raw vegetables, or they may be transformed into a main dish. In this case, you just have to add one or more of the following ingredients to the vegetables you have chosen:
- pasta,
- legumes,
- grains,
- nuts and seeds,
- eggs or milk products.

Fresh herbs such as basil, parsley, and mint, when in season, bring out the flavor of vegetable salads as well as of

salad dressings wonderfully well. In winter use frozen or dried herbs, or, better still, herbs which you grow indoors.

Spinach Salad

4 cups (1 L) spinach
1 green pepper, cut into strips
2 green onions, chopped
3 carrots, grated
1/2 cup (125 ml) sunflower seeds

1/2 cup (125 ml) parsley, finely chopped
1/2 cup (125 ml) cheese, grated
Sesame salt

- Tear up the spinach leaves with your fingers and add the other ingredients.

- Sprinkle with a garlic salad dressing and sesame salt.

Fresh Summer Salad

2 large tomatoes, cubed
1 cup (250 ml) cottage cheese
1/2 cup (125 ml) walnuts,
1/2 cup (125 ml) fresh parsley, chopped

1 tablespoon (15 ml) lemon juice
1 teaspoon (5 ml) oregano
Lettuce leaves
Olive oil

- Gently mix the first 6 ingredients and arrange on the lettuce leaves.

- Drizzle with olive oil, if desired.

Red, Green, and Yellow Salad

2 cobs corn, cooked or uncooked
2 tomatoes, cubed

1 green pepper, cubed
Lettuce leaves

- Remove the kernels of corn from the cobs. Add the tomatoes and green pepper.

- Serve on lettuce leaves and sprinkle with a garlic dressing.

SALADS

Cucumbers with Yogurt   *Serves 2*

1 English cucumber, cut into thin
  slices
1/2 cup (125 ml) yogurt
2 green onions, finely chopped

1/4 teaspoon (1 ml) sea salt
1/4 teaspoon (1 ml) dill
A few mint leaves, chopped
Paprika

- Mix together the yogurt, green onions, salt, dill, and mint in a medium-size bowl.

- Add the slices of cucumber and toss.

- Sprinkle with paprika. Cover and refrigerate.

Serve with rice, millet, or bulgur.

Greek Salad   *Serves 2*

1 cucumber, cut into pieces
1 tomato, cubed
1 onion, cut into slices

1/2 cup (125 ml) feta cheese
8 black olives
1/2 teaspoon (2 ml) basil

- Mix the ingredients together gently, and drizzle with a trickle of olive oil and lemon juice.

VARIATIONS:

- Grate the feta cheese and lay it on top of the mixture.

- Replace the feta cheese with tofu.

- Encircle with alfalfa sprouts and sliced mushrooms.

- Replace the cucumber with avocado and serve on romaine lettuce.

Red Cabbage Salad   *Serves 6*

3 cups (750 ml) red cabbage,
  grated
1 teaspoon (5 ml) caraway seeds
2 tablespoons (30 ml) sunflower oil
Juice of 1/2 lemon

1/2 teaspoon (2 ml) basil
1/2 teaspoon (2 ml) sea salt
1/2 cup (125 ml) pineapple juice
  or crushed pineapple

- Mix all the ingredients together well and let stand for a while before serving. Really tasty.

Bountiful Salad

1 head Boston lettuce
1 small cauliflower, finely grated

1 red pepper, cubed
2 tablespoons (30 ml) fresh parsley

- Wash and spin-dry the lettuce. Place it around the perimeter of an attractive salad bowl.

- Place the grated cauliflower and the cubed red pepper in the center.

- Garnish with parsley and serve with a delicate green salad dressing.

Colorful Salad   *(see photo)*

2 medium-sized beets
1 small turnip

2 carrots
Alfalfa sprouts

- Wash and scrub the vegetables.

- Finely grate all of them.

- Layer the grated vegetables in a glass bowler, if your bowl is opaque, set aside a portion of each vegetable to be used later as a decoration.

- Garnish with alfalfa sprouts and serve with home-made mayonnaise and sesame salt.

SALADS

Zucchini and Arame

Seaweeds, those vegetables of the sea, are easy to prepare and rich in minerals.

3 zucchini, coarsely grated
1/2 red pepper, cubed

1/2 red pepper, cut into strips
1/4 cup (60 ml) arame seaweed

- Wash and soak the arame seaweed for 15 minutes.

- Mix in with the other ingredients and decorate with strips of red pepper, placed in the form of a star.

Serve with nutritional yeast dressing.

NOTE: Several varieties of seaweed make excellent salads. Simply wash, soak, drain and serve. Soak dulse for 5 minutes, arame for 15 minutes, and hijiki for 20 minutes. Delicious as a vegetable side dish.

Avocado Salad

1 avocado
1 green onion
1 stalk celery

1 tomato
1 teaspoon (5 ml) lemon juice
Garlic dressing

- Cut up all the ingredients. Add the lemon juice and the dressing, to taste.

- Place in the center of a salad bowl and encircle with alfalfa sprouts.

VARIATION: Cut the avocado into halves and stuff with the other chopped vegetables.

Jerusalem Artichoke Salad

2 cups (500 ml) Jerusalem
   artichokes
1 stalk celery, finely chopped

1 green onion, chopped
1 teaspoon (5 ml) celery seeds
1 teaspoon (5 ml) seaweed powder

- Mix together the vegetables and the seasonings. Add some mayonnaise and sesame salt. Garnish with fresh parsley.

Apple and Beet Salad

1 1/2 cups (375 ml) cooked beets,
   cubed
1/3 cup (75 ml) parsley, finely
   chopped

1 cup (250 ml) apples, cut into
   cubes and sprinkled with lemon
   juice

Dressing:

1/4 cup (60 ml) safflower oil
1 clove garlic, crushed
1 teaspoon (5 ml) lemon juice

1 teaspoon (5 ml) honey
1 teaspoon (5 ml) tamari soy sauce
1/2 teaspoon (2 ml) basil

- Prepare the dressing.

- Mix together all the ingredients in a salad bowl.

- Let sit briefly before serving. Decorate the perimeter of the bowl with chicory leaves.

VARIATIONS:

- Cut the apples and beets into slices.

- Replace the apples and beets with cooked, cubed potatoes and cooked, sliced leeks. Serve with the same dressing but leave out the honey.

SALADS

SALAD IDEAS

- **When in season, flowers add beauty and color to salads: nasturtiums, cow vetches, roses, clover, etc.**

- Steamed green beans, mushrooms, and finely chopped parsley, with olive oil and lemon juice.

- Green cabbage cut into strips, green peppers, onions, and apples, with mayonnaise.

- Cooked potatoes, rutabaga, chives, and parsley, with mayonnaise.

- Lettuce, tomatoes, and mushrooms, with green parsley dressing.

- Spinach, hard-boiled eggs, and croutons, with yellow mayonnaise.

- Chicory, apples, and walnuts, with nutritional yeast dressing.

- Grated carrots, apples, cottage cheese, and chives.

- Chinese cabbage, black olives, and parsley, with garlic dressing.

- Cubed tomatoes and a lot of very finely chopped parsley, with garlic dressing.

- Potatoes, green onions, and red and green peppers, with mayonnaise.

- Avocado, spinach, green onions, and tomatoes, with garlic dressing.

- Raw leeks, chopped into fine strips, and black olives on Boston lettuce, with yogurt dressing.

- Onions and mushrooms marinated in the sauce from the " Marinated Tofu " recipe.

- Radishes, lettuce, and watercress.

- Cottage cheese, apples, and nuts.

- Grated carrots, apples, celery, grapes, sunflower seeds, and mint, with lemon juice and mayonnaise.

- Turnip, yellow squash (butternut squash, pumpkin), and beets, finely grated and arranged in rainbow fashion on a bed of parsley and spinach.

- Grated carrots and kohlrabi, and soaked hijiki seaweed served on romaine lettuce.

- Greens (lettuce and watercress), avocado, sliced cucumbers, small tomatoes, croutons, and parmesan cheese, with garlic dressing.

Love Those Sprouts!

SHOULD BE EATEN RAW IN LARGE QUANTITIES!

Delightful Salad

2 cups (500 ml) carrots, grated	1/2 cup (125 ml) wheat sprouts
1 apple, cut into pieces	1/2 cup (125 ml) raisins

Mix together thoroughly, and serve with mayonnaise or yogurt dressing.

Pretty Julie's Salad

2 cups (500 ml) bean sprouts	1 green pepper, cut into short strips
1/2 package spinach	2 cups (500 ml) cooked rice
1 cup (250 ml) celery, diced	1 cup (250 ml) sunflower seeds
2 green onions	1 cup (250 ml) mushrooms

Mix together all the ingredients and serve with garlic dressing.

SPROUTS

- Alfalfa sprouts, finely grated carrots, and finely chopped parsley.

- Mung bean sprouts, lentil sprouts, arame seaweed, and green onions.

- Your favorite sprouts with lettuce or cabbage.

- Mung bean sprouts, macaroni, peppers, and spinach.

- Wheat sprouts and finely grated beets, garnished with parsley.

- Alfalfa and radish sprouts, pieces of avocado, tomatoes, and feta cheese.

- Alfalfa sprouts, sunflower sprouts, tomatoes, and lettuce.

- Alfalfa sprouts, kernels of corn, grated carrots.

- Wheat and fenugreek sprouts, with grated pumpkin.

Sprouts may be eaten raw in salads, in sandwiches, or in juices (after being put through the blender), or added to grain dishes. They may also be eaten warm, but not really cooked, in dishes such as chop suey and chow mein.

To learn about why and how to make sprouts, consult the chapter dealing with sprouts in the " Theory Book "section.

Chop Suey with Vegetables

2 onions, chopped	1 apple, cut into pieces
3 carrots, julienne	4 cups (1 L) mung or other bean
2 stalks celery, cut into pieces	sprouts
1 tablespoon (15 ml) safflower oil	Basil and tamari soy sauce, to taste

- Heat a wok and add the oil. When the oil is hot, brown first the onions, and then add the celery and carrots. Sauté for a few minutes while stirring.

- If the vegetables are still too crisp, add a bit of water, cover, and cook for 5 minutes.

- When the vegetables are just right, add the apples and sprouts, mix well, and season. Keep the sprouts crisp.

Serve hot with bread and cheese.

VARIATION: Add tofu cubes to the vegetables.

Alfalfa Juice

1 cup (250 ml) orange, pineapple, or tomato juice

1/2 cup (125 ml) alfalfa sprouts
1 tablespoon (15 ml) parsley

- Put through the blender. It's delicious!

Salad Dressings

MAYONNAISE

Making your own mayonnaise is economical, fast, and simple. Try it and you will see!

In the Blender or Food Processor

1 egg, whole
Juice from 1/2 lemon or 2 tablespoons (30 ml) lemon juice
1 green onion
1/4 cup (60 ml) fresh parsley

1/2 teaspoon (2 ml) Dijon or
   dry mustard (optional)
1 cup (250 ml) safflower oil
A pinch of sea salt
A dash of paprika

- All the ingredients should be at room temperature.

- Break the egg into a blender or a food processor. Add all the other ingredients except the oil.

- Mix at the slowest speed, while slowly pouring in the oil. Makes 1 cup (250 ml) of mayonnaise.

It is easy to double the quantities of this recipe. It will keep for a week in a jar in the refrigerator.

By Hand

2 egg yolks
1/2 teaspoon (2 ml) Dijon mustard
Juice from 1/2 lemon or
  2 tablespoons (30 ml) lemon juice

A pinch of sea salt
1 cup (250 ml) safflower or
  sunflower oil

- **All the ingredients should be at room temperature.**

- Put the egg yolks, mustard, and salt into a cone-shaped bowl, and mix together well with a whisk.

- Add half the oil, drop by drop, while whipping at the same time.

- Add the lemon juice and continue pouring in the rest of the oil, whipping constantly.

Makes a thick mayonnaise in 10 minutes. Keeps well in the refrigerator.

Serve on bread, in salads, as a dip, etc.

VARIATIONS:

- **White Mayonnaise:** Leave out the green onion and the parsley.

- **Yellow Mayonnaise:** Add 1 teaspoon (5 ml) of curry and a pinch of cayenne pepper.

- **Red Mayonnaise:** Add 1 tablespoon (15 ml) of tomato paste.

Garlic Salad Dressing

This dressing serves as the main ingredient in a multitude of recipes!

2 cloves garlic (or more for garlic lovers)	3/4 cup (200 ml) olive or other oil
1/4 teaspoon (1 ml) salt	1/2 teaspoon (2 ml) tarragon
2 tablespoons (30 ml) lemon juice	1/2 teaspoon (2 ml) basil
	1 teaspoon (5 ml) parsley

- Press the garlic and add the other ingredients. Whip the ingredients by hand, or combine them in a blender; their texture will be different. Let stand for a while before serving.

VARIATIONS:

- **Unique Dressing:** Add 1/4 cup (60 ml) of fresh basil.

- **Nutritional Yeast Dressing:** Add 2 tablespoons (30 ml) of nutritional yeast and 1 tablespoon (15 ml) of tamari soy sauce.

- ***Picante* Dressing:** Add 1 tablespoon (15 ml) of hot mustard.

You can create great dressings in a blender. Depending on the inspiration of the moment, add your choice of feta cheese, cucumber, tomato, radish, parsley, etc.

Yogurt Salad Dressing

1 cup (250 ml) plain yogurt
1 clove garlic, crushed
1 tablespoon (15 ml) tamari soy sauce

1 teaspoon (5 ml) tarragon
1 teaspoon (5 ml) basil
1 tablespoon (15 ml) olive oil

- Mix together thoroughly.

VARIATIONS:

- Add green onion, parsley, and dill for their flavor and color.

- Add a beet cube or some beet powder to get a superb pink dressing.

- Add pieces of red pepper.

- 1 cup (250 ml) of yogurt, 1 thinly sliced cucumber, 3 tablespoons (45 ml) fresh mint.

When prepared in a blender, yogurt dressings become runny; they thicken when left to sit in the refrigerator.

Green Parsley Dressing

1 egg
2 teaspoons (10 ml) lemon juice
1 teaspoon (5 ml) honey
1 clove garlic
1 cup (250 ml) parsley, chopped

A pinch of tarragon
1/2 teaspoon (2 ml) sea salt
1/4 cup (60 ml) safflower oil
1/4 cup (60 ml) water
1/2 cup (125 ml) sour cream

- Put the first 7 ingredients into the blender.

- Slowly add the oil, while whipping at low speed.

- Add the water and the sour cream. Mix.

- Add a bit of water, if the mixture is too thick.

- Correct the seasoning, if necessary.

Tahini Salad Dressing*

2 tablespoons (30 ml) tamari soy sauce
1/2 cup (125 ml) tahini (sesame butter)

3/4 cup (200 ml) sunflower oil
3/4 cup (200 ml) cold water
1/4 cup (60 ml) lemon juice

- Mix together the tamari, the oil, and the tahini in the blender.

- Slowly add the cold water and the lemon juice.

* This recipe comes from *Le Commensal*, a vegetarian restaurant on St. Denis St. in Montreal, Quebec, Canada.

VARIATION: You can heat the dressing and serve it on croquettes, pâtés, felafels, etc.

Apricot Nectar Dressing

1 egg
1 clove garlic
1 lemon (4 tablespoons of juice)

1/2 teaspoon (2 ml) sea salt
1/2 teaspoon (2 ml) basil
2 cups (500 ml) apricot nectar

Whip the first 5 ingredients in a blender and slowly add the nectar, as you do oil, when making mayonnaise.

SALAD DRESSINGS

IDEAS FOR IRRESISTIBLE DRINKS

- *Pina Colada:* 4 cups (1 L) orange juice, 4 cups (1 L) pineapple juice, 1 cup (250 ml) yogurt, and a few drops of coconut essence. Mix together in the blender. Serve in goblets. Decorate with a mint leaf or a strawberry.

- **Ginger Water:** 4 cups (1 L) water, a 3-inch (7 cm) piece of ginger (grated), 1 sliced lemon, 1 tablespoon (15 ml) honey. Mix together and let sit over night in the refrigerator.

- **Sparkling Mauve Punch:** Combine 1 part orange juice, 1 part apple juice, 1 part grape juice, and 2 parts sparkling mineral water in a large bowl with fruit and ice.

- **Fruit Punch:** Combine 2 parts orange juice, 1 part white grape juice, 1 part apple juice, purple and green grapes cut into halves, and mint leaves.

- **Very Green Juice:** 1 cup (250 ml) orange juice, 1 tablespoon (15 ml) yogurt, 1 teaspoon (5 ml) powdered spirulina.

- **Fresh Tomato Juice:** Combine some ripe tomatoes, a pinch of salt, and a hint of lemon juice in the blender. Strain to remove the seeds, if necessary.

- **Vegetable Juice:** Choose some vegetables and run them through the juicer. Beets provide a superb color.

- **Rich Milk:** In the blender, combine 1 cup (250 ml) of soy milk, 1 egg yolk, 1 teaspoon (5 ml) of nutritional yeast, and 1 teaspoon (5 ml) of molasses.

- **Fruit Milkshake:** In the blender, combine soy milk with frozen strawberries and/or frozen bananas, and a bit of honey or a few dates.

- **Carob Milkshake:** Combine a glass of milk and 1 teaspoon (5 ml) of carob in the blender. Add a banana and 1 teaspoon (5 ml) of honey, if desired.

- **Strawberry and Yogurt Milkshake:** In the blender, combine 1 cup (250 ml) of strawberries (or blueberries or raspberries), 1 cup (250 ml) of yogurt, 1 cup (250 ml) of milk, 1 tablespoon (15 ml) of honey. Children love this drink. Add 1/2 banana to make a creamier milkshake.

- **Almond Milkshake:** Combine 1 cup (250 ml) of almonds with 3 cups (750 ml) of water in the blender. It is preferable to presoak the almonds. Strain if necessary. Use the pulp in a fruit salad.

- **Additional Ingredients:** If desired you may choose to add 1 or 2 of the following: nut butter, nutritional yeast, milk powder, wheat germ, egg yolk, etc.

A FEW IDEAS TO REPLACE SWEETS FROM THE CONVENIENCE STORE DURING THE SUMMER:

Popsicles:

- Juice.
- Fruit purée and yogurt.
- Fruit jelly and yogurt.
- Frozen juice and yogurt.

Slush:

Combine equal quantities of ice cubes and juice in the food processor.

Home-made Soda Pop:

Combine juice and sparkling mineral water.

Ice Cream:

See the " Espresso Ice Cream " recipe.

CHAPTER 4

Vegetables and Squash

Vegetables are found in the greater part of our meals as a side dish. When cooked just right, they remain crisp.

Look back at the chapter in the " Theory Book " section dealing with vegetables, and particularly at the part dealing with how to cook them.

To provide stimulation for the appetite, it is a good idea to vary the way you cut vegetables and cook them.

Vegetables à l'étouffée
(steam-cooked without water)   *Serves 4-6*

2 onions, coarsely chopped	1 potato, cut into pieces
2 carrots, cut into sticks	1 parsnip, sliced diagonally
1/2 turnip, cut into strips	1 leek, cut into rounds

- Heat a thick-bottomed cast-iron saucepan (enamelled or not) with a tight lid, and pour in 2 tablespoons (30 ml) of

water to begin the cooking process. When the water begins to steam, add the onions first and then the other vegetables.

- Season with salt, basil, and a bit of thyme.

- Cover and cook over low heat until the vegetables are tender, 10-30 minutes, depending on the size and type of vegetables.

Chinese Vegetables *Serves 4-6 (see photo)*

2 onions, chopped
2 cloves garlic, finely chopped
A 1-inch (2.5 cm) piece fresh
  ginger root, finely chopped
1 green pepper, cut into wide
  strips
2 carrots, julienne

1 cup (250 ml) snow peas or broccoli
2 tablespoons (30 ml) safflower oil
1/2 cup (125 ml) water
3 tablespoons (45 ml) tamari soy
  sauce
2 tablespoons (30 ml) lemon juice
1 teaspoon (5 ml) arrowroot
Almonds, split

- Pour the oil into a wok and brown the onions. Add the garlic and ginger.

- Place the onions around the perimeter of the wok and sauté the other vegetables one at a time, beginning with the least tender: broccoli, carrots, green peppers, and peas.

- Mix together the water, tamari soy sauce, lemon juice, and arrowroot. Add the mixture to the vegetables.

- Cook until thickening occurs, stirring constantly. The vegetables will take on a shiny appearance.

- Garnish with the almonds.

Serve over rice or as a side dish.

Steamed Broccoli

WHAT COULD BE SIMPLER AND GREENER!

1 bunch broccoli (florets and stalk)	Olive or safflower oil
Lemon juice	Fresh parsley, finely chopped

- Wash the broccoli under a stream of water, being careful to separate each stem.

- Cut the stalk into fine slices. Leave the small stems and the florets whole.

- When the water comes to a boil, place the broccoli in a steamer basket and steam for a few minutes. Broccoli should remain crisp and very green.

- Sprinkle on some lemon juice, oil, and parsley.

NOTE: Because of its nutritional value, broccoli should be included regularly on the menu.

1 cup (250 ml) of steamed broccoli contains the following:

- **5 g of protein.**
- **140 mg of vitamin C.**
- **132 mg of calcium.**
- **iron, fiber, chlorophyll, etc.**

Spinach au gratin

QUICK AND TASTY!

Spinach or Swiss chard	Lemon juice
Tamari soy sauce	Strong cheddar cheese

- Steam the spinach for 1 minute.

- Put half the spinach into a baking dish, sprinkle on a few drops of tamari sauce and a trickle of lemon juice, and cover with grated cheddar cheese.

- Begin the operation again, finishing with the cheese.

VEGETABLES

- Sprinkle with paprika and bake at 400°F (200°C) for 10 minutes.

Baked Potatoes and Onions   *Serves 4-6*

3 potatoes, sliced
3 onions, sliced
1 teaspoon (5 ml) tamari soy
  sauce

Olive oil
2 tablespoons (30 ml) parsley,
  chopped
1 teaspoon (5 ml) chives

- In a glass baking dish, lay the vegetables alternately one on top of the other in layers.

- Drizzle with oil and a few drops of tamari sauce, and season.

- Cover and bake at 350°F (180°C) for 30 minutes.

Serve as a side dish. If desired, you can arrange this dish au gratin towards the end of the baking period.

VARIATION: Add medallions of green peppers or zucchini.

Garlic Mushrooms   *Serves 4*

2 cups (500 ml) mushrooms,
  thickly sliced
3 tablespoons (45 ml) lemon juice
1 tablespoon (15 ml) safflower oil
1 onion, finely chopped

3 cloves garlic, finely chopped
1/2 cup (125 ml) parsley, chopped
1/2 teaspoon (2 ml) tamari soy
  sauce
1/2 teaspoon (2 ml) basil

- Sprinkle the slices of mushroom with lemon juice and set aside.

- Heat the oil and sauté the onion and garlic.

- Add the mushrooms. Cook over low heat for 5 minutes.

- Add the parsley and the seasonings, and mix.

Serve hot as a side dish, or over buckwheat or pasta.

Ratatouille *Serves 4*

3 onions, cut into thin strips
2 cloves garlic, finely chopped
1 eggplant, cubed
2 green peppers, cut into strips
3 zucchini, cut into medallions
4 tomatoes, cut into pieces

1 tablespoon (15 ml) tamari soy
  sauce
1 teaspoon (5 ml) tarragon
1/2 teaspoon (2 ml) seaweed
  powder

- Brown the onion and garlic in a bit of oil in a thick-bottomed saucepan with a heavy cover.

- Add the other vegetables, season, cover, and cook over low heat for about 20 minutes. The vegetables will cook in their own steam without water.

Serve with a grain and/or a legume.

VARIATION: Bake au gratin or add cubes of tofu to make this dish into a main course.

Potato Pancakes *Serves 4*

3 medium-sized potatoes,
  washed
1 small onion, finely chopped
1/2 teaspoon (2 ml) seaweed
  powder
1/2 teaspoon (2 ml) basil

1/3 cup (75 ml) whole wheat flour
2 tablespoons (30 ml) nutritional
  yeast
2 eggs, lightly beaten
1/4 teaspoon (1 ml) nutmeg

- Grate the potatoes.

- Add the other ingredients.

- Cook on both sides in an oiled frying pan, or bake at 375°F (190°C) for 20 minutes.

This is a quick, delicious meal. Serve with broccoli and steamed carrot sticks.

VEGETABLES

Corn on the Cob

- Set the oven grill at medium height, lay the corn on it, leaving the husk on, and bake at 350°F (180°C) for 20 minutes. Then peel away the husks from the cob and enjoy the flavor.

- **Or**, steam it with the husk on. In order to conserve as much of the corn's nutritional value as possible, avoid cooking it in water.

VARIATIONS:

- Try eating fresh corn raw, on the cob or off the cob, when it is in season. You can add it to salads.

- Cobs of corn can be put into a plastic bag and frozen raw, with the husks left on. To cook, place them on a grill in the oven and bake for 30 minutes. When prepared in this way they keep their succulent flavor.

French Fries in the Oven

For Those Who Can't Resist!

- Cut the potatoes into French fries.

- Pour 1 tablespoon (15 ml) oil onto a baking tray, .

- Spread out the potatoes on the tray, turning them over, so that they are coated on all sides.

- Bake at 350°F (180°C), turning them over from time to time, until golden brown.

Vegetable Pie *Serves 4-6*

1 or 2 rolled-out pastry crusts
3 cups (750 ml) assorted vegetables

2 cups (500 ml) béchamel sauce
Chives, thyme, sea salt

- Cut the vegetables into small cubes or thin slices.

- Place the vegetables in a whole wheat pastry crust. Add the béchamel sauce. Season to taste.

- Cover with another pastry crust or some grated cheese.

- Bake at 350°F (180°C) for 30 minutes.

VARIATION: Cut the pastry into a circle or triangle, garnish, and fold the edges over for a touch of variety.

Onion Pie *Serves 4*

A 9-inch (23 cm) pie crust
2 1/2 cups (625 ml) onions,
chopped
1/4 teaspoon (1 ml) thyme
1 tablespoon (15 ml) safflower oil
2 tablespoons (30 ml) wheat flour
3/4 cup (200 ml) Gruyère cheese,
grated

2 eggs, beaten
1 cup (250 ml) soy milk
2 teaspoons (10 ml) tamari soy
sauce
1/2 teaspoon (2 ml) seaweed
powder
A pinch of nutmeg

- Preheat the oven to 450°F (230°C).

- Brown the onions and thyme in the oil over low heat for 10 minutes.

- Sprinkle the bottom of the pie shell with flour. Then add half the onions and some cheese.

- Mix the rest of the ingredients together well. Pour into the pie shell.

- Bake at 450°F (230°C) for 10 minutes, reduce heat to 350°F (180°C), and bake for another 20 minutes.

Apples and Cabbage *Serves 4*

3 apples
1/2 head red cabbage
1 tablespoon (15 ml) safflower oil

1/4 teaspoon (1 ml) caraway seeds
Sesame salt

- Peel the apples (if not organically grown) and cut them into pieces. Cut the cabbage into nice big strips.

- Heat the oil and sauté the cabbage with the caraway seeds for 5 minutes. Add the apples and cook for another 10 minutes.

Sprinkle with sesame salt and serve as a vegetable side dish.

Sautéed Onions and Carrots *Serves 4*

2 onions, sliced into medallions
2 carrots, coarsely grated
1 tablespoon (15 ml) safflower oil

Nutritional yeast
Tamari soy sauce or sesame salt

- Heat the oil and sauté the onions until tender. Add the carrots for just a few moments to heat them up.

- Season with a sprinkling of nutritional yeast, and a few drops of tamari sauce or a pinch of sesame salt.

VARIATIONS:

You may replace the carrots with the following:

- Beets. They are colorful and tasty.
- Rutabaga. It tastes like fries.
- Cabbage, cut into strips. It is delicious.

Italian-style Eggplant

1 eggplant, sliced into medallions
1 green pepper, cubed
Tomato paste or home-made
    tomato sauce

6 mushrooms, sliced
Basil, parsley
Cheddar cheese

- Cut the eggplant into medallions.

- Place them on an oiled baking tray. Spread on a thin layer of tomato paste or, better still, of your own home-made tomato sauce.

- Garnish with vegetables as you would small pizzas. Season.

- Cover with cheese and bake at 350°F (180°C) for 10-15 minutes.

Serve with a grain such as millet or bulgur.

VARIATIONS:

- Place in a pie shell, add onions, cut into medallions, and bake.

- Since eggplant is a fall vegetable, you may replace it with squash or rutabaga, when it is not in season.

Sautéed Tomatoes with Eggplant

4 tomatoes	2 cloves garlic
1 eggplant	1 teaspoon (5 ml) basil
Wheat flour	1/4 teaspoon (1 ml) thyme
1 cup (250 ml) mushrooms	Tamari soy sauce
2 green onions	

- Cut the eggplant into cubes and dust with flour.

- Slice the mushrooms and tomatoes. Chop the green onions and garlic.

- Place the slices of tomato in a baking dish.

- Sauté the eggplant in a bit of oil. Place some on the center of each slice of tomato.

- Brown the mushrooms, green onions, garlic, and herbs.

- Place the mixture around the eggplant on the sliced tomatoes. Sprinkle on a bit of tamari sauce.

- Bake at 325°F (160°C) for 10 minutes.

This it makes a delicious dish with a superb appearance.

VARIATION: Cover with cooked rice, slices of tomato, and grated cheese. Prepare au gratin and you will have a delicious dish of moussaka.

Stuffed Eggplant or Squash

1 eggplant, cut in half lengthwise	1 tablespoon (15 ml) safflower oil
1 onion, chopped	2 slices bread, cubed
1 green pepper, cubed	**or** 1/2 cup (125 ml) cooked millet
1 stalk celery, finely cut	1/2 cup (125 ml) cheese, grated
3 tomatoes, cut into pieces	Basil, salt, and paprika

- Empty out the eggplant, leaving 1/4 inch (1 cm) of flesh.

- Heat the oil, add the onion, and brown.

Vegetables, Nuts and Seeds

Grains

Legumes

Desserts

- Add the celery, green pepper, tomatoes, and chopped eggplant pulp.

- Cook for 5 minutes. Mix with bread or cooked millet.

- Season well. Fill both halves of the eggplant with the mixture.

- Cover with cheese and bake at 350°F (180°C) for 20 minutes.

Delicious Spaghetti Squash

1 spaghetti squash	1/2 teaspoon (2 ml) tamari soy sauce
1/2 teaspoon (2 ml) basil	1/2 teaspoon (2 ml) nutritional yeast

- Cut the squash into halves. Remove the seeds and dry them. They are delicious to eat.

- Steam the squash, or cook it in a saucepan in a bit of water, or bake it at 300°F (150°C), until the flesh can be removed with a fork, like spaghetti noodles. Cooking time varies with the size of the squash. If overcooked, the pulp will turn into a purée.

- Remove the flesh of the squash, and season.

Serve as is, in the squash itself, or bathe in the dressing of your choice and serve in a bowl.

289

My Boyfriend's Sautéed Zucchini *Serves 2-3*

1 large onion, chopped
1 zucchini, cut into half moons
1 clove garlic, finely chopped
1 tablespoon (5 ml) olive oil

3-4 tomatoes, cut into cubes
1 teaspoon (5 ml) tamari soy sauce
1/2 teaspoon (2 ml) thyme

- Heat the oil and brown the onion.

- Add the garlic and zucchini, and sauté for 5 minutes.

- Add the tomatoes and seasonings, and cook a little over low heat.

It is easy, fast, and economical. Serve over rice with a salad.

VARIATIONS:

- Add large cubes of tofu or a cooked legume and you will have a substantial dish!

- Super Simple Zucchini: Wash and cut the zucchini lengthwise, brush it with a bit of oil, and cover with garlic powder, pieces of tomato, and parmesan cheese. Bake on the bottom shelf of the oven at the broil setting for 10 minutes. Serve with a tomato, parsley, and garlic salad, and a piece of quiche.

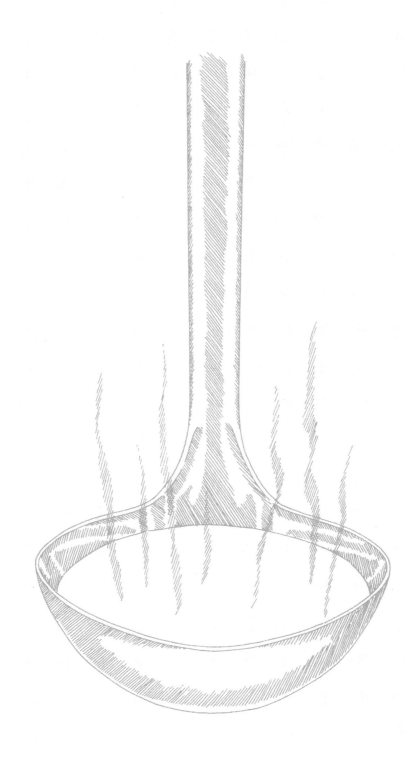

CHAPTER 5

Soups

SOUPS

- Allow you to use the food that you have on hand.

- Fit well into a lunch box meal.

- Are easy to prepare.

- Stimulate your creativity.

There are different kinds of soups:

- **Light soup**, made with a miso or vegetable stock base, and enhanced with small cubes of cooked vegetables or tofu. This soup should be served at the beginning of the meal.

- **Thick, velvety cream soup**, made with a raw or cooked vegetable base, which is puréed and thickened with milk or cream and a bit of flour. This soup is also served at the beginning of the meal.

- **Hearty soup**, a meal on its own. It is made with a

vegetable, cooked grain and/or legume, or pasta base. This soup is served as a main course.

STOCKS

To make soups that are delightful and unforgettable, you should pay special attention to the stock. Here are some suggestions to help you cook up a good stock.

- Keep any liquid that contains nutritive elements: water used to steam vegetables or pasta, mint tea, etc.

- Keep all the healthy leftovers that you remove when preparing vegetables: tips of carrots or beans, parsley stems, celery leaves, pea pods, etc. When you have accumulated a large enough quantity, wash them and put them into cold water in a large saucepan. Add onions and herbs, and bring to a boil. Simmer for 45 minutes. Cool and pour off the stock. Keep in the refrigerator (for 3 days) or in the freezer.

- You can make stock in the same way, using the vegetables themselves: 4 carrots, 1 celery stalk with the leaves, 1 onion, 1 green pepper, parsley and herbs, to taste, for example.

- Sauté some onions, garlic, celery, and herbs (basil, thyme, marjoram), before adding stock to them. They add a great deal of flavor.

- Miso and tamari sauce heighten the flavor. Add them 5 minutes before the stock has finished cooking.

- Excellent concentrated soup stocks, made from dehydrated vegetables and herbs, are available on the market.

Here are various suggestions for preparing soups:

- Cut the vegetables into large chunks and steam them.

SOUPS

Purée them in the blender with the cooking water and add to a béchamel sauce or milk. Season well.

- Cook the vegetables in stock until crisp. Add some cooked legumes and simmer for about 10 minutes. Serve with some tasty bread.

- To thicken soup, add some rice, millet, pasta, etc.

- To make soup creamier, all you have to do is to put part of it through the blender and add some of the resulting purée to the soup.

- To add color, flavor, and nutritional value to soup, put part of it into the blender, and add some parsley, chervil, or alfalfa sprouts.

- Try something new: raw soup which can be prepared in five minutes. Using the standard blade in a food processor, chop different vegetables as finely as possible (broccoli stems, carrots, etc.). Add heated stock, and 2 cooked potatoes to thicken. Season and serve!

- Powdered milk, when added to soup at the very end of the cooking period, will increase the nutritional value in terms of calcium, protein, etc.

Any garnish will add extra nutritional value and a touch of novelty to soups. Here are a few suggestions for garnishing soups:

- Grated cheese.

- Garlic croutons and/or 1 teaspoon (5 ml) of nutritional yeast.

- Sprouts, which should be added at the last minute.

- Small cubes of tofu.

- A spoonful of yogurt (particularly good in a green soup or

beet soup!) and/or a fine slice of radish, cut in the form of a flower.

- Sunflower seeds.

- A fine slice of lemon and/or fresh parsley.

- Mint leaves or chopped chives.

Miso Soup   *Serves 4*

1 small leek, finely chopped	1 teaspoon (5 ml) oil
1 leaf Chinese cabbage, cut into fine strips	8 ounces (225 g) tofu, cubed
	3 cups (750 ml) stock
1 carrot, cut into star-shaped pieces or sticks	2-3 tablespoons (30-45 ml) miso

- In a thick cast-iron saucepan, heat the oil and brown the vegetables. Add the tofu and stir for a few minutes.

- Add the stock, bring to a boil, and simmer for 20 minutes.

- Remove from the heat. Dilute the miso in about 1/2 cup (125 ml) stock and then blend into the soup.

Serve hot. Decorate with green onions.

VARIATIONS:

- Reduce the quantity of vegetables and tofu, and make into a comforting consommé.

- Add some grated ginger, sautéed mushrooms, etc.

SOUPS

Vegetable Soup *Serves 6*

1 onion, chopped
2 cloves garlic, finely chopped
2 stalks celery, cut into pieces
2 potatoes, cubed
2 carrots, cut in half lengthwise
   and sliced
4 cups (1 L) stock

2 cups (500 ml) tomato purée
1 1/2 teaspoons (7 ml) sea salt
1/2 teaspoon (2 ml) marjoram
1/2 teaspoon (2 ml) basil
1/4 teaspoon (1 ml) thyme
1 tablespoon (15 ml) parsley, dried

- Sauté the onion, garlic, and celery in a bit of oil.

- Add the vegetables and cook in the stock until crisp (about 15-30 minutes, depending on the size).

- Add the tomatoes and herbs, and cook for another 5 minutes.

Serve with a fresh parsley garnish.

Squash Soup *Serves 4-6*

1 squash (butternut or other)
2 stalks celery, finely sliced
4 cloves garlic, finely chopped
1 tablespoon (15 ml) tamari soy
   sauce

1 tablespoon (15 ml) safflower oil
1 teaspoon (5 ml) basil
1 teaspoon (5 ml) chives
2 green onions, finely chopped

- Wash the squash and cut it into large chunks, unpeeled. Steam.

- Sauté the celery and garlic, and add the herbs.

- Put the squash through the blender with the cooking water, and add the other ingredients.

- Correct the consistency and the seasoning, if necessary.

Serve, garnished with green onions.

Cream of Broccoli *Serves 4*

1 whole broccoli
3 tablespoons (45 ml) flour
3 tablespoons (45 ml) oil
2 cups (500 ml) soy milk, or stock

1 teaspoon (5 ml) seaweed powder
1 tablespoon (15 ml) tamari soy
  sauce
1/2 teaspoon (2 ml) basil

- Steam the broccoli.

- Make a béchamel sauce out of the flour, oil, and liquid. Season.

- Put the broccoli and sauce through the blender, until they are creamy in consistency.

VARIATIONS:

- **Cream of Cauliflower:** Use cauliflower instead of broccoli.

- **Cream of Celery:** Use onions, celery, and potatoes.

- **Cream of Leek:** Use leeks and potatoes.

- **Cream of Carrot:** Use carrots, onions, and a bit of cooked rice.

Onion Soup *Serves 4*

4 onions, cut into pieces
4 cloves garlic, finely chopped
1 tablespoon (15 ml) safflower oil
4 cups (1 L) stock
1/2 teaspoon (2 ml) basil

1/4 teaspoon (1 ml) marjoram
1/4 teaspoon (1 ml) thyme
2 tablespoons (30 ml) tamari soy
  sauce, or miso

- Sauté the onions and garlic in the oil for a few minutes.

- Add the stock and seasonings, and cook for 15 minutes.

- Serve with garlic croutons and, if desired, au gratin.

When served au gratin after a plentiful salad, this dish makes a simple, nutritious meal.

Garlic Croutons

- Toast some slices of bread in the toaster or in the oven.

- While they are still warm, rub them with one clove, or a few cloves, of garlic. The garlic will penetrate into the bread. In this way you will avoid butter or oil!

- Cut into croutons and serve.

VARIATION: For very dry croutons, cut the slices of bread into cubes and toast them in the oven at 150°F (95°C) until dry and crusty. They keep well.

Borsch *Serves 4-5*

4 beets	1/2 teaspoon (2 ml) tarragon
2 potatoes	2 tablespoons (30 ml) lemon juice
1/2 cup (125 ml) yogurt	(optional)

- Steam the vegetables, leaving the skins on.

- Peel, if necessary, and put through the blender with some stock until you obtain the desired consistency. Add tarragon and lemon juice.

- Add the yogurt. Decorate with a chopped green onion, a bit of yogurt, and a thin slice of lemon. Serve.

VARIATION: Replace the potatoes with cucumbers.

Gazpacho Cold Soup: *Serves 8*

Uncommonly refreshing! Prepare this soup ahead of time and let it sit for at least 5 hours in the refrigerator.

4 tomatoes
1 green pepper
1 cucumber
1 stalk celery
1 small onion
2 or more cloves garlic, finely
  chopped
Tomato juice, to cover

1 tablespoon (15 ml) fresh basil
1 tablespoon (15 ml) fresh parsley
1 tablespoon (15 ml) fresh mint
1/2 teaspoon (2 ml) thyme
1/2 teaspoon (2 ml) tarragon
3 tablespoons (45 ml) lemon juice
2 tablespoons (30 ml) olive oil
A pinch of cayenne pepper

- Wash and finely chop the vegetables. Cover with the tomato juice.

- Add the other ingredients. Correct the seasoning and consistency to suit your taste.

- Refrigerate for a few hours and serve.

Lentil Soup *Serves 6* (see photo)

2 onions, chopped
2 cloves garlic, finely chopped
2 carrots, cut in half lengthwise
  and sliced
1 stalk celery, cut into pieces
1 tablespoon (15 ml) safflower oil

4 cups (1 L) stock
1 cup (250 ml) lentils, washed
1 large can stewed tomatoes, with
  the juice
1/2 teaspoon (2 ml) savory
1/2 teaspoon (2 ml) thyme

- Sauté the onions and garlic in a large saucepan. Add the carrots, celery, and herbs, and cook for a few minutes.

- Add the stock, lentils, and tomatoes. Bring to a boil.

- Simmer over medium heat for 45 minutes. Before serving, adjust the seasoning, if necessary. Garnish with fresh parsley and some finely chopped green onion.

Serve with bread and cheese.

Green Split Pea Soup *Serves 4*

1 onion, chopped
2 cloves garlic, finely chopped
1 carrot, sliced into medallions
1 tablespoon (15 ml) safflower oil
1 cup (250 ml) split peas, washed

6 cups (1.5 L) stock
1 teaspoon (5 ml) basil
1/2 teaspoon (2 ml) thyme
1 tablespoon (5 ml) miso, or tamari
   soy sauce

- Sauté the onion, garlic, and carrot in the oil.

- Add the split peas, stock, and herbs. Cook for 1 hour.

- Add the miso or soy sauce and serve.

Barley Soup

- Add 1 cup (250 ml) of precooked barley to the vegetable soup recipe. Adjust the consistency.

   or

- Soak some barley and cook it for 1 hour in a large quantity of water. Add your choice of vegetables and herbs, season, and let simmer for 30 minutes. It's so easy!

Potato and Kasha Soup *Serves 8*

8 cups (2 L) stock
6 potatoes, cubed
2 large onions, finely chopped
2 stalks celery, cubed
1/2 cup (125 ml) kasha (roasted
   buckwheat)
2 teaspoons (10 ml) basil

1 teaspoon (5 ml) thyme
1 tablespoon (15 ml) tamari soy
   sauce
Fresh parsley and 1 green onion
1 cup (250 ml) milk
   or 1/3 cup (75 ml) milk powder

- Bring the vegetables, kasha, and herbs to a boil in the stock. Lower the heat, cover, and let simmer for 20-30 minutes, or until the potatoes are tender.

- Add the tamari sauce, parsley, green onion, and milk, and simmer for 5 minutes.

CHAPTER 6

Sauces and Dips

In general, sauces are used to increase the pleasure we derive from the flavor of the food we eat. They also allow us to mask the flavor of foods whose taste we find less pleasing.

However, using sauces should not become a habit, nor should sauces become indispensable to the pleasure of eating. Serve them only occasionally.

A trickle of oil or a bit of lemon juice, and some finely chopped parsley can easily replace a sauce. And don't forget that thorough mastication allows saliva to penetrate and soften any food we eat—as long as we apply ourselves to the task!

Sauces of all Sorts

Basic Ingredients:

LIQUID:

- Milk, soy milk, milk derived from nuts, whey.

- Cooking stock from vegetables.

- Various herbal teas.

- Fruit juices (for desserts).

THICKENING AGENT:

- Flour (wheat, buckwheat, etc.).

- Starch.

FATS: Oil or butter, for flavor and texture (optional).

SEASONINGS: Garlic, onion, herbs, spices, etc.

An explanation of how to prepare each recipe is provided.

Béchamel Sauce

4 tablespoons (60 ml) safflower oil
4 tablespoons (60 ml) wheat or
  other flour
2 cups (500 ml) warm milk

1/2 teaspoon (2 ml) tarragon
1/4 teaspoon (1 ml) salt
A pinch of nutmeg

- Heat the oil over low heat in a saucepan or a skillet.

- Add the flour and stir to thicken, until the mixture becomes a light reddish brown color.

- Add the warm milk slowly, while stirring vigorously with a whisk, and bring close to the boiling point over medium heat. Stir until thick.

- Season and let simmer for 10-15 minutes.

- Let sit for a few moments before serving.

Sauce which has been properly thickened should not be lumpy. However, if lumpiness should occur, put the sauce through a blender, a food processor, or a sieve.

SAUCES AND DIPS

VARIATIONS:

- Increasing or reducing the quantity of liquid or flour will change the consistency of the sauce. One , two, or three tablespoons of flour, respectively, per cup (250 ml) of liquid will produce thin, medium, or thick sauce.

- Using warm milk to make sauces is recommended. However, you may also use cold milk, in which case you must stir vigorously in order to avoid lumpiness.

- **Cheese Sauce:** When your sauce is ready, add some grated cheese, stir until it melts, and add your choice of herbs.

- **Onion and/or Garlic Sauce:** Sauté some onions and garlic in oil, add flour, stir, add the milk, and cook until thickening occurs.

- **Tomato, Broccoli, Spinach, or Other Sauce:** Add 1 cup of vegetable purée per cup of sauce. If you add 2 cups of purée per cup of sauce, you will have a delicious vegetable cream soup. Season and cook for 5 minutes over low heat.

- **Sauce without Fat:** Toast the flour lightly. Add the milk little by little, while stirring constantly, or blend the flour into the milk in a pot, while stirring vigorously. Bring to a boil over medium heat, while stirring.

- **Mushroom Sauce:** Use the same ingredients as you would to make a béchamel sauce. Sauté the mushrooms in the oil, add the flour, stir, add the milk, and cook until thickening occurs.

Don't Forget!

Garlic, onion, and grated ginger root will enhance the flavor of most of your sauces. First sauté these ingredients in oil, then add flour, and proceed as usual.

Brown Gravy *(see photo)*

2 tablespoons (30 ml) safflower oil
2 tablespoons (30 ml) flour
1 cup (250 ml) water or warm
  stock

2 tablespoons (30 ml), or more,
  tamari soy sauce
1/4 teaspoon (1 ml) basil
Parsley

- Heat the oil. Add the flour and roast lightly over low heat.

- Add the water or warm stock, while stirring vigorously with a whisk. Bring to a boil over medium heat.

- Season with tamari sauce and basil, and decorate with chopped parsley.

Serve hot over croquettes, potatoes, or a grain.

VARIATIONS:

- **Onion Gravy:** Sauté 1 chopped onion in some oil and proceed as above.

- **Green Onion and/or Garlic Gravy:** Proceed as in the onion gravy recipe, replacing the onion with garlic and/or green onions.

- **Tamari-Tahini Gravy:** Add 1 tablespoon (15 ml) of tahini at the very end of the preparation. Mix in well and serve on bread, pancakes, croquettes, etc.

- Replace the flour with 1 tablespoon (15 ml) of starch per cup (250 ml) of liquid. Sauté the onion, add the water, and heat. Dissolve the starch in the tamari sauce, pour into the water, and cook until thickening occurs, while stirring constantly.

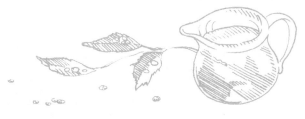

Simple Tomato Sauce

EASY TO PREPARE AND SIMPLY DELICIOUS.

2 tablespoons (30 ml) olive oil	1 bay leaf
1 onion, chopped	4 cups (1 L) fresh, blanched,
3 cloves garlic, finely chopped	or canned tomatoes
1 1/2 teaspoons (7 ml) oregano	1 teaspoon (5 ml) salt
1/2 teaspoon (2 ml) basil	

- Sauté the onion in the olive oil for 5 minutes. Add the garlic and brown for 2 minutes.

- Add the oregano, basil, and bay leaf. Cook for 1 minute.

- Crush the tomatoes and add them to the other ingredients, along with the salt.

- Simmer over low heat for at least 30 minutes. Adjust the seasoning, to taste.

VARIATIONS:

- To obtain a creamy tomato sauce, for garnishing fresh pasta, for example, add about 1 cup (250 ml) of thick, seasoned béchamel sauce and a pinch of cinnamon.

- To obtain a more nutritious sauce, add cooked buckwheat, a cooked legume, coarsely ground seeds or nuts, finely chopped parsley, etc.

Ginger Sauce

Accompanies chop suey or chow mein.

1 cup (250 ml) stock or water	1 teaspoon (5 ml) fresh ginger
3 tablespoons (45 ml) tamari soy	root, grated
sauce	1 tablespoon (15 ml) arrowroot
1/2 teaspoon (2 ml) curry	

- In a saucepan mix together all the ingredients except the arrowroot.

- Blend the arrowroot into a bit of cold water and add it to the mixture.

- Heat, while stirring, until the sauce thickens.

Yogurt Sauce

Serve with felafels in a pita bread.

1 cup (250 ml) yogurt
1 teaspoon (5 ml) dill seeds
3 cloves garlic, crushed

1 tablespoon (15 ml) tahini
1 tablespoon (15 ml) sunflower oil

Mix all the ingredients together.

Guacamole: Avocado Dip

SUPERB AND REFRESHING!

2 ripe avocados, peeled
3 tablespoons (45 ml) lemon juice
1 tomato, finely chopped
1 green onion, finely chopped

2 cloves garlic, finely chopped
1/4 teaspoon (1 ml) chili powder
A pinch of cayenne pepper

- Purée the avocado and lemon juice with a whisk, or in the blender.

- Add the other ingredients and mix together.

Surround with alfalfa sprouts and radishes, and serve with a side dish of raw vegetables, or on toast.

Tahini Dip

1/2 cup (125 ml) tahini
4 tablespoons (60 ml) water
2 tablespoons (30 ml) lemon juice

2 cloves garlic, crushed
1/2 teaspoon (2 ml) tamari soy
  sauce

- Alternately add the water and lemon juice to the tahini in small quantities.

- Whip vigorously with a fork to emulsify.

- When the mixture is thick and creamy, add the garlic and tamari sauce.

The President's Cottage Dip

1 cup (250 ml) cottage cheese
1/2 cup (125 ml) mayonnaise
2 tablespoons (30 ml) lemon juice
1 umeboshi plum (optional)
2 cloves garlic

1/4 teaspoon (1 ml) celery seeds
A pinch of cayenne pepper
Tarragon and caraway seeds,
  to taste

- Put all the ingredients through the blender. Garnish with a green onion, if desired.

Serve with raw vegetables.

Zucchini Dip

1 cup (250 ml) zucchini, finely
  grated
1 onion, very finely chopped
1/4 cup (60 ml) parsley, finely
  chopped
2 tablespoons (30 ml) lemon juice

1 clove garlic, finely chopped
1/2 teaspoon (2 ml) tamari soy
  sauce
1/2 teaspoon (2 ml) basil
1/2 cup (125 ml) mayonnaise
  (approximately)

- Mix together all the ingredients and add enough mayonnaise to obtain the desired consistency.

Serve with raw vegetables and a few crackers.

CHAPTER 7

Nuts and Seeds

Roasted Sunflower Seeds

1 cup (250 ml) sunflower seeds   A few drops of tamari soy sauce

- Wash the sunflower seeds and dry them in a hot cast-iron skillet.
- Roast them until they brown slightly.
- Put them into a bowl and season with a few drops of tamari sauce.

Serve as a snack or add them to a salad.

Gomashio: Sesame Salt   *(see photo)*

DELICIOUS, NUTRITIOUS, AND VERSATILE.

It may be used in sandwiches, salads, and on cooked vegetables.

It may be kept in a glass jar in the refrigerator.

1 cup (250 ml) whole sesame seeds   1 teaspoon (5 ml) sea salt

- Wash the seeds well.

- Heat a cast-iron skillet. Add the sesame seeds. Dry them and roast them, while stirring.

- When the seeds are lightly browned, add the salt and roast for an extra minute.

- Cool and grind with a *suribachi* (Japanese mortar) or in the blender.

Soaked Nuts

- Make a habit of soaking 2 tablespoons (30 ml) of nuts or seeds before going to bed.

- Eat them whole or puréed at breakfast time, or keep them for lunch or a snack. Add them to your salad. This is a nutritious habit!

NOTE:

- Nuts and seeds that have been soaked are pleasant to chew and easier to digest.

- Nuts with shells, when soaked for two days, taste like fresh nuts.

Emulsified Nut Butters

When prepared as emulsions, nut butters take on a pleasant texture and are easier to digest.

Peanut, almond, sesame   Warm water
butter, etc.

- Using a fork or a food processor whip the desired quantity of nut butter, adding a little bit of water at a time.

- Beat well until you obtain a smooth cream.

Serve immediately with bread, on pancakes, or with fruit.

Depending on how much water you use, you will obtain a spread, a sauce for dipping fruit, or a salad dressing.

Emulsified nut butters are easy to make and so delicious!

They should be prepared in small quantities. They do not keep for a long time.

VARIATION: Add some honey and you will have a delicious icing for a cake.

Vegetable Pâté *Serves 6 (see photo)*

Excellent as a spread or with raw vegetables.

3/4 cup (200 ml) whole wheat flour
1/2 cup (125 ml) sunflower seeds, ground
2 tablespoons (30 ml) lemon juice
1/3 cup (75 ml) safflower or sunflower oil
1 clove garlic, finely chopped
2/3 cup (175 ml) nutritional yeast
2 onions, finely chopped

1 carrot, finely chopped
1 stalk celery, finely chopped
1 raw potato, grated
4 tablespoons (60 ml) tamari soy sauce
1 teaspoon (5 ml) basil
1/2 teaspoon (2 ml) thyme
1/4 teaspoon (1 ml) sage
1 cup (250 ml), or less, hot water

- Finely chop all the vegetables with a knife or in the food processor.

- Mix the ingredients together thoroughly.

- Spread out into a mold to a thickness of about 1 1/2 inches (4 cm).

- Bake at 350°F (180°C) for 45-60 minutes.

- Cool and take out of the mold.

Meatless Balls *Serves 6* *(see photo)*

1 cup (250 ml) rolled oats
1 cup (250 ml) sunflower seeds
1/2 cup (125 ml) breadcrumbs
3 tablespoons (45 ml) wheat germ
1 large onion, finely chopped
1 egg, preferably organic
1 teaspoon (5 ml) nutritional yeast
5 ounces (150 g) tofu

3 tablespoons (45 ml) oil
2 cloves garlic
1 teaspoon (5 ml) tamari soy sauce
1 teaspoon (5 ml) thyme
2 teaspoons (10 ml) basil
1 teaspoon (5 ml) 4 spices
1 teaspoon (5 ml) savory

- Grind up the rolled oats and sunflower seeds.

- Mix together the first 5 ingredients in a large bowl.

- Mix together the egg, yeast, tofu, oil, garlic, tamari sauce, and seasonings in the food processor. Blend thoroughly with the other ingredients in a large bowl.

- Form into small balls (or croquettes).

- Cook for 15-20 minutes in onion gravy, or bake on a cookie sheet.

Serve as is with potatoes and other root vegetables, or with a grain.

VARIATION: Cook the balls in tomato sauce and serve over pasta.

NUTS AND SEEDS

CHAPTER 8

Bread
Piecrusts
Quiches and
Sandwiches
Pancakes and
Crêpes

BREAD

Bread is a staple food in our daily diet. We eat a lot of it, either to accompany another dish, or in the form of sandwiches. It is essential, therefore, to know all the steps involved in how to make it. This knowledge will enable us to better evaluate its quality.

For many people, replacing white bread with whole wheat bread is the first step on the road towards a healthy diet.

315

The Quality of Bread

- Bread must have a wholesome color, aroma and consistency.

- The quality of the processes involved in producing its basic ingredients (cultivation, harvesting, etc.) as well as that of the methods used in their transformation (using real millstones to grind up the flour, the cooking process, etc.) determine the quality of the final product.

The Characteristics of Modern Bread

- Contains wheat grains which are grown non-organically.

- Flour used to make it undergoes refining which removes the bran and the germ.

- Made of grains milled industrially on metal grindstones, which heat the grains and oxidize them.

- Baked too quickly.

- Filled with chemical additives: about thirty are authorized.

- Enriched with synthetic vitamins, while the very refining process it has undergone has deprived it of many of its nutritional elements!!!

Modern bread is a degenerate and degenerating product. Look for suppliers of wholesome bread or make it yourself.

INGREDIENTS OF WHOLESOME BREAD:

Flour

- Use whole wheat flour with an extraction rate of 85%.

- Freshly stone-ground.

- The flavor of freshly milled flour is incomparable!

- Use organic hard wheat flour, which contains more gluten and minerals than soft wheat flour (pastry flour).

Mills with Stone Grindstones

- Heat up more slowly and, hence, do not oxidize the wheat as much.

- Do not accept unripened or damp grains.

- Are used to grind up grains only.

Mills with Metal Grindstones

- Heat up rapidly and, therefore, oxidize the wheat.

- Accept unripened grains and grains of lesser quality.

- Are used to grind up grains, nuts, and legumes.

Flour Mixtures for Bread

To make bread, use at least 60% hard wheat flour.

Hard wheat and rye contain more gluten than other grains. Gluten is a protein which gives bread its elasticity.

- 75% hard wheat flour - 25% buckwheat flour. Makes darker bread with a richer flavor.

- 40% hard wheat flour - 60% rye flour. Gives bread a delicious flavor and a denser texture.

- 80% hard wheat flour - 20% soy flour. Gives bread a nutty flavor and provides a complete protein.

- 80% hard wheat flour - 20% oat flour. Makes light, spongy bread (Use oats in the form of flour or flakes.)

- 80% hard wheat flour - 20 % okara or soy pulp. Gives bread a more grainy texture.

GIVE FREE REIN TO YOUR IMAGINATION!

Oil

- Don't use too much oil–just enough to make the inside of the bread soft: 1/4 cup per 9-10 cups of flour is enough.

- Use high quality, non-hydrogenated oil. Corn oil gives bread a good flavor.

Honey

- Yeast needs to feed on simple sugars in order to release carbon dioxide (CO_2), which allows the bread dough to rise.

- Use very little–just enough to feed the yeast. Use unpasteurized honey.

- 1/4 cup per 9-10 cups of flour makes slightly sweet bread.

Salt

- Helps the bread dough to rise. Regularizes the effect of the yeast. Improves the flavor.

- The dough does not rise as quickly, when you use too much salt.

- Use sea salt.

Water

- It is preferable to use spring water.

- The water must be warm: 110°F (46°C). Water which is too hot kills the yeast, and cold water slows down its action.

- Water may be partly or completely replaced by milk.

- When using milk, you must heat it to just over the boiling point, in order to kill the bacteria which might interfere with the action of the yeast, and then let it cool. Milk gives bread a higher protein content.

- Cooking stocks or vegetable stocks may be used in combination with water or they may replace it. They add vitamins, minerals, and flavor.

Other Ingredients Which May Be Added to Bread, When It Is Kneaded for the Last Time:

- Mashed potatoes make bread lighter and give it a sweet flavor (1/2 cup per 2 cups of flour).

- Powdered milk increases the nutritional value of bread (1-2 tablespoons per cup of flour).

- Precooked grains (millet, kasha, barley, rice) give bread a pleasant texture (1/2 cup per 2 cups of flour).

- Okara is good for completing the protein in the wheat (1/2 cup per 2 cups of flour).

- Roasted or unroasted sunflower seeds add to the nutritional value and flavor of bread (1/2-1 cup per loaf).

- Nutritional yeast also increases the nutritional value and flavor of bread (1 tablespoon per cup of flour).

- Herbs (oregano, marjoram, thyme, basil) give bread an unforgettable aroma (quantities according to taste).

- Grated cheese may be added to the dough (1/2-1 cup per loaf)

- Eggs make bread lighter and add nutritional value (1 egg per 4 cups of flour).

- Finely chopped garlic (to taste).

- Caraway seeds are usually used in conjunction with rye flour to make rye bread. Their flavor is well worth discovering.

- Raisins along with cinnamon and nuts to make raisin bread (quantities according to taste).

- Wheat sprouts, when added to bread, give it a crunchy texture (1/2-1 cup per loaf).

Don't Forget!

- You can prepare bread according to the inspiration of the moment and the ingredients that you have on hand. One or several of the ingredients may vary. This list is only a guide to help you make bread with a pleasing aroma and texture.

- In order to be well digested and assimilated, bread must be well masticated and impregnated with saliva, because the digestion of starch begins in the mouth. Remember?

A RECIPE FOR BREADMAKING

Yeast Bread

5 cups (1.2 L) lukewarm water	12 cups (3 L) hard wheat bread flour
1/4 cup (60 ml) honey	**or** 8-10 cups (2– 2.5 L) hard wheat
2 tablespoons (30 ml) yeast	flour and 2-4 cups (0.5– 1 L) of any
1/2 cup (125 ml) corn oil	other flour (soy, buckwheat, rye,
2 tablespoons (30 ml) sea salt	oat, etc.)

This recipe makes **4 loaves of bread** or **8 large pizza crusts**. Quantities may be doubled.

1. Dissolve the honey in the warm water (110°F/46°C). Sprinkle in the yeast. Make sure that all the granules of yeast come in contact with the water.

   NOTE:
   - After a few minutes the yeast will become active. The granules will burst, and frothing will occur. This is a sign that the yeast is alive. If the yeast does not become active, throw away the whole mixture and begin again with new yeast.

   - Continue with the recipe, as soon as the yeast be-

comes active. The longer you wait, the more the yeast becomes exhausted. Never wait longer than 20 minutes.

2. Add the oil, the salt, and 1 cup (250 ml) of flour. Continue to add the flour, 1 cup at a time, while stirring vigorously.

   Stir in a circular pattern, pulling the dough back towards yourself. Lift the spoon out of the dough, in order to introduce air into the mixture and develop the elasticity of the gluten (wheat protein).

   When half the quantity of flour has been added, the dough should be thick and elastic.

3. Add the rest of the flour gradually, until the dough stops sticking to the bowl.

   NOTE: At this stage you may place the dough in a covered container, put it in the refrigerator for 8-10 hours, and continue the next day; or, you may freeze it and continue another day.

4. Place the dough on a well-floured board or counter, and knead it.

5. Knead firmly with the palms of your hands, but do not tear the dough. Turn the ball of dough 1/4 of a turn with each cycle, stretch it a bit, and draw it back towards yourself, folding it over in two.

   NOTE:
   - When kneading a large quantity of dough, work with a movement that involves your whole body, placing one foot slightly in front of the other. This posture will prevent tension in your shoulders or arms.

   - When the dough seems to expand by itself, and pressing on it with your finger tips hardly leaves a mark, you have kneaded it enough!

6. Oil a large bowl. Don't forget that the dough will double in volume. Place the ball of dough in the bowl and turn it over several times, so that it becomes coated with oil. Cover with an oiled piece of waxed paper and a damp or dry cloth, depending on the level of humidity in the room. Always cover dough which is in the process of rising: otherwise, the top surface will form a crackled crust, and there will be hard brown particules inside the bread, after baking.

7. Let the dough rise in a warm place where there are no drafts. Yeast bread rises well between 70° and 80° F (18° and 20°C).

8. After an hour and a half, the dough should have doubled in volume. Dough which has risen enough collapses, when you push your fist into it. If it has not risen enough, it will spring back and rise again very rapidly.

9. Divide the dough into a number of balls of equal size, according to how many loaves you wish to make. Cut it with a knife or with the side of your hand. Do not tear the dough.

10. Knead each ball once again for about 5 minutes.If desired, you may blend in some seeds, cheese, raisins, etc. Cover and let sit for 15 minutes on a floured counter. This short rest period will ensure that your bread has a fine, light texture.

11. Flatten all of the balls and form them into loaves, by hand, or with a pastry roller. The roller technique is simple and makes bread with no air pockets in it.

    You just have to flatten the balls of dough into rectangles of the same length as your loaf pans, and then roll them like jellyrolls.

    Each time you roll the dough, fold the ends in to the center and press the two together with the sides of your hands,

sealing them, so that the dough does not come apart during baking. Otherwise you will end up with a sort of spiral-shaped loaf instead of bread with a fine texture.

12. Place each loaf in a well-oiled pan and cover. Let rise for about an hour. The dough has risen enough, when your finger hardly leaves a mark in it. Whole wheat bread dough doubles in volume, whereas white bread dough may rise to triple its height.

   If the dough seems to have risen too much—your finger will leave a clear mark and the dough will tend to collapse —you will have to take it out of the pan, form it into a loaf once again, and allow it to rise. This time it will rise very quickly in 20 to 30 minutes. Keep an eye on it. Dough that has risen too much makes bread which collapses in the oven and crumbles more easily.

13. Bake in a preheated oven at 350°F (180°C) for 45 minutes. When bread is cooked, tapping on the crust will produce a hollow sound. An experienced cook knows that bread is done by its aroma. If bread is insufficiently cooked, it will collapse when it cools.

14. After taking your bread from the oven, remove it from the pan, lay it on its side on a baking rack, and wait patiently for it to cool before slicing.

VARIATION:

- Instead of making ordinary loaves of bread, you can have fun making different forms such as braids, small balls, sticks, pita breads, etc. Watch over the bread during baking.

   Note: 2 cups of flour per loaf for small bread pans
   3 cups of flour per loaf for large bread pans

FREEZING RAW DOUGH

- Raw bread dough can be formed into loaves and frozen just before it rises for the last time in the bread pan.

- All you have to do is place it on a piece of oiled waxed paper and put it into a plastic bag, which you then close tightly without letting in any air.

Baking

- Take the dough out of the freezer the night before baking and place it in a well-oiled bread pan. Cover, let rise, and bake.

Why Should Raw Bread Dough Not Be Eaten?

- Yeast is a microscopic mushroom which develops in a warm, humid environment, from 80°-115°F (26°-43°C) and can cause digestive problems. It is destroyed during baking.

Why Should Bread Not Be Eaten Right from the Oven?

- Yeast feeds on simple sugars and produces carbon dioxide (CO_2). When this gas passes through the gluten, it makes bread rise. Letting bread cool allows the CO_2 to dissipate, before the bread is eaten.

Pizza Dough

The "Yeast Bread" recipe makes 8 pizza crusts, 14 inches (35 cm) in diameter. Take advantage of this opportunity to freeze some in advance, or reduce the quantities to suit your needs.

- Follow the steps in the "Yeast Bread" recipe until the bread has risen for the first time (step 8).

- Roll out the dough and divide it up according to the number of pizza pans you have. Do not knead it.

- Roll it out quite thin, that is to a thickness of about 1 inch (2-3 cm).

- Place the dough in an oiled pan, prick it here and there with a fork, and bake at 400°F (200°C) for 7 minutes.

- Freeze, if desired, or cover with tomato sauce, raw or sautéed vegetables, tofu, cheese, etc.

- Return to the oven and bake at 400°F (200°C) for 15 minutes.

NOTE: Pizza dough may be frozen raw or baked (7 minutes).

Ultra Easy Bread (or Pizza Dough) *(see photo)*

This recipe makes 2 small loaves. It may be doubled or tripled. It's fast and tasty!

2 cups (500 ml) lukewarm water
1 1/2 tablespoons (20 ml) honey
1 tablespoon (15 ml) yeast
4 tablespoons (60 ml) corn oil

2 teaspoons (10 ml) sea salt
4 cups (1 L) hard wheat flour
  (bread flour)

- Dissolve the honey in the lukewarm water and sprinkle with the yeast. Stir slightly, so that all the granules of yeast come into contact with the water.

- Let sit for 10 minutes. The yeast will expand.

- In a large bowl, mix together the oil and salt. Then add the yeast and stir a bit. Add 2 cups (500 ml) hard wheat flour (bread flour). Stir.

- Add 1 egg (optional).

- Stir 200 strokes, to develop the elasticity of the gluten and to introduce some air into the mixture.

- Add the rest of the flour. Mix well. The dough will be stickier than that of traditional bread.

- Cover the bowl and let the dough rise for either 1 hour at room temperature, or 8 hours in the refrigerator.

- Heat the oven to 350°F (180°C).

- Flour your working surface well, lay the dough on it, sprinkle it with flour, and divide it into two parts with the help of a knife.

- Knead each loaf lightly for about 5 minutes, or just long enough to blend in the flour and to take away the stickiness from the dough.

- With a sharp knife, make an incision in the form of a cross on the top of each loaf.

- Lay both loaves on a cookie sheet, which you have sprinkled with flour or cornmeal to prevent them from sticking. You may also bake the 2 loaves in oiled bread pans.

- Bake at 350°F (180°C) for 45-50 minutes.

NOTE: When mixing the dough or while kneading it, you may blend in some seeds, wheat sprouts, garlic, raisins, etc.

This recipe makes delicious bread, pizza crust, or pita bread easily and quickly, since it only rises once.

Pita Bread

Pita bread comes from the Middle East and is made from a traditional bread recipe. After it has risen the first time, you simply have to form the dough into small rounds and cook them quickly at high temperature, so that they puff up and then collapse afterwards, forming pockets, which may be used for fillings.

2 1/2 cups (625 ml) lukewarm water	2 tablespoons (30 ml) corn oil
2 tablespoons (30 ml) honey	1 tablespoon (15 ml) sea salt
1 tablespoon (15 ml) yeast	6 cups (1.5 L) hard wheat flour

- Dissolve the honey in 1/2 cup (125 ml) lukewarm water.

- Sprinkle with yeast, stir a little, and let sit for 10 minutes.

- Pour the yeast mixture into a large bowl. Add the rest of the water, the oil, and 3 cups (750 ml) flour.

- Mix well with a wooden spoon, until the mixture is supple and elastic.

- Add the salt and the rest of the flour gradually, while stirring well.

- Knead for 10 minutes. The dough should be firm and supple, but not hard.

- Place the dough in an oiled bowl. Then daub it with a bit of oil, and cover.

- Put the bowl in a warm place and let it sit for about 1 hour, until the dough has doubled in volume.

- Heat the oven to 450°F (230°C).

- Punch down the dough and separate it into 24 balls the size of a large egg. Let sit for 10 minutes under a dry cloth.

- With the help of a rolling pin, flatten the balls into uniform 1/4-inch (1-cm) thick rounds. Flour the rolling pin, if the rounds are sticky.

- Place the pitas on an unoiled cookie sheet, and bake them on the lowest shelf of the oven for 5 minutes, or until they have risen. If they brown on the bottom before they brown on the top, turn them over.

or

- Pitas may also be cooked in a cast-iron skillet, or on a small grill, placed 1 inch (3 cm) above the burner element of an electric stove. The temperature should be kept between medium and high.

- Lay the pitas on the grill or in the skillet for 1 minute. Turn them with a spatula, being careful not to puncture them. Balloons should appear after 1 or 2 minutes.

- Turn the pitas over and they will puff up without any difficulty.

- Cook them for at least 2 minutes on each side.

- If you serve them immediately, wrap the cooked pitas in a damp cloth to keep them soft.

- They are also soft and delicious, when reheated in the oven in aluminum foil.

Storage:

- Seal tightly in a plastic bag, and place in the refrigerator or in the freezer.

Ideas for Garnishes:

- Cut the pitas in half, open them up, and garnish with the following:
    - any sort of salad;
    - yogurt, cucumbers, and tomatoes;
    - tofu dip and cubes of green pepper;
    - eggs, onions, and black olives;
    - hummus or felafels, alfalfa sprouts, etc.

Open them up and break them into two halves. Garnish like a pizza.

This is also a recipe for traditional bread. It may be used to make small, individual rolls, 3 small loaves of bread, 2 large loaves, or pizza crusts.

Piecrust Dough Made with Oil

Healthful, quick, and easy, these dough recipes make delicious, slightly crisp pie crusts.

Basic Principles

Ingredients: pastry flour, oil, water, and salt.

- To make good dough, the oil and water must be very well emulsified, that is, mixed together very well with a fork, a whisk, or a blender.

- Corn and safflower oil produce the best results.

- Oil-based pastry doughs should be rolled out thin between two sheets of waxed paper.

NOTE:

- In order to obtain dough which is easy to work with, pastry flour, and not bread flour, should be used.

- This kind of dough should be used immediately, because the oil will have a tendency to separate out. Otherwise, it should be frozen.

Piecrust Dough Made with Corn Oil

This recipe makes a 9-inch (23-cm) piecrust. You can make your dough with your fingers right in the pie plate, or you can roll it out between 2 sheets of waxed paper.

1 cup (250 ml) pastry flour
1/4 teaspoon (1 ml) salt

1/4 cup (60 ml) corn oil
1/4 cup (60 ml) cold water

- Mix together the flour and salt in a pie plate.

- Pour the oil and water into a measuring cup and emulsify well by stirring vigorously with a fork.

- Make a well in the center of the flour and pour the liquid mixture into it. Gradually blend the flour with the liquid.

- Finish with your fingers, pressing out the dough uniformly around the pie plate and onto the top of the outer edges.

- Press the contour with a fork and prick the bottom a bit.

- Bake at 425°F (220°C) for 7 minutes, or fill and bake, following the instructions for the recipe you are making.

AN EASY, EFFICIENT PRINCIPLE!

- When making the crust for a whole pie, including a top crust, you should press the edges firmly together. Make a handsome edging, using your fingers or a fork.

- Brushing the top crust with some egg yolk, before baking, will give it a golden brown color and a shiny lustre.

- Cut up the leftovers into various forms and put them onto the top crust, to transform your pie into a chef-d'oeuvre.

For two 9-inch (23 cm), or four smaller piecrusts:

2 cups (500 ml) pastry flour
1/2 teaspoon (2 ml) sea salt

1/2 cup (125 ml) corn oil
1/2 cup (125 ml) cold water

For four 9-inch (23 cm), or eight smaller piecrusts :

4 cups (1 L) pastry flour
1 teaspoon (5 ml) sea salt

1 cup (250 ml) corn oil
1 cup (250 ml) cold water

Light, Oil-based Pastry Dough

For three 9-inch (23 cm) piecrusts, or 2 piecrusts of the same size, complete with the tops.

3 cups (750 ml) pastry flour, sifted
1/2 teaspoon (2 ml) sea salt
1/2 cup (125 ml) corn oil

1/2 cup (125 ml) cold water
1 egg, lightly beaten
1 tablespoon (15 ml) lemon juice

- Mix together the flour and salt in a bowl.

- Mix together the oil, water, egg, and lemon juice, and pour into the center of the flour mixture.

- Gradually blend the flour mixture into the liquid and form the resulting mixture into a ball with your hands.

- Let the dough cool in the refrigerator for 15-30 minutes before rolling it (optional).

- Divide and roll on a lightly floured surface or between 2 sheets of waxed paper.

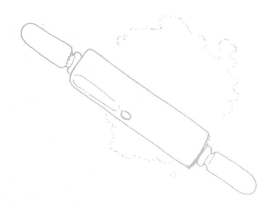

331

Breadcrumb Piecrust

3 slices whole wheat bread
1/4 cup (60 ml) powdered milk
1 tablespoon (15 ml) nutritional
   yeast

2 tablespoons (30 ml) rolled oats
1/4 cup (60 ml) oil
1 tablespoon (15 ml) honey

- Make the bread into crumbs with the blender.

- Mix the other ingredients together in a 9-inch (23 cm) pie plate.

- Blend in the bread and press the mixture right out over the edge of the pie plate.

- Bake or garnish, depending on the recipe.

This piecrust is delicious for fruit or cheese pies. For vegetable pies or quiches, replace the honey with water.

Rice Piecrust

2 cups (500 ml) cooked rice

- With your fingers, press the rice into a 9-inch (23 cm) pie plate

- Push the rice right out, up, and onto the top edge of the pie plate. This is very attractive, once the pie is cooked.

NOTE: Put your hands into ice-cold water to prevent the grains from sticking to them.

IDEAS FOR FILLINGS:

- Quiche.

- Lentil or tomato purée.

- Cooked vegetables with a béchamel sauce, etc.

VARIATION: Replace the rice with barley or millet.

Cheese Quiche

3 eggs
1 cup (250 ml) soy (or other) milk
1/2 teaspoon (2 ml) sea salt
1/4 teaspoon (1 ml) nutmeg

1 teaspoon (5 ml) basil
1 tablespoon (15 ml) wheat flour
1 cup (250 ml) Gruyère cheese

- Beat the eggs. Add the milk and seasonings. Mix well.

- Grate the cheese, blend in the flour, and mix together well.

- Put the cheese and the egg mixture into a rice piecrust, or some other type of piecrust. Sprinkle with paprika.

- Bake at 375°F (190°C) for 10 minutes and at 325°F (170°C) for about another 25 minutes.

Quiches are quick and easy to prepare and are always a favorite with the family. They are delicious, hot or cold.

VARIATIONS:

- Using the cheese quiche as a starting point, you can give infinite variety to the composition of your quiches, by incorporating different vegetables and seasonings into them. Try the following:

- **Spinach Quiche:** Steam the spinach.

- **Leek Quiche:** Sauté the leeks with garlic beforehand. Garnish with tomatoes.

- **Broccoli Quiche:** Steam the broccoli until tender and cut into pieces.

- **Green Pepper and Tomato Quiche:** Sauté the green pepper with garlic. Add tomato and basil.

IDEAS FOR SANDWICHES

For delightful, nutritious, varied lunches and quick meals.

- Tofu spread, alfalfa sprouts, and finely chopped carrot.

- Hummus, tomato, and alfalfa sprouts with yogurt or tahini sauce.

- Hummus, cubes of green pepper, and lettuce.

- Tofu and peanut butter spread, and sliced bananas and apples.

- Sliced tomatoes and avocado, nutritional yeast, and radish sprouts.

- Slices of tofu, strips of black olive and Chinese cabbage.

- Legume purée and lettuce.

- Ricotta cheese, finely chopped beet, and alfalfa sprouts.

- Scrambled eggs, red pepper, and green onion.

- Radish sprouts and ricotta cheese.

- Vegetable pâté and lettuce.

You can make excellent sandwiches using whole wheat, rye, or other bread, and a mayonnaise or nut butter spread (peanut, almond, etc.).

For Hot Sandwiches

Here are some suggestions for dishes which are nutritious and quick to prepare, when you are lacking in time and energy.

- **Pizza Sandwich:** Garnish a slice of bread with tomato sauce, green pepper, a slice of tomato, and oregano. Bake au gratin on a cookie sheet.

- **Mushroom Bread:** Sauté some mushrooms with garlic,

CHAPTER 9

Desserts

Rhubarb and Date Purée

- Cut up some rhubarb into pieces and cook over low heat in a bit of water.

- When you can easily reduce the rhubarb to a pulp, add the desired quantity of dates, after cutting them cut up into pieces. For example: 1/3 dates to 2/3 rhubarb.

- Cook a little longer to break down the dates.

Serve at breakfast time on bread or crêpes, with some yogurt.

VARIATION: For use as a pie filling. When cooking, thicken with some starch dissolved in a bit of water.

Date Sauce

12 pitted dates   1/2 cup (125 ml) water or apple juice

- Wash the dates and soak them overnight.

- Put them through the blender with the water used for soaking.

- Add 1 teaspoon (5 ml) of lemon juice, if desired.

The dates may also be liquefied directly in the blender, without soaking.

Serve with yogurt or fruit, or on a muffin or a piece of cake to replace the icing.

Prune Butter

- Wash the prunes and then soak them in water for at least 8 hours.

- Pit them and put them through the blender with the water used for soaking or with juice.

VARIATIONS:

- Put through the blender with an apple and/or a few nuts.

- The quantity of liquid used will determine the consistency: butter, mousse, or sauce.

- Try using dried pears, peaches, or apricots for variety.

NOTE: Use dried fruits marked N. S./N. F. (non-sulfurated, non-fumigated). These home-made purées are good substitutes for jam and icing. Serve on sliced bananas or in a fruit cup, in alternate layers with yogurt or " Tofu Whipped Cream ".

Avocado Sauce

1 or 2 ripe avocados   1/2 cup (125 ml) apple juice
2 tablespoons (30 ml) honey

- Put the ingredients through the blender. That's all there is to it.

Serve over fruit or cakes and decorate with coconut or some seeds. You can add a banana to give the sauce more body.

DESSERTS

VARIATION:

- **Avocado Mousse:** Add more fruit and less liquid. For example: 1 avocado and 1 apple, or 1 avocado and 1 banana. Put through the blender with a bit of juice, if necessary. Makes a delightful, uplifting snack.

Fresh Fruit Mousse *Serves 4*

6 very ripe peaches
4 oranges or 4 bananas
1 tablespoon (15 ml) orange peel
2 tablespoons (30 ml) honey

2 tablespoons (30 ml) lemon juice
2 cups (500 ml) yogurt
Chopped nuts

- Peel the fruit, and put it through the blender or the food processor along with the orange peel, honey, and lemon juice.

- Add the yogurt and pour into fruit cups. Garnish with the chopped nuts. Refrigerate for a few hours.

Fruit Salad

- Cut up three varieties of fruit, according to the season. In winter and spring: apples, bananas, and grapes (cut in two, with the seeds removed). In summer and fall, you can choose from a variety of different fruits.

- Place in a large bowl, sprinkle on some apple juice, and cover with coconut and a few pinches of cinnamon.

VARIATIONS:

- If you use pineapple, serve your fruit salad in the hollowed-out pineapple shell.

- In summer, make melon salads and serve in the melon shell.

- For an exotic touch, add a few drops of essence of coconut or essence of passion fruit.

- In winter, create salads using acidic fruits: oranges, mandarines, pineapple, etc. Garnish with chopped nuts.

Apple, Date, and Sesame Butter Salad *Serves 4*

4 apples
1 tablespoon (15 ml) sesame
  butter or tahini

1/2 cup (125 ml) N. S./N. F. dates
1 tablespoon (15 ml) yogurt

- Cut the apples into cubes, chop the dates, and add them to the apples.

- Add the sesame butter and yogurt, and blend well.

VARIATIONS:

- Add walnuts and sunflower seeds.

- Use other fruit such as bananas, pears, etc.

- Put the mixture through the blender to obtain a creamy sauce.

Baked Stuffed Apples *Serves 4*

4 apples
1/2 cup (125 ml) raisins
1/4 cup (60 ml) sesame butter

1 tablespoon (15 ml) honey
1/2 teaspoon (2 ml) cinnamon

- Wash and core the apples.

- Mix together the raisins, sesame butter, honey, and cinnamon.

- Place the apples in an oiled baking dish and fill the center of each apple with the raisin mixture.

- Cover and bake at 350°F (180°C) for 25-30 minutes.

VARIATIONS:

- Peel the apples, sprinkle them with lemon juice, stuff them, and place them whole on a square piece of pie

DESSERTS

dough. Then fold the dough back up over the apples. Bake at 400°F (200°C).

- Cut up the apples into pieces, mix with the other ingredients, and place on a square piece of pastry dough. Then fold the dough over into a triangle. Seal the edges well and bake at 400°F (200°C), until the crust is golden brown.

Serve hot or cold at breakfast or as a snack.

Carob Bananas *Makes 8 popsicles*

4 bananas   Chopped nuts
1/2 cup (125 ml) carob powder   Coconut

• Cut the bananas in two or three pieces, depending on their length.

• Push a popsicle stick into each piece of banana and dip in the carob powder, which has been dissolved in a bit of water. If desired, you can add 1 teaspoon (5 ml) of honey.

• Roll the " Carob Bananas " in the finely chopped nuts and coconut.

• Place on a cookie sheet and put in the freezer for a few hours.

Serve as a snack or as a special treat for children.

Espresso Ice Cream

4 ripe bananas

• Peel the bananas. Place them in plastic bags in the freezer for at least 24 hours.

• Cut the frozen bananas into pieces and put them through the blender or the food processor. Add a bit of yogurt to start the process. Makes soft ice cream.

VARIATIONS:

- You may purée the fruits before freezing. In this case, the recipe makes hard ice cream. Before serving take out of the freezer a little bit ahead of time to allow the ice cream to soften up slightly.

- Add pieces of nuts.

- Use other varieties of fruit such as peaches. Peel and freeze. Fruit other than bananas will yield ice cream with the consistency of sherbet.

- Use any dried fruit as a garnish, alone or in a mixture.

Raw Fruit Pie *(see photo)*

SUPERB, DELICIOUS AND UNUSUAL!

3/4 cup (200 ml) sunflower seeds, roasted	1/2 cup (125 ml) raisins 1/2 cup (125 ml) coconut

- Put the ingredients through the food processor and press the mixture into a pie plate to form a crust. If the mixture doesn't hold together, add a bit of juice or oil to thicken, and let freeze for at least one hour before garnishing.

- Cut up fruit that is in season (3 varieties). Place the fruit in a frozen piecrust.

- Cover generously with yogurt and decorate with fruit.

Serve as a dessert or at breakfast.

VARIATION: Use " Tofu Whipped Cream " instead of yogurt.

Banana and Cottage Cheese Pie

1 cup (250 ml) cottage cheese
2 ripe bananas
1 cup (250 ml) plain yogurt

1/4 cup (60 ml) wheat flour
1 tablespoon (15 ml) honey

- Put all the ingredients through the blender.

- Pour into an unbaked piecrust. The "Breadcrumb Piecrust" recipe is delicious for this pie.

- Bake at 350°F (180°C) for 30 minutes, until the center is firm.

Serve cold, garnished with nuts or sliced bananas.

Date Surprise

Dates, almonds, and apple juice.

- Grind up the almonds and blend in the apple juice until you obtain a paste.

- Pit the dates and stuff them with the paste!

Carob Candy   *(see photo)*

1/2 cup (125 ml) peanut butter
1/4 cup (60 ml) carob powder

1/4 cup (60 ml) flax seeds, ground
1/4 cup (60 ml) honey

- Mix together well and form into small balls.

- Roll in coconut and/or chopped walnuts. Refrigerate.

VARIATIONS:

- To make peanut butter candy, replace the carob with milk powder.

- Add walnuts or rolled oats.

- Finely chop some dried fruit and add it to the candy.

- Use different kinds of seeds: sesame, sunflower, pump-kin, etc.

Raisin Squares *Makes 10*

Filling

2 cups (500 ml) organic, N.S./N.F. Thompson raisins

- Wash the raisins, cover them with water, and let them soak for 2 to 8 hours.

- Put them through the blender with a bit of the water used for soaking, until you obtain a thick paste.

Crust

1 1/3 cups (325 ml) pastry flour
1 3/4 cups (450 ml) rolled oats
1/3 cup (75 ml) honey

2/3 cup (175 ml) safflower oil
2 apples, cut into slices

- Thouroughly mix together the flour, rolled oats, and honey.

- Blend in the oil, until the mixture has a granulated texture.

- Press half of the mixture into an oiled 8– x 8– inch (20– x 20– cm) cake pan.

- Cover with a sliced apple, then with the raisin filling,finishing off with the remaining apple. Cover with the rest of the crust mixture.

- Bake at 350°F (180°C) for 45 minutes. Cut into squares.

DESSERTS

Carrot Squares *(see photo)*

1 cup (250 ml) carrots, grated	1/2 cup (125 ml) apples, grated
1/2 cup (125 ml) raisins	1 cup (250 ml) wheat flour
1 egg, beaten	1/4 teaspoon (1 ml) sea salt
1/2 cup (125 ml) dates, chopped	

- Soak the raisins in just enough lukewarm water to cover.

- Mix together all the ingredients and moisten sufficiently with the water used for soaking.

- Place the mixture in an oiled baking dish.

- Bake at 350°F (180°C) for 30 minutes.

- Let cool and cut into squares.

Serve as a snack or put into your lunch boxes.

Sugar-Free Fruit Squares* *Makes 16*

1 1/2 cups (375 ml) oatmeal	1/4 cup (60 ml) currants
1/2 cup (125 ml) wheat pastry flour	1/4 cup (60 ml) apricots, chopped
1/3 cup (75 ml) coconut, grated	1/3 cup (75 ml) sunflower oil
1/2 cup (125 ml) dates, chopped	3/4 cup (200 ml) puréed bananas
1/2 cup (125 ml) figs, chopped	or apple sauce

- Mix together all the ingredients in the order indicated.

- Press into an oiled 8– x 8– inch (20– x 20– cm) cake pan.

- Bake at 350°F (180°C) for 20 minutes.

- Cut into 2-inch (5 cm) squares in the baking dish, while the preparation is still hot.

* This recipe comes from *Le Mille-Feuille*, a vegetarian restaurant on Ste-Foy St. in Quebec city, Quebec, Canada.

Apple Jelly

2 tablespoons (30 ml) powdered agar   4 cups (1 L) apple juice
  or 4 tablespoons (60 ml) agar flakes

- Soak the agar in the apple juice for 5 minutes, so that it will dissolve better.

- Bring to a boil, reduce the heat and cook, stirring constantly, until the agar is completely dissolved.

- If you use frozen juice, dissolve the agar in water only, bring to a boil, and then add the frozen concentrate. In this way you will avoid heating the pulp for no reason.

- Pour into a jelly mold or into fruit cups. Let cool a little at room temperature and then refrigerate.

VARIATIONS:

- When making jelly that you want to remove from the mold, cool in ice water. If desired, add fruit when semi-firm and refrigerate. To remove from the mold, run a knife around the inside edge of the mold, put it into hot water for a few moments, and turn it upside down on a plate.

- Color the apple juice with beet powder or beet juice to obtain lovely red jelly. Add some strawberries. Superb!

- When semi-firm, whip, along with some yogurt, and freeze in popsicle trays or some other container. Delicious!

DESSERTS

Apple Cookies *Makes 36* (**see photo**)

1/2 cup (125 ml) oil
1/2 cup (125 ml) honey
2 eggs
1 3/4 cups (425 ml) whole wheat
  pastry flour
1/2 cup (125 ml) rolled oats
1/2 teaspoon (2 ml) sea salt

1 1/2 teaspoons (7 ml) baking
  powder
1/4 teaspoon (1 ml) cinnamon
1/2 cup (125 ml) raisins
1 cup (250 ml) nuts, chopped
1 1/2 cups (375 ml) apples, finely
  chopped or grated

- Heat the oven to 350°F (180°C).

- Beat together the oil and honey until creamy in texture.

- Add the eggs and mix well.

- Mix together all the other ingredients in a large bowl. Add the liquid ingredients. Mix well.

- Using a spoon, place the mixture on a lightly oiled cookie sheet and bake for 12-15 minutes.

Granola Bars

3 cups (750 ml) rolled oats
1 cup (250 ml) whole wheat
   pastry flour
1/2 teaspoon (2 ml) baking
   powder
1/3 cup (75 ml) oil

1/3 cup (75 ml) water
1 cup (250 ml) honey
1 teaspoon (5 ml) vanilla
1/2 to 1 cup (125 to 250 ml) raisins
1/4 teaspoon (1 ml) sea salt
A pinch of cinnamon

- Heat the oven to 350°F (180°C).

- Oil a cookie sheet.

- Mix together all the dry ingredients in a large bowl.

- In another bowl, mix together the liquid ingredients. Add them to the dry mixture. Mix well.

- Spread out the mixture on a cookie sheet and bake for about 15 minutes or until the top is a light golden brown.

- Let cool before cutting.

Tofu Whipped Cream

1/2 cup (125 ml) cashews
   or sesame butter
8 ounces (225 g) tofu

2 tablespoons (30 ml) honey
1 teaspoon (5 ml) vanilla
Some liquid

- Grind up the nuts in the blender. Add the tofu, honey, and vanilla. Use soft tofu for best results.

- Add a bit of liquid (apple juice, milk, or water) to facilitate mixing and whip until you obtain a thick, smooth cream.

Serve with fresh fruit or jelly.

This recipe can also be used for icing cakes. Add some beet powder to get pink icing.

Cake or Muffin Icing

Use powdered milk instead of icing sugar.

1/2 cup (125 ml) powdered milk
2 tablespoons (30 ml) milk
2 tablespoons (30 ml) oil

1 tablespoon (15 ml) honey
1 teaspoon (5 ml) vanilla

- Mix together the milk, oil, honey, and vanilla. Add the powdered milk.

- Whip until the mixture is creamy. Add some liquid, if necessary.

VARIATIONS:

- **Carob Icing:** Add 3 tablespoons (45 ml) of carob.

- **Spicy Icing:** Add cinnamon, nutmeg, and 4-spices to taste.

- **Pink Icing:** Add beet juice or beet powder.

- **Fruit Icing:** Replace the milk with fruit juice, and orange or lemon peel.

- **Coconut Icing:** Add coconut.

- **Tofu Icing:** Use the " Tofu Whipped Cream " recipe.

- **Non-Dairy-Product Icing:** Use soy milk powder and soy milk or juice.

- **Peanut Butter (or Other Nut Butter) Icing:** Add honey to the " Emulsified Nut Butters " recipe.

NOTES

" Theory Book " Section

CHAPTER 1 **Progressive Changes**
1.　Linda R. Pim, *Nos aliments empoisonnés*, 1986, p. 19.

CHAPTER 3 **The Needs of the Body**
1.　Société canadienne du cancer, «Le cancer et le régime alimentaire», brochure, 1986.
2.　*Jane Brody's Nutrition Book*, 1987, p. 150.
3.　*Médecine moderne du Canada*, revue, février 1987, p. 150.
4.　Scheider, *La nutrition*, 1984, p. 69.
5.　Scheider, *La nutrition*, 1984, p. 80.
6.　Jean de Trémollières, *Les bases de l'alimentation*,1984, p. 170.
7.　Scheider, *La nutrition*, 1984, p. 110.
8.　Scheider, *La nutrition*, 1984, p. 116.
9.　Scheider, *La nutrition*, 1984, p. 116.
10.　Santé et Bien-être social Canada, «Apports nutritionnels recommandés pour les Canadiens-nes», 1983.
11.　Dr C. Kousmine, *Soyez bien dans votre assiette*, 1980, p. 149.

CHAPTER 4 **The Digestive System**
1.　Scheider, *La nutrition*, 1984, p. 178.

CHAPTER 6 **Grains**
1.　Claude Aubert, *Une autre assiette*, 1979, p. 151.
2.　*Médecine moderne du Canada*, revue, février 1987, p. 14.
3.　Linda R. Pim, *Additive Alert*, 1981, p. 35.

CHAPTER 7 **Legumes**
1.　W. Shurtleff and A. Aoyagi, *The Book of Miso*, 1983.

CHAPTER 9 **Sprouts**
1.　F. et R. Hurd, *Ten Talents*, 1968, p. 291.
2.　Claude Aubert, *Une autre assiette*, 1979, p. 150.
3.　Michèle Caya, *Découvrez les graines germées*, 1982, p. 37.

INDEX OF CHARTS, TABLES, AND ILLUSTRATIONS

TABLE OF CONTENTS "Theory Book" Section

TABLE OF CONTENTS " Recipe Book " Section

356

357

BIBLIOGRAPHY

Alpha Santé. *Les secrets d'une bonne alimentation*, Collection.

ANDRÉ, J. *L'équilibre nutritionnel du végétarien*, Paris, Louvain, 1985.

AUBERT, C. *Une autre assiette*, Paris, Debard, 1979.

BAKER, E. et E. *The Uncook Book*, Drelwood Publications, 1980.

BESSETTE, C. *La gastronomie végétarienne*, Dossier A.P.R.A.S., 1986.

BRODY, J. *Jane Brody's Nutrition Book*, Bantam, 1987.

BROWN, E. *Tassajara Cooking*, Berkeley, Shambala, 1973.

CARON, C. *L'eau et la santé*, Québec, Dossier A.P.R.A.S., 1986.

CHELF HUDON, V. *La grande cuisine végétarienne*, Québec, Stanké, 1985.

CAYA, M. *Découvrez les graines germées*, Nature et Progrès, 1982.

FAELTEN, S. et les rédacteurs du magazine Prevention. *Minerals for Health*, Rodale Press, 1981.

HAMEL MONGEAU, S. *Le Kéfir*, Québec, Dossier A.P.R.A.S., 1986.

HURD F. et R. *Ten Talents*, Hurd, 1968.

KIRSCHMANN, J. et L. DUNNE. *Nutrition Almanac*, McGraw Hill, 1984.

KOUSMINE, C. *Soyez bien dans votre assiette jusqu'à 80 ans et plus*, Tchou, 1980.

KRAUSE, M. et M. HUNSCHER. *Nutrition et diétothérapie*, HRW, 1978.

MAGARINOS, H. *Cuisine pour une vie nouvelle*, Paris, Debard, 1982.

Médecine moderne du Canada, revue, février 1987.

MOORE LAPPÉ, F. *Diet for a Small Planet*, 10th Anniversary Edition, New York, Ballantine, 1982.

PIM, R. L. *Additive Alert*, Double Day, 1981.

PIM, R. L. *Nos aliments empoisonnés*, Québec-Amérique, 1986.

PASSEBECQ, A. et J. *Cours d'alimentation de santé*, Vie et Action.

ROBERTSON, L., C. FLINDERS et B. RUPPENTHAL. *The New Laurel's Kitchen*, Ten Speed Press, 1986.

ROBINSON, C. H. *Normal and Therapeutic Nutrition*, 15e édition, Macmillan.

ROSNAY, S. et J. de. *La Malbouffe*, Paris, Seuil, 1981.

SANTÉ ET BIEN-ÊTRE SOCIAL CANADA, «Apports nutritionnels recommandés», Approvisionnements et Services Canada, 1992.

SANTÉ ET BIEN-ÊTRE SOCIAL CANADA, «Le manuel du guide alimentaire canadien» (révision), 1992.

SCHEIDER, W. *La nutrition*, McGraw Hill, 1985.

SHURTLEFF, W. and A. AOYAGI. *The Book of Miso*, Ten Speed Press, 1983.

Société canadienne du cancer, «Le cancer et le régime alimentaire», brochure, 1986.

SPENCE and MASON, *Human Anatomy and Physiology*, 2nd Edition, Benjamin/Cummings Publishing, 1983.

SCHMIDT, G. *Alimentation dynamique*, Triades, 1977.

TRASH, A. et C. *Nutrition for vegetarians*, Trash Publications, 1982.

TRÉMOLLIÈRES, J., Y. SERVILLE, R. JACQUOT et H. DUPIN. *Les bases de l'alimentation*, E.S.F., 1984.

TRÉMOLLIÈRES, J., Y. SERVILLE, R. JACQUOT et H. DUPIN. *Les aliments*, E.S.F., 1968.

United States Department of Agriculture, *Handbook of the Nutritional Contents of Foods*, Dover.

WHITNEY, E. and E. HAMILTON. *Understanding Nutrition*, 4th Edition, West, 1987.

WIGMORE, A. *The Hippocrates Diet and Health program*, Avery Publishing Group Inc., 1984.

This book was printed
on recycled paper.

PRINTED IN CANADA

BIBLIOGRAPHY

Alpha Santé. *Les secrets d'une bonne alimentation*, Collection.

ANDRÉ, J. *L'équilibre nutritionnel du végétarien*, Paris, Louvain, 1985.

AUBERT, C. *Une autre assiette*, Paris, Debard, 1979.

BAKER, E. et E. *The Uncook Book*, Drelwood Publications, 1980.

BESSETTE, C. *La gastronomie végétarienne*, Dossier A.P.R.A.S., 1986.

BRODY, J. *Jane Brody's Nutrition Book*, Bantam, 1987.

BROWN, E. *Tassajara Cooking*, Berkeley, Shambala, 1973.

CARON, C. *L'eau et la santé*, Québec, Dossier A.P.R.A.S., 1986.

CHELF HUDON, V. *La grande cuisine végétarienne*, Québec, Stanké, 1985.

CAYA, M. *Découvrez les graines germées*, Nature et Progrès, 1982.

FAELTEN, S. et les rédacteurs du magazine Prevention. *Minerals for Health*, Rodale Press, 1981.

HAMEL MONGEAU, S. *Le Kéfir*, Québec, Dossier A.P.R.A.S., 1986.

HURD F. et R. *Ten Talents*, Hurd, 1968.

KIRSCHMANN, J. et L. DUNNE. *Nutrition Almanac*, McGraw Hill, 1984.

KOUSMINE, C. *Soyez bien dans votre assiette jusqu'à 80 ans et plus*, Tchou, 1980.

KRAUSE, M. et M. HUNSCHER. *Nutrition et diétothérapie*, HRW, 1978.

MAGARINOS, H. *Cuisine pour une vie nouvelle*, Paris, Debard, 1982.

Médecine moderne du Canada, revue, février 1987.

MOORE LAPPÉ, F. *Diet for a Small Planet*, 10th Anniversary Edition, New York, Ballantine, 1982.

PIM, R. L. *Additive Alert*, Double Day, 1981.

PIM, R. L. *Nos aliments empoisonnés*, Québec-Amérique, 1986.

PASSEBECQ, A. et J. *Cours d'alimentation de santé*, Vie et Action.

ROBERTSON, L., C. FLINDERS et B. RUPPENTHAL. *The New Laurel's Kitchen*, Ten Speed Press, 1986.

ROBINSON, C. H. *Normal and Therapeutic Nutrition*, 15e édition, Macmillan.

ROSNAY, S. et J. de. *La Malbouffe*, Paris, Seuil, 1981.

SANTÉ ET BIEN-ÊTRE SOCIAL CANADA, «Apports nutritionnels recommandés», Approvisionnements et Services Canada, 1992.

SANTÉ ET BIEN-ÊTRE SOCIAL CANADA, «Le manuel du guide alimentaire canadien» (révision), 1992.

SCHEIDER, W. *La nutrition*, McGraw Hill, 1985.

SHURTLEFF, W. and A. AOYAGI. *The Book of Miso*, Ten Speed Press, 1983.

Société canadienne du cancer, «Le cancer et le régime alimentaire», brochure, 1986.

SPENCE and MASON, *Human Anatomy and Physiology*, 2nd Edition, Benjamin/Cummings Publishing, 1983.

SCHMIDT, G. *Alimentation dynamique*, Triades, 1977.

TRASH, A. et C. *Nutrition for vegetarians*, Trash Publications, 1982.

TRÉMOLLIÈRES, J., Y. SERVILLE, R. JACQUOT et H. DUPIN. *Les bases de l'alimentation*, E.S.F., 1984.

TRÉMOLLIÈRES, J., Y. SERVILLE, R. JACQUOT et H. DUPIN. *Les aliments*, E.S.F., 1968.

United States Department of Agriculture, *Handbook of the Nutritional Contents of Foods*, Dover.

WHITNEY, E. and E. HAMILTON. *Understanding Nutrition*, 4th Edition, West, 1987.

WIGMORE, A. *The Hippocrates Diet and Health program*, Avery Publishing Group Inc., 1984.

This book was printed
on recycled paper.

PRINTED IN CANADA